IBM Cognos 10 Report Studio Cookbook

Second Edition

Over 100 recipes that will show you how to use IBM Cognos 10 Report Studio to build creative, stunning, and sophisticated reports

Ahmed Lashin

Abhishek Sanghani

[PACKT] enterprise

PUBLISHING

professional expertise distilled

BIRMINGHAM - MUMBAI

IBM Cognos 10 Report Studio Cookbook
Second Edition

First published: May 2010

Second edition: August 2013

Production Reference: 1200813

Published by Packt Publishing Ltd.
Livery Place
35 Livery Street
Birmingham B3 2PB, UK.

ISBN 978-1-84968-820-8

www.packtpub.com

Cover Image by Vivek Sinha (vs@viveksinha.com)

Credits

Authors

Ahmed Lashin

Abhishek Sanghani

Reviewers

Ramesh Parcha

João Patrão

Acquisition Editor

Joanne Fitzpatrick

Lead Technical Editor

Dayan Hyames

Technical Editors

Jalasha D'costa

Menza Mathew

Zafeer Rais

Amit Ramadas

Project Coordinators

Arshad Sopariwala

Venitha Cutinho

Proofreader

Paul Hindle

Indexers

Rekha Nair

Monica Ajmera Mehta

Production Coordinator

Shantanu Zagade

Cover Work

Shantanu Zagade

About the Authors

Ahmed Lashin is a highly motivated Information Technology (IT) professional with more than nine years of experience, most of it in the Business Intelligence and data warehousing domains. His core skills include a full set of BI tools, ETL, and data warehousing tools such as IBM Cognos, IBM DataStage, SAP BusinessObjects, Microsoft SQL Server BI SSIS, SSAS, and SSRS. Through his experience, he has been exposed to many industries such as banking and finance, oil and gas, education, and the automotive industry.

Currently, Ahmed is working as a Business Intelligence Lead in one of IBM's major global partners. He is also an IBM Certified Cognos Solution Expert.

This is Ahmed's first technical book. He is maintaining a technical blog at `http://www.alashin.net`. You can get in touch with him at `ahmed@alashin.net`.

I would like to thank my beloved wife Esraa for all the encouragement and support she has given me. I would also like to thank my mother and my family.

I would like also to thank my partner Abhishek for his great work and his valuable comments. With your work, Cognos is much more fun.

A special thanks to Packt Publishing for their efforts. I am sure that I wouldn't have been able to complete this book without their support.

Abhishek Sanghani was born in India and attended Mumbai University, where he majored in Computer Engineering. He began his career in 2004 as a Business Intelligence and Cognos Consultant, and has worked with leading IT and financial services companies since then.

He pursued Finance Management along with his work in the field of Cognos and BI, successfully progressing and winning awards and certifications year-on-year. Presently, he is working in the United Kingdom, utilizing his skills of Cognos, SQL, BI, and data warehousing. In his free time, he writes technical blogs and also provides training/seminars on demand.

He first authored *Packt Publishing's* book *IBM Cognos 8 Report Studio Cookbook,* which was well received worldwide. He has recently composed a video course called *IBM Cognos 10 Report Studio Fundamentals*, which is available on the www.packtpub.com website for download as well as online streaming.

> I would like to thank Ahmed for giving a new life and avatar to my Cookbook, making it suitable for Cognos v10.x. I am sure, this new book with its new content, easy-to-understand recipes, real-life examples, and v10 sample codes, will prove very useful to Report Studio users, project managers, developers, and business analysts.
>
> I would also like to thank the whole Packt Publishing team for all the hard work and support. On a personal note, I would also like to thank my loving wife Dolly for the encouragement and for putting up with my IT nonsense at the dinner table.

About the Reviewers

Ramesh Parcha graduated with a degree in Mechanical Engineering from Gulbarga University and has been working in the IT industry for over 13 years now. He is presently working in *NTTDATA* as a Project Manager.

He has been working with IBM Cognos BI products since 2006.

Earlier in his career, he worked for SETKHAM, SIS Inoftech, and Dataformix Technologies, USA. He has worked on a few other books such as *IBM Cognos Framework Manager, Video Course on IBM Cognos 10 Report Studio*, and *IBM Cognos 8 Report Studio Cookbook*.

> It was a great pleasure reviewing this book and I would sincerely like to thank Dayan and Arshad.

João Patrão is a technology leader with expertise in mobile development, application integration aligned with business and strategic goals, multi-disciplinary team management, and project delivery. As the IT Director of *SUMA*, he has built a responsive and proactive IT organization, with improvements to service delivery, standardization, and business/systems performance.

With a strong orientation to strategic and business objectives, he always looks for innovation and integration of different methods and technologies to create new solutions that can maximize the talent and the resources of the organization.

He has a background in Engineering and Computer Science at Instituto Superior Técnico (IST Lisbon) and has an Executive MBA from EGP-University of Porto Business School.

www.PacktPub.com

Support files, eBooks, discount offers and more

You might want to visit www.PacktPub.com for support files and downloads related to your book.

Did you know that Packt offers eBook versions of every book published, with PDF and ePub files available? You can upgrade to the eBook version at www.PacktPub.com and as a print book customer, you are entitled to a discount on the eBook copy. Get in touch with us at service@packtpub.com for more details.

At www.PacktPub.com, you can also read a collection of free technical articles, sign up for a range of free newsletters and receive exclusive discounts and offers on Packt books and eBooks.

http://PacktLib.PacktPub.com

Do you need instant solutions to your IT questions? PacktLib is Packt's online digital book library. Here, you can access, read and search across Packt's entire library of books.

Why Subscribe?

- Fully searchable across every book published by Packt
- Copy and paste, print and bookmark content
- On demand and accessible via web browser

Free Access for Packt account holders

If you have an account with Packt at www.PacktPub.com, you can use this to access PacktLib today and view nine entirely free books. Simply use your login credentials for immediate access.

Instant Updates on New Packt Books

Get notified! Find out when new books are published by following @PacktEnterprise on Twitter, or the *Packt Enterprise* Facebook page.

I would like to dedicate this book to my beloved wife Esraa. Thank you for being you.

—Ahmed Lashin

I am dedicating this book to the smiling addition to my life, my daughter Siyara.

—Abhishek Sanghani

Table of Contents

Preface

IBM Cognos Report Studio is widely used for creating and managing business reports in medium to large-scale companies. It is simple enough for any business analyst, power user, or developer to pick up and start developing basic reports. However, when it comes to developing more sophisticated, fully functional business reports for wider audiences, report authors will need guidance.

This book helps you to understand and use all the features provided by the new version of IBM Cognos 10 Report Studio to generate impressive deliverables. It will take you from being a beginner to a professional report author. It bridges the gap between the basic training provided by manuals or trainers and the practical techniques learned over years of practice.

What this book covers

Chapter 1, Report Authoring Basic Concepts, introduces you to some fundamental components and features that you will be using in most of the reports. This is meant to bring all readers on the same page before moving on to advanced topics. It covers filters, sorting, aggregations, formatting and conditional formatting, and so on.

Chapter 2, Advanced Report Authoring, introduces you to the advanced techniques required to create more sophisticated report solutions that meet demanding business requirements. It covers cascaded prompts, master-detail queries, conditional blocks, defining drill links, and overriding the drill links. The most distinguishing recipe in this chapter is *Writing back to the database*.

Chapter 3, Using JavaScript Files – Tips and Tricks, explains how to manipulate the default selection, titles, visibility, and so on when the prompt page loads. It also explains how to add programmability like validating the prompt selection before submitting the values to the report engine. A favorite recipe in this chapter is *Creating a variable width bar chart using JavaScript*. The recipes in this chapter open a whole new avenue for you to progress on.

Chapter 4, The Report Page – Tips and Tricks, shows some techniques to break boundaries and provides some features in reports that are not readily available in the Studio. It also talks about showing images dynamically (traffic lights), handling missing images, dynamic links to external websites (for example, Google Maps), alternating drill links, showing tooltips on reports, minimum column width, and merged cells in Excel output.

Chapter 5, Working with XML, shows you how to edit the report outside the Studio by directly editing the XML specifications. The recipes in this chapter show you how to save time and quickly change references to old items, copy and paste the drill parameter mappings, and introduce you to important XML tags. The most intriguing recipe in this chapter is *A hidden gem in XML – row level formatting*.

Chapter 6, Writing Printable Reports, gives you tips and shows you the options available within the Studio to make the reports printable, as business reports need to be printed. This is often ignored during technical specification and development.

Chapter 7, Working with Dimensional Models, explains how when reports are written against a dimensional data source (or a dimensionally modeled relational schema), a whole new style of report writing is needed. You can use dimensional functions, slicers, and others. Also, filtering and zero suppression are done differently. This chapter talks about such options (as dimensional data sources are becoming popular again).

Chapter 8, Working with Macros, shows you that even though macros are often considered a framework modeler's tool, they can be used within Report Studio as well. These recipes will show you some very useful macros around security, string manipulation, and prompting.

Chapter 9, Using Report Studio Efficiently, shows you the Studio options and development practices to get the best out of Report Studio. It will include discussions about Studio options, setting time-outs, capturing the real query fired on a database, handling slow report validation, customizing classes, and so on.

Chapter 10, Working with Active Reports, introduces you to a new and powerful tool available in IBM Cognos 10 Report Studio called Active Reports. Active Reports allows you to create highly interactive and easy-to-use reports. You will learn some techniques that will change the way your reports look.

Chapter 11, Charts and New Chart Features, shows you how to use advanced features in charts available in IBM Cognos Report Studio. These features are based on the new charting engine that was introduced in IBM Cognos Version 10.

Chapter 12, More Useful Recipes, is an assorted platter of useful recipes, meant to show more workarounds, tricks, and techniques.

Chapter 13, Best Practices, shows you how to achieve code commenting, version controlling, regression testing, and so on. It will also show you some useful practices you should cultivate as standard during development.

Appendix, Recommendations and References, covers topics that are very useful for a Cognos report developer such as version controlling, Cognos mash-up service, and Cognos Go Office.

What you need for this book

IBM Cognos Report Studio 10 (10.1 to 10.2) or any later version.

Who this book is for

If you are a Business Intelligence or MIS Developer (programmer) working on Cognos Report Studio who wants to author impressive reports by putting to use what this tool has to offer, this book is for you. You could also be a Business Analyst or Power User who authors your own reports and who wants to look beyond the conventional features of Report Studio 10.

This book assumes that you can do basic report authoring, are aware of the Cognos architecture, and are familiar with Studio.

Conventions

In this book, you will find a number of styles of text that distinguish between different kinds of information. Here are some examples of these styles, and an explanation of their meaning.

Code words in text are shown as follows: "We can include other contexts through the use of the include directive".

A block of code is set as follows:

```
<script>
function img2txt(img) {
txt = img.alt;
img.parentNode.innerHTML=txt;}
</script>
```

When we wish to draw your attention to a particular part of a code block, the relevant lines or items are set in bold:

```
<script>
function img2txt(img) {
txt = img.alt;
img.parentNode.innerHTML=txt;}
</script>
```

New terms and **important words** are shown in bold. Words that you see on the screen, in menus or dialog boxes for example, appear in the text like this: "Clicking on the **Next** button moves you to the next screen".

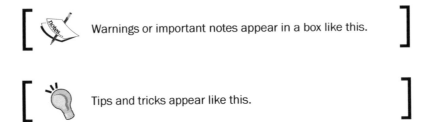

Warnings or important notes appear in a box like this.

Tips and tricks appear like this.

Reader feedback

Feedback from our readers is always welcome. Let us know what you think about this book—what you liked or may have disliked. Reader feedback is important for us to develop titles that you really get the most out of.

To send us general feedback, simply send an e-mail to feedback@packtpub.com, and mention the book title via the subject of your message.

If there is a book that you need and would like to see us publish, please send us a note in the **SUGGEST A TITLE** form on www.packtpub.com or e-mail suggest@packtpub.com.

If there is a topic that you have expertise in and you are interested in either writing or contributing to a book on, see our author guide on www.packtpub.com/authors.

Customer support

Now that you are the proud owner of a Packt book, we have a number of things to help you to get the most from your purchase.

Errata

Although we have taken every care to ensure the accuracy of our content, mistakes do happen. If you find a mistake in one of our books—maybe a mistake in the text or the code—we would be grateful if you would report this to us. By doing so, you can save other readers from frustration and help us improve subsequent versions of this book. If you find any errata, please report them by visiting http://www.packtpub.com/support, selecting your book, clicking on the **let us know** link, and entering the details of your errata. Once your errata are verified, your submission will be accepted and the errata will be uploaded on our website, or added to any list of existing errata, under the Errata section of that title. Any existing errata can be viewed by selecting your title from http://www.packtpub.com/support.

Piracy

Piracy of copyright material on the Internet is an ongoing problem across all media. At Packt, we take the protection of our copyright and licenses very seriously. If you come across any illegal copies of our works, in any form, on the Internet, please provide us with the location address or website name immediately so that we can pursue a remedy.

Please contact us at copyright@packtpub.com with a link to the suspected pirated material.

We appreciate your help in protecting our authors, and our ability to bring you valuable content.

Questions

You can contact us at questions@packtpub.com if you are having a problem with any aspect of the book, and we will do our best to address it.

1

Report Authoring Basic Concepts

In this chapter, we will cover the following:

- ▶ Summary filters and detail filters
- ▶ Sorting grouped values
- ▶ Aggregation and rollup aggregation
- ▶ Implementing if-then-else in filters
- ▶ Formatting data – dates, numbers, and percentages
- ▶ Creating sections
- ▶ Hiding columns in crosstabs
- ▶ Prompts – display value versus use value

Introduction

In this chapter, we will cover some fundamental techniques that will be used in your day-to-day life as a Report Studio author. In each recipe, we will take a real-life example and see how it can be accomplished. At the end of the chapter, you will learn several concepts and ideas which you can mix-and-match to build complex reports. Though this chapter is called *Report Authoring Basic Concepts*, it is not a beginner's guide or a manual. It expects the following:

- ▶ You are familiar with the Report Studio environment, components, and terminologies
- ▶ You know how to add items on the report page and open various explorers and panes
- ▶ You can locate the properties window and know how to test run the report

Based on my personal experience, I will recommend this chapter to new developers with two days to two months of experience. If you have more experience with Report Studio, you might want to jump to the next chapter.

In the most raw terminology, a report is a bunch of rows and columns. The aim is to extract the right rows and columns from the database and present them to the users. The selection of columns drive what information is shown in the report, and the selection of rows narrow the report to a specific purpose and makes it meaningful. The selection of rows is controlled by **filters**. Report Studio provides three types of filtering: **detail**, **summary**, and **slicer**. **Slicers** are used with dimensional models and will be covered in a later chapter (*Chapter 7, Working with Dimensional Models*). In the first recipe of this chapter, we will cover when and why to use the detail and summary filters.

Once we get the correct set of rows by applying the filters, the next step is to present the rows in the most business-friendly manner. Grouping and ordering plays an important role in this. The second recipe will introduce you to the sorting technique for grouped reports.

With grouped reports, we often need to produce subtotals and totals. There are various types of aggregation possible. For example, average, total, count, and so on. Sometimes, the nature of business demands complex aggregation as well. In the third recipe, you will learn how to introduce aggregation without increasing the length of the query. You will also learn how to achieve different aggregation for subtotals and totals.

The fourth recipe will build upon the filtering concept you have learnt earlier. It will talk about implementing the `if-then-else` logic in filters. Then we will see some techniques on data formatting, creating sections in a report, and hiding a column in a crosstab.

Finally, the eighth and last recipe of this chapter will show you how to use prompt's **Use Value** and **Display Value** properties to achieve better performing queries.

The examples used in all the recipes are based on the **GO Data Warehouse (query)** package that is supplied with IBM Cognos 10.1.1 installation. These recipe samples can be downloaded from the Packt Publishing website. They use the relational schema from the **Sales and Marketing (query) / Sales (query)** namespace.

The screenshots used throughout this book are taken from Cognos Version 10.1.1 and 10.2.

Summary filters and detail filters

Business owners need to see the sales quantity of their product lines to plan their strategy. They want to concentrate only on the highest selling product for each product line. They would also like the facility to select only those orders that are shipped in a particular month for this analysis.

In this recipe, we will create a list report with product line, product name, and quantity as columns. We will also create an optional filter on the Shipment Month Key. Also, we will apply correct filtering to bring up only the top selling product per product line.

Getting ready

Create a new list report based on the GO Data Warehouse (query) package. From the **Sales (query)** namespace, bring up **Products / Product line**, **Products/Product**, and **Sales fact / Quantity** as columns, the way it is shown in the following screenshot:

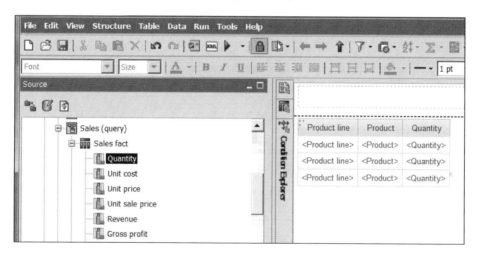

How to do it...

Here we want to create a list report that shows product line, product name, and quantity, and we want to create an optional filter on Shipment Month. The report should also bring up only the top selling product per product line. In order to achieve this, perform the following steps:

1. We will start by adding the optional filter on Shipment Month. To do that, click anywhere on the list report on the Report page. Then, click on **Filters** from the toolbar.

2. In the **Filters** dialog box, add a new detail filter. In the **Create Filter** screen, select **Advanced** and then click on **OK** as shown in the following screenshot:

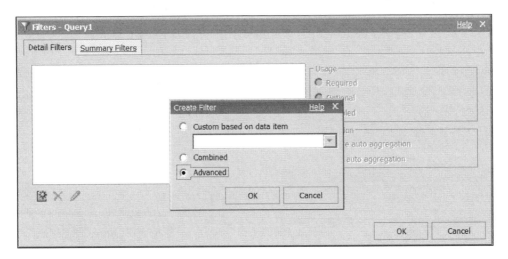

3. By selecting **Advanced**, we will be able to filter the data based on the fields that are not part of our list table like the Month Key in our example as you will see in the next step.

4. Define the filter as follows:

```
[Sales (query)].[Time (ship date)].[Month key (ship date)]
= ?ShipMonth?
```

5. Validate the filter and then click on **OK**.

6. Set the usage to **Optional** as shown in the following screenshot:

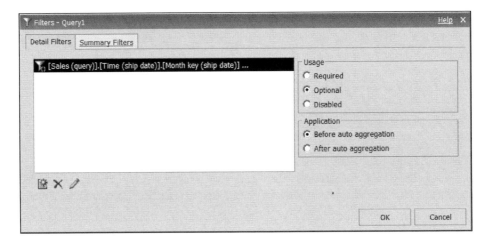

7. Now we will add a filter to bring only the highest sold product per product line. To achieve this, select **Product line** and **Product** (press *Ctrl* and select the columns) and click on the group button from the toolbar. This will create a grouping as shown in the following screenshot:

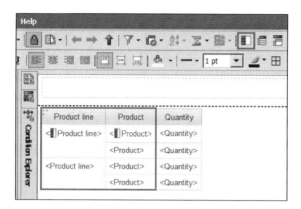

8. Now select the list and click on the filter button again and select **Edit Filters**. This time go to the **Summary Filters** tab and add a new filter. In the **Create Filter** screen, select **Advanced** and then click on **OK**.

9. Define the filter as follows:

   ```
   [Quantity] = maximum([Quantity] for [Product line]).
   ```

10. Set usage to **Required** and set the scope to **Product** as shown in the following screenshot:

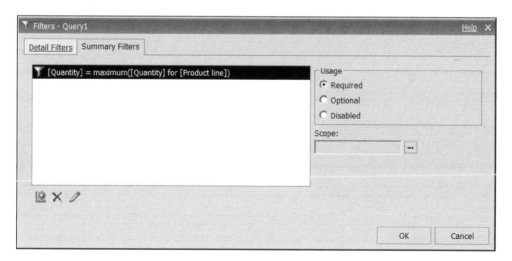

11. Now run the report to test the functionality. You can enter `200401` as the Month Key as that has data in the Cognos supplied sample.

How it works...

Report Studio allows you to define two types of filters. Both work at different levels of granularity and hence have different applications.

The detail filter

The detail filter works at the lowest level of granularity in a selected cluster of objects. In our example, this grain is the **Sales entries** stored in **Sales fact**. By putting a detail filter on Shipment Month, we are making sure that only those sales entries which fall within the selected month are pulled out.

The summary filter

In order to achieve the highest sold product per product line, we need to consider the aggregated sales quantity for the products.

If we put a detail filter on quantity, it will work at sales entry level. You can try putting a detail filter of `[Quantity] = maximum([Quantity] for [Product line])` and you will see that it gives incorrect results.

So, we need to put a summary filter here. In order to let the query engine know that we are interested in filtering sales aggregated at product level, we need to set the **SCOPE** to **Product**. This makes the query engine calculate `[Quantity]` at product level and then allows only those products where the value matches `maximum([Quantity]` for `[Product line])`.

There's more...

When you define multiple levels of grouping, you can easily change the scope of summary filters to decide the grain of filtering.

For example, if you need to show only those products whose sales are more than 1000 and only those product lines whose sales are more than 25000, you can quickly put two summary filters for code with the correct **Scope** setting.

Before/after aggregation

The detail filter can also be set to apply after aggregation (by changing the application property). However, I think this kills the logic of the detail filter. Also, there is no control on the grain at which the filter will apply. Hence, Cognos sets it to before aggregation by default, which is the most natural usage of the detail filter.

See also

- The *Implementing if-then-else in filtering* recipe

Sorting grouped values

The output of the previous recipe brings the right information back on the screen. It filters the rows correctly and shows the highest selling product per product line for the selected shipment month.

For better representation and to highlight the best-selling product lines, we need to sort the product lines in descending order of quantity.

Getting ready

Open the report created in the previous recipe in Cognos Report Studio for further amendments.

How to do it...

In the report created in the previous recipe, we managed to show data filtered by the shipment month. To improve the reports look and feel, we will sort the output to highlight the best-selling products. To start this, perform the following steps:

1. Open the report in Cognos Report Studio.
2. Select the **Quantity** column.
3. Click on the **Sort** button from the toolbar and choose **Sort Descending**.
4. Run the report to check if sorting is working. You will notice that sorting is not working.
5. Now go back to Report Studio, select **Quantity**, and click on the **Sort** button again. This time choose **Edit Layout Sorting** under the **Other Sort Options** header.

6. Expand the tree for **Product line**. Drag **Quantity** from **Detail Sort List** to **Sort List** under **Product line** as shown in the following screenshot:

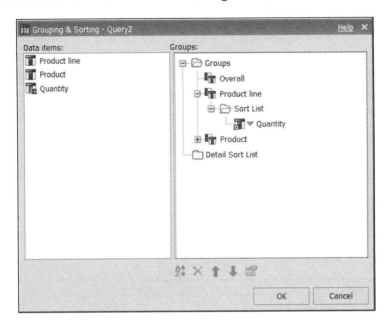

7. Click on the **OK** button and test the report. This time the rows are sorted in descending order of **Quantity** as required.

How it works...

The sort option by default works at the detailed level. This means the non-grouped items are sorted by the specified criteria within their own groups.

Here we want to sort the product lines that are grouped (not the detailed items). In order to sort the groups, we need to define a more advanced sorting using the **Edit Layout Sorting** options shown in this recipe.

There's more...

You can also define sorting for the whole list report from the **Edit Layout Sorting** dialog box. You can use different items and ordering for different groups and details.

You can also choose to sort certain groups by the data items that are not shown in the report. You need to bring only those items from source (model) to the query, and you will be able to pick it in the sorting dialog.

Aggregation and rollup aggregation

Business owners want to see the unit cost of every product. They also want the entries to be grouped by product line and see the highest unit cost for each product line. At the end of the report, they want to see the average unit cost for the whole range.

Getting ready

Create a simple list report with **Products / Product line**, **Products/Product**, and **Sales fact / Unit cost** as columns.

How to do it...

In this recipe, we want to examine how to aggregate the data and what is meant by rollup aggregation. Using the new report that you have created, this is how we are going to start this recipe:

1. We will start by examining the **Unit cost** column. Click on this column and check the **Aggregate Function** property.
2. Set this property to **Average**.
3. Add grouping for **Product line** and **Product** by selecting those columns and then clicking on the **GROUP** button from the toolbar.
4. Click on the **Unit cost** column and then click on the **Summarize** button from the toolbar. Select the **Total** option from the list.
5. Now, again click on the **Summarize** button and choose the **Average** option as shown in the following screenshot:

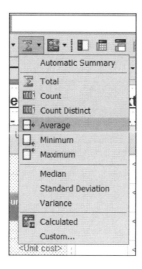

6. The previous step will create footers as shown in the following screenshot:

7. Now delete the line with the **<Average (Unit cost)>** measure from **Product line**. Similarly, delete the line with the **<Unit cost>** measure from **Summary**. The report should look like the following screenshot:

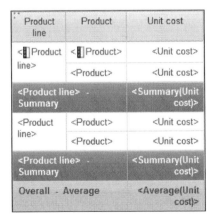

8. Click on the **Unit cost** column and change its **Rollup Aggregate Function** property to **Maximum**.

9. Run the report to test it.

How it works...

In this recipe, we have seen two properties of the data items related to aggregation of the values.

The aggregation property

We first examined the aggregation property of unit cost and ensured that it was set to average. Remember that the unit cost here comes from the sales table. The grain of this table is sales entries or orders. This means there will be many entries for each product and their unit cost will repeat.

We want to show only one entry for each product and the unit cost needs to be rolled up correctly. The aggregation property determines what value is shown for unit cost when calculated at product level. If it is set to **Total**, it will wrongly add up the unit costs for each sales entry. Hence, we are setting it to **Average**. It can be set to **Minimum** or **Maximum** depending on business requirements.

The rollup aggregation property

In order to show the maximum unit cost for product type, we create an aggregate type of footer in step 4 and set the **Rollup Aggregation** to **Maximum** in step 8.

 Here we could have directly selected **Maximum** from the **Summarize** drop-down toolbox. But that creates a new data item called **Maximum (Unit Cost)**. Instead, we ask Cognos to aggregate the number in the footer and drive the type by rollup aggregation property. This will reduce one data item in query subject and native SQL.

Multiple aggregation

We also need to show the overall average at the bottom. For this we have to create a new data item. Hence, we select unit cost and create an **Average** type of aggregation in step 5. This calculates the **Average (Unit Cost)** and places it on the product line and in the overall footer.

We then deleted the aggregations that are not required in step 7.

There's more...

The rollup aggregation of any item is important only when you create the aggregation of **Aggregate** type. When it is set to automatic, Cognos will decide the function based on the data type, which is not preferred.

It is good practice to always set the aggregation and rollup aggregation to a meaningful function rather than leaving them as automatic.

Implementing if-then-else in filters

Business owners want to see the sales quantity by order methods. However, for the **Sales Visit** type of order method, they want a facility to select the retailer.

Therefore, the report should show quantity by order methods. For the order methods other than **Sales Visit**, the report should consider all the retailers. For **Sales Visit** orders, it should filter on the selected retailer.

Getting ready

Create a simple list report with **Order method / Order method type** and **Sales fact / Quantity** as columns. Group by **Order method** to get one row per method and set the **Aggregation** for quantity to **Total**.

How to do it...

In this recipe, we need to create a filter that will be used to select the retailer if the **Order method** is **Sales Visit**. We will check what will happen if we use the if then else construction inside the filter and how to overcome any problems with the following steps:

1. Here we need to apply the retailer filter only if **Order method** is **Sales Visit**. So, we start by adding a new detail filter.

2. Define the filter as follows:

    ```
    if ([Order method type]='Sales visit') then ([Sales (query)].
    [Retailers].[Retailer name] = ?SalesVisitRetailer?).
    ```

3. Validate the report. You will find multiple error messages.

4. Now change the filter definition to:

    ```
    (([Order method type]='Sales visit') and ([Sales (query)].
    [Retailers].[Retailer name] = ?SalesVisitRetailer?)) or ([Order
    method type]<>'Sales visit').
    ```

5. Validate the report and it should be successful.

6. Run the report and test the data.

How it works...

The if else construct works fine when it is used in data expression. However, when we use it in a filter, Cognos often doesn't like it. It is strange because the filter is parsed and validated fine in the expression window and if else is a valid construct.

The workaround for this problem is to use and...or clauses as shown in this recipe. The if condition and corresponding action item are joined with the and clause. The else part is taken care of by the or operations with the reverse condition (in our example, Order Method <> 'Sales Visit').

There's more...

You need not use both and and or clauses all the time. The filtering in this example can also be achieved by this expression:

```
-([Sales (query)].[Retailers].[Retailer name] = ?SalesVisitRetailer?)
```

or

```
([Order method]<>'Sales visit')
```

Depending on the requirement, you need to use only or, only and, or the combination of and...or.

Make sure that you cover all the possibilities.

Formatting data – dates, numbers, and percentages

Virtually all reports involve displaying numerical information. It is very important to correctly format the numbers. In this recipe, we will create a report which formats dates, numbers, and percentages.

Date transformation and formatting are important in business reports. We will see two ways of displaying **MONTH-YEAR** from the Shipment Date Key. We will apply some formatting to a numeric column and will also configure a ratio to be displayed as a percentage.

Getting ready

Create a simple list report with **Products / Product line**, **Products / Product type**, and **Time (ship date) / Date (ship date)** as columns from the **Sales (query)** namespace.

Also, add **Quantity, Unit price**, and **Unit cost** from the **Sales fact Query Subject**.

Create a grouping on **Product line** and **Product type**.

How to do it...

In this recipe, we will check how to apply different formats on the data items.

1. We will start by formatting the date column we have (check in Cognos 8).

2. Select the **Time (ship date)** / **Date (ship date)** column and open **Data Format** from the **Properties** pane. Open the **Data Format** dialog box by clicking on the **Browse** button next to the **Data Format** property.

3. Choose the format type **Date**, set **Date Style** to **Medium**, and set **Display Days** to **No**, as shown in the following screenshot:

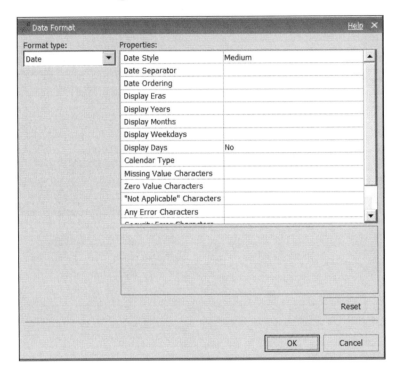

4. Now select the **Quantity** column in the report. Choose **Data Format** from property and open the dialog box again.

5. This time select **Number** as the type and set the different properties as required. In our example recipe, we will set the **Number of Decimal Points** to **2** and use **brackets () as a Negative Sign Symbol**.

6. Finally, we will add the ratio calculation to the report. For that, add a new query calculation and define it as follows:

```
[Unit price]/[Unit cost]
```

7. Select this column and from the **Data Format** property dialog box, set it as **Percent**. Choose % as the **Percentage Symbol** and set the **Number of Decimal Places** to **2**. Also, set the **Divide by Zero Characters** to **N/A**.

8. Run the report to test it.

How it works...

In this recipe, we are trying multiple techniques. We are checking how dates can be formatted to hide certain details (for example, days) and how to change the separator. Also, we have tested formatting options for numbers and the percentage.

Date format

Here, we started by setting the data format for the **Month Year** column as **date** for display purposes. We have set the display days to **No** as we only want to display **MONTH-YEAR**.

Numerical format

This is straightforward. The quantity column is displayed with two decimal points and negative numbers are displayed in brackets as this is what we have set the data formatting to.

The % margin

The ratio of unit price to unit cost is calculated by this item. Without formatting, the value is simply the result of a division operation. By setting the data format to **Percent**, Cognos automatically multiplies the ratio by 100 and displays it as a percentage.

There's more...

Please note that ideally the warehouse stores a calendar table with a **Date** type of field; this is made available through the Framework model. Also, we are assuming here that you need to see the shipment month. So, you want to see the **MONTH-YEAR** format only and we are hiding the days.

Using the data format options, you can do a lot of things. Assume that you don't have a date field in your data source but instead you have just a date key and you want to display the year and month as we did in our recipe. For that, create a new query calculation and use the following expression:

```
[Sales (query)].[Time (ship date)].[Day key (ship date)]/10000
```

Now set the **Data Format** to **Number** with the following options:

  ▸ Set the **No of decimal places** field to **2**
  ▸ Set the **Decimal separator** to -
  ▸ Set **Use thousand separator** to **No**

Run the report to examine the output. You will see that we have gotten rid of the last two digits from the day key and the year part is separated from the month part by a hyphen. This is not truly converted to **MONTH-YEAR**, but conveys the information as shown in the following screenshot:

Product line	Product type	Date (ship date)	MonthYear2	Quantity	Unit price	Unit cost	Ratio
Camping Equipment	Cooking Gear	Jan 2004	2004-01	155,066.00	44.56	25.95	172%
		Jan 2004	2004-01	43,604.00	41.02	24.76	166%
		Jan 2004	2004-01	17,994.00	79.68	47.10	169%
		Jan 2004	2004-01	3,263.00	46.42	25.63	181%
		Jan 2004	2004-01	1,088.00	3.66	0.85	431%
		Jan 2004	2004-01	2,592.00	82.99	49.47	168%
		Jan 2004	2004-01	4,149.00	22.81	14.33	159%
		Jan 2004	2004-01	5,800.00	26.86	17.19	156%
		Jan 2004	2004-01	478.00	54.93	34.97	157%
		Feb 2004	2004-02	411.00	66.77	46.38	144%
		Feb 2004	2004-02	1,571.00	23.80	15.93	149%
		Feb 2004	2004-02	96,456.00	45.20	26.09	173%
		Feb 2004	2004-02	37,947.00	52.55	30.39	173%
		Feb 2004	2004-02	37,992.00	39.68	22.34	178%
		Feb 2004	2004-02	15,894.00	44.48	27.14	164%
		Feb 2004	2004-02	10,536.00	68.78	40.58	169%
		Feb 2004	2004-02	15,119.00	67.25	43.79	154%
		Feb 2004	2004-02	6,811.00	54.46	27.70	197%
		Feb 2004	2004-02	2,278.00	47.00	30.45	154%
		Feb 2004	2004-02	3,236.00	51.29	33.00	155%

The advantage here is that the numerical operation is faster than converting the numerical key to DATE. We can use similar techniques to cosmetically achieve the required result.

Creating sections

Users want to see the details of orders. They would like to see the order number and then a small table showing the details (product name, promotion, quantity, and unit sell price) within each order.

Getting ready

Create a simple list report with **Sales order / Order number**, **Products / Product**, **Sales fact / Quantity**, and **Sales fact / Unit sale price** as columns.

How to do it...

Creating sections in a report is helpful to show a data item as the heading of a section. When you run the report, separate sections appear for each value. There is a way to reconstruct the report, and this is how to do it:

1. Click on the **Order number** column. Hit the **Section** button on the toolbar as shown in the following screenshot:

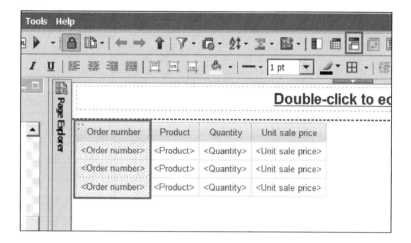

2. You will see that Report Studio automatically creates a header for **Order number** and moves it out of the list.

3. Notice that the **Order number** field is now grouped as shown in the following screenshot:

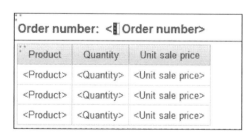

4. Run the report to test it.

How it works...

The information we are trying to show in this report can also be achieved by normal grouping on order number. That will bring all the related records together. We can also set an appropriate group/level span and sorting for better appearance.

However, in this recipe, I want to introduce another feature of Report Studio called **section**.

When you create a section on a column, Report Studio automatically does the following:

- ▸ It creates a new list object and moves the current report object (in our case, the existing list) inside that. This is report nesting. Both the inner and outer objects use the same query.
- ▸ It creates grouping on the column selected for section, which is **Order number** in this case. It also creates a group header for that item and removes it from the inner list.
- ▸ It formats the outer list appropriately. For example, hiding the column title.

There's more...

Some of the advantages of creating sections are as follows:

1. As mentioned earlier, Report Studio does a lot of the work for you and gives you a report that looks more presentable. It makes the information more readable by clearly differentiating different entities; in our case, different orders. You will see mini-lists or tables, one for each **Order number**, as shown in the following screenshot:

2. As the outer and inner queries are the same, there is no maintenance overhead.

> ▸ The *Creating a nested report – defining the master-detail relationship* recipe in *Chapter 2, Advanced Report Authoring*

Hiding columns in crosstabs

Users want to see sales figures by periods and order method. We need to show monthly sales and the yearly total sales. The year should be shown in the **Year total** row and not as a separate column.

Getting ready

Create a crosstab report with **Sales fact** / **Quantity** as a measure. Drag **Time/Year** and **Month** on rows, **Order method** / **Order method type** on column as shown in the following screenshot, and create aggregation on measure:

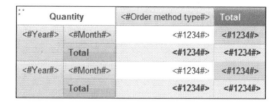

Add a total for the **Month** and **Order method type** then define appropriate sorting if required.

How to do it...

In this recipe, we want to hide the year from the crosstab and show it only in the report as a year total. To do this, perform the following steps:

1. First, let's identify the issue. If you run the report as it is, you will notice that the year is shown to the left of the months. This consumes one extra column. Also, the yearly total doesn't have a user friendly title as shown in the following screenshot:

Quantity		Fax	Telephone	Mail	E-mail	Web	Sales visit	Special	Total
2012	September	27,499	38,064	526	37,050	1,981,004	86,973		2,171,116
	February	29,376	44,974	28,100	43,337	1,943,343	145,864		2,234,994
	January	27,435	55,613	7,913	32,927	1,536,501	153,751	2,539	1,816,679
	August	25,324	62,001	538	24,865	1,967,747	90,213	372	2,171,060
	November	8,239	37,326	647	40,717	1,943,112	80,697		2,110,738
	April	18,567	53,730	19,448	36,894	1,767,412	131,971	1,135	2,029,157
	October	30,948	67,931	1,205	45,074	1,954,052	144,222		2,243,432
	March	19,551	80,643	10,727	13,382	1,818,226	93,205	7,380	2,043,114
	June	33,076	89,531	16,887	42,176	2,222,216	115,187	391	2,519,464
	July	10,002	48,463	6,502	37,677	1,887,573	135,596		2,125,813
	December	9,044	38,513	819	31,048	2,035,793	126,429	63	2,241,709
	May	10,173	67,878	26,307	23,902	1,997,152	107,360	1,742	2,234,514
	Total	249,234	684,667	119,619	409,049	23,054,131	1,411,468	13,622	25,941,790
2010	December	36,482	274,401	30,177	112,578	1,154,802	183,539	45,820	1,837,799
	February	68,025	362,630	45,286	246,832	628,555	236,249	19,914	1,607,491
	March	76,427	340,363	59,902	163,708	767,058	229,202	28,691	1,665,351
	November	57,006	307,864	28,665	109,995	1,002,751	150,371	32,826	1,689,478
	June	57,082	406,120	49,635	212,068	905,745	195,526	32,637	1,858,813
	January	41,558	373,573	61,037	246,150	545,897	299,605	36,396	1,604,216
	July	92,102	275,612	34,616	150,439	869,339	306,237	22,338	1,750,683

2. We will start by updating the title for the yearly total row. Select the **<Total(Month)>** crosstab node. Change its **Source Type** to **Data Item Value** instead of **Data Item Label** and choose **Year** as the **Data Item Value**.

3. Run the report and check that the yearly total is shown with the appropriate year as shown in the following screenshot:

Quantity		Fax	Telephone	Mail	E-mail	Web	Sales visit	Special	Total
2012	September	27,499	38,064	526	37,050	1,981,004	86,973		2,171,116
	February	29,376	44,974	28,100	43,337	1,943,343	145,864		2,234,994
	January	27,435	55,613	7,913	32,927	1,536,501	153,751	2,539	1,816,679
	August	25,324	62,001	538	24,865	1,967,747	90,213	372	2,171,060
	November	8,239	37,326	647	40,717	1,943,112	80,697		2,110,738
	April	18,567	53,730	19,448	36,894	1,767,412	131,971	1,135	2,029,157
	October	30,948	67,931	1,205	45,074	1,954,052	144,222		2,243,432
	March	19,551	80,643	10,727	13,382	1,818,226	93,205	7,380	2,043,114
	June	33,076	89,531	16,887	42,176	2,222,216	115,187	391	2,519,464
	July	10,002	48,463	6,502	37,677	1,887,573	135,596		2,125,813
	December	9,044	38,513	819	31,048	2,035,793	126,429	63	2,241,709
	May	10,173	67,878	26,307	23,902	1,997,152	107,360	1,742	2,234,514
2012		**249,234**	**684,667**	**119,619**	**409,049**	**23,054,131**	**1,411,468**	**13,622**	**25,941,790**
2010	December	36,482	274,401	30,177	112,578	1,154,802	183,539	45,820	1,837,799
	February	68,025	362,630	45,286	246,832	628,555	236,249	19,914	1,607,491
	March	76,427	340,363	59,902	163,708	767,058	229,202	28,691	1,665,351
	November	57,006	307,864	28,665	109,995	1,002,751	150,371	32,826	1,689,478
	June	57,082	406,120	49,635	212,068	905,745	195,526	32,637	1,858,813
	January	41,558	373,573	61,037	246,150	545,897	299,605	36,396	1,604,216
	July	92,102	275,612	34,616	150,439	869,339	306,237	22,338	1,750,683

4. Now we need to get rid of the year column on the left edge. For that, click on the **Unlock** button in the Report Studio toolbar. The icon should change to an open lock (unlocked).

5. Now select the **<#Year#>** text item (not the whole cell) and delete it.

6. Select the empty crosstab node left after deleting the text. Change its **Padding** to **0** pixels in all directions.

7. Run the report and you will see the following screenshot:

Quantity	Fax	Telephone	Mail	E-mail	Web	Sales visit	Special	Total
September	27,499	38,064	526	37,050	1,981,004	86,973		2,171,116
February	29,376	44,974	28,100	43,337	1,943,343	145,864		2,234,994
January	27,435	55,613	7,913	32,927	1,536,501	153,751	2,539	1,816,679
August	25,324	62,001	538	24,865	1,967,747	90,213	372	2,171,060
November	8,239	37,326	647	40,717	1,943,112	80,697		2,110,738
April	18,567	53,730	19,448	36,894	1,767,412	131,971	1,135	2,029,157
October	30,948	67,931	1,205	45,074	1,954,052	144,222		2,243,432
March	19,551	80,643	10,727	13,382	1,818,226	93,205	7,380	2,043,114
June	33,076	89,531	16,887	42,176	2,222,216	115,187	391	2,519,464
July	10,002	48,463	6,502	37,677	1,887,573	135,596		2,125,813
December	9,044	38,513	819	31,048	2,035,793	126,429	63	2,241,709
May	10,173	67,878	26,307	23,902	1,997,152	107,360	1,742	2,234,514
2012	249,234	684,667	119,619	409,049	23,054,131	1,411,468	13,622	25,941,790
December	36,482	274,401	30,177	112,578	1,154,802	183,539	45,820	1,837,799
February	68,025	362,630	45,286	246,832	628,555	236,249	19,914	1,607,491
March	76,427	340,363	59,902	163,708	767,058	229,202	28,691	1,665,351
November	57,006	307,864	28,665	109,995	1,002,751	150,371	32,826	1,689,478
June	57,082	406,120	49,635	212,068	905,745	195,526	32,637	1,858,813
January	41,558	373,573	61,037	246,150	545,897	299,605	36,396	1,604,216
July	92,102	275,612	34,616	150,439	869,339	306,237	22,338	1,750,683

As you can see the year column on the left is now successfully hidden.

How it works...

When we want to hide an object in Report Studio, we often set its **Box Type** property to **None**. However, in this case, that was not possible.

Try setting the **Box Type** of the year column to **None** and run the report. It will look like the following screenshot:

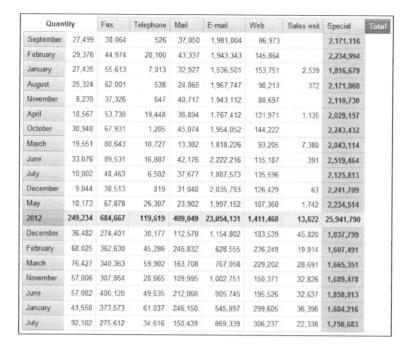

Quantity		Fax	Telephone	Mail	E-mail	Web	Sales visit	Special	Total
September	27,499	38,064	526	37,050	1,981,004	86,973		2,171,116	
February	29,376	44,974	28,100	43,337	1,943,343	145,864		2,234,994	
January	27,435	55,613	7,913	32,927	1,536,501	153,751	2,539	1,816,679	
August	25,324	62,001	538	24,865	1,967,747	90,213	372	2,171,060	
November	8,239	37,326	647	40,717	1,943,112	80,697		2,110,738	
April	18,567	53,730	19,448	36,894	1,767,412	131,971	1,135	2,029,157	
October	30,948	67,931	1,205	45,074	1,954,052	144,222		2,243,432	
March	19,551	80,643	10,727	13,382	1,818,226	93,205	7,380	2,043,114	
June	33,076	89,531	16,887	42,176	2,222,216	115,187	391	2,519,464	
July	10,002	48,463	6,502	37,677	1,887,573	135,596		2,125,813	
December	9,044	38,513	819	31,048	2,035,793	126,429	63	2,241,709	
May	10,173	67,878	26,307	23,902	1,997,152	107,360	1,742	2,234,514	
2012	249,234	684,667	119,619	409,049	23,054,131	1,411,468	13,622	25,941,790	
December	36,482	274,401	30,177	112,578	1,154,802	183,539	45,820	1,837,799	
February	68,025	362,630	45,286	246,832	628,555	236,249	19,914	1,607,491	
March	76,427	340,363	59,902	163,708	767,058	229,202	28,691	1,665,351	
November	57,006	307,864	28,665	109,995	1,002,751	150,371	32,826	1,689,478	
June	57,082	406,120	49,635	212,068	905,745	195,526	32,637	1,858,813	
January	41,558	373,573	61,037	246,150	545,897	299,605	36,396	1,604,216	
July	92,102	275,612	34,616	150,439	869,339	306,237	22,338	1,750,683	

As you can see, the cells have shifted to the left leaving the titles out of sync. This is most often the problem when Report Studio creates some merged cells (in our case, for the aggregations).

The solution to this is to format the column in such a way that it is hidden in the report as we have seen in this recipe.

There's more...

This solution works best in HTML output. The Excel output still has a column on the left with no data in it.

You might need to define the background color and bordering as well so as to blend the empty column with either the page background on the left or the month column on the right.

Prompts – display value versus use value

In order to achieve the best performance with our queries, we need to perform filtering on the numerical key columns. However, the display values in the prompts need to be textual and user friendly.

In this recipe, we will create a filter that displays the product line list (textual values) but actually filters on the numerical codes (Product_Line_Code).

Getting ready

Create a simple list report with **Products/Product** and **Sales fact / Quantity** as columns.

How to do it...

In this recipe, we will create a prompt and examine the differences between using the display value and the use value.

1. Open **Page Explorer** and click on the **Prompt Pages** folder. Drag a new page from **Toolbox** under **Prompt Pages**.

2. Double-click on the newly created prompt page to open it for editing.

3. From the toolbox, drag **Value Prompt** to the prompt page. This will open a wizard.

4. Set the prompt name to `ProductLine` and then click on **Next** as shown in the following screenshot:

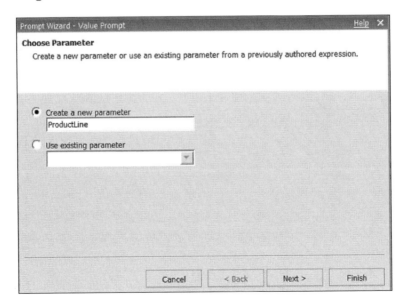

5. Keep the **Create a parameterized filter** option checked. For **Package item**, choose **Sales (query) / Products / Product line code**. Click on **Next** as shown in the following screenshot:

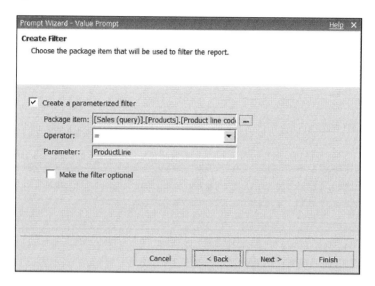

6. Keep the **Create new query** option checked. Give the query name as `promptProductLine`.

7. Under **Value to display**, select **Sales (query) / Products / Product line**.

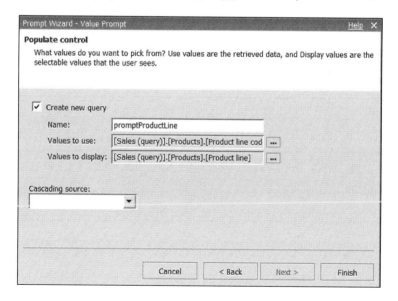

8. Click on the **Finish** button. Run the report to test it.

How it works...

When you drag a prompt object from **Toolbox**, Report Studio launches the prompt wizard.

In the first step, you choose the parameter to be connected to the prompt. It might be an existing parameter (defined in the query filter or framework model) or a new one. In this recipe, we chose to create a new one.

Then, you are asked whether you want to create a filter. If there is already a filter defined, you can uncheck this option. In our example, we are choosing this option and creating a filter on **Product line code**. Please note that we have chosen the numerical key column here. Filtering on a numerical key column is a standard practice in data warehousing as it improves the performance of the query and uses the index.

In the next step, Report Studio asks where you want to create a new query for the prompt. This is the query that will be fired on the database to retrieve prompt values. Here we have the option to choose a different column for the display value.

In our recipe, we chose **Product line** as the display value. **Product line** is the textual or descriptive column that is user friendly. It has one-to-one mapping with the **Product line code**. For example, Camping Equipment has a product line code of 991.

Hence, when we run the report, we see that the prompt is populated by Product line names, which makes sense to the users. Whereas if you examine the actual query fired on the database, you will see that filtering happens on the key column; that is, Product line code.

There's more...

You can also check the generated SQL from Report Studio.

In order to do that, navigate to the **Tools | Show Generated SQL/MDX** option from the menu as shown in the following screenshot:

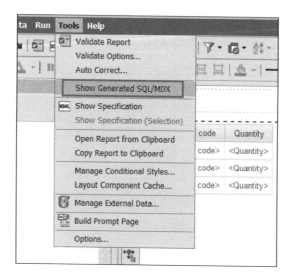

It will prompt you to enter a value for the product line code (which is proof that it will be filtering on the code).

Enter any dummy number and examine the query generated for the report. You will see that the Product line code (key column) is being filtered for the value you entered.

So, now you know how the prompt display values and use values work.

If you ever need to capture the prompt value selected by the user in expressions (which you will often need for conditional styling or drill-throughs), you can use the following two functions:

> **ParamDisplayValue (parameter name)**: This function returns the textual value which represents the display value of the prompt. In our example, it will be the product line that was selected by the user.

> **ParamValue (parameter name)**: This function returns the numeric value which represents the use value of the prompt. In our example, it will be the Product line code for the product line selected by the user.

2
Advanced Report Authoring

In this chapter, we will cover the following:

- ▶ Adding cascaded prompts
- ▶ Creating a nested report – defining the master-detail relationship
- ▶ Writing back to the database
- ▶ Adding conditional formatting
- ▶ Formatting negative values
- ▶ Playing with conditional styles
- ▶ Using conditional blocks – many reports in one
- ▶ Defining drill-through from crosstab intersection
- ▶ Overriding crosstab intersection drill-through definitions

Introduction

Now as you have implemented the recipes in *Chapter 1, Report Authoring Basic Concepts* or read through them, I am confident that we are on the same page about the fundamental techniques of report authoring.

Now you know how filtering, sorting, and aggregation work. You also know how to apply data formatting, create sections, and hide columns. You are also now aware of how to add new prompts and select appropriate options in the prompt wizard.

Based on this understanding, we will now move on to some advanced topics; including cascaded prompts, nested reports, and conditional blocks. We will also examine some techniques around drill-through links. These will enable you to create professional reports as required in the current industrial environment.

Adding cascaded prompts

Business owners want to see sales made by employees. They also want the facility to limit the report to a certain region, country, or employee.

When they select a region, they would like the country pick-list to automatically reduce to the countries falling in that region. Similarly, the employee pick-list should also reduce when they pick a country.

Getting ready

Create a simple list report with **Employee name** (from the **Employee by region** query subject) and **Quantity** (from **Sales fact**).

Define appropriate grouping and sorting for **Employee name** and ensure that aggregations for **Quantity** are correctly set.

How to do it...

In this recipe we will build three prompts for **Region, Country,** and **Employee**. We will create a relationship between these prompts by making them cascading prompts. So if you change the value selected in one prompt, the data in the other prompts should change accordingly. To do this, perform the following steps:

1. We will start by creating detailed filters on the report query. Select the list report and open the filters dialog by clicking on the **Filters** button and then click on **Edit Filters**.

2. Add three detailed filters as follows:

    ❑   `[Employee name]=?Employee?`

    ❑   `[Sales (query)].[Employee by region].[Country]=?Country?`

    ❑   `[Sales (query)].[Employee by region].[Branch region]=?Region?`

3. Define all filters as **Optional** as shown in the following screenshot:

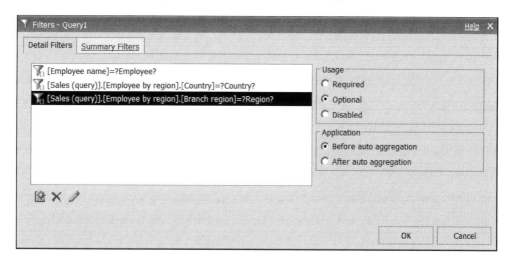

4. Now create a new prompt page. We will start by adding a prompt for **Region**.

5. Drag a new value prompt. In the prompt wizard, choose the existing parameter **Region** for it. Choose to create a new query called `Regions` for this parameter.

6. Click on the **Finish** button.

7. Now add another value prompt. Choose the existing parameter **Country** for this, and create a new query called **Countries**. On the same page, choose **Region** under the **Cascading source** as shown in the following screenshot:

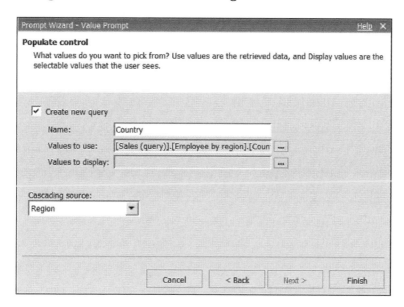

8. Similarly, add the third and last value prompt for employee. Choose **Employee** as a parameter, **Employees** as the query name, and **Country** for the **Cascading source**.

9. Select the **Region** prompt and set its **Auto-Submit** property to **Yes**. Do the same for the **Countries** prompt.

10. Run the report to test it.

How it works...

In our case, users may run the report for the whole company, select a particular region, select a region and country combination, or go all the way down to employees. We want to allow them to submit the selections at any stage. That is why we created three filters and kept them all as optional.

Even if it was mandatory for the users to select an employee, we would have kept filters for country and region. The reason is that one employee might have done sales in different countries/regions. By keeping those filters, we would ensure that the report fetches data for that employee for the selected region/country only.

Cascaded source

When we set the cascaded source property, Report Studio ensures two things. Firstly, the prompt is disabled until the cascaded source is satisfied. Secondly, when re-prompted and the cascade source is populated, the prompt values are filtered accordingly.

In our case, the **Countries** prompt remains disabled until a valid value for region is submitted. Similarly, the employee list is disabled until a valid value is submitted for countries.

There's more...

In step 9, we set the **Auto-Submit** property to **Yes** for the prompts.

Auto-Submit

When the Auto-Submit property is set to **Yes**, the prompt value is automatically submitted when the user selects one. This enables the dependent prompt to be correctly filtered and enabled.

In our recipe, **Auto-Submit** for **Region** is set to **Yes**. Hence, when you select a region, the value is automatically submitted and the **Country** prompt is enabled with the correct values populated.

This action can also be performed by a **Reprompt** button. In that case, Auto-Submit is not required.

See also

▸ The *Prompts – display value versus use value* recipe in *Chapter 1, Report Authoring Basic Concepts*

Creating a nested report – defining the master-detail relationship

Users want to see product lines, products, and corresponding unit costs. For every product, they also want to see the trend of sales over the last year.

We need to produce a list report with the required information and nest a line chart within it to show the sales trend.

Getting ready

Create a simple list report based on the **Sales (query)** namespace. Pull **Products / Product line**, **Products/Product** and **Sales fact / Unit cost** in the list.

How to do it...

To complete this recipe, we need to create a relationship between the list report created and a chart report that will be embedded into it. We can do this by defining a master-detail link between them.

1. We already have a list report that shows the product lines, products, and corresponding unit costs. Please make sure that appropriate sorting and aggregations are applied to the columns.

2. Now we will add a nested **Chart** object to show the sales trend for each product.

3. Drag a new **Chart** object from the **Toolbox** pane into the report as a column as shown in the following screenshot:

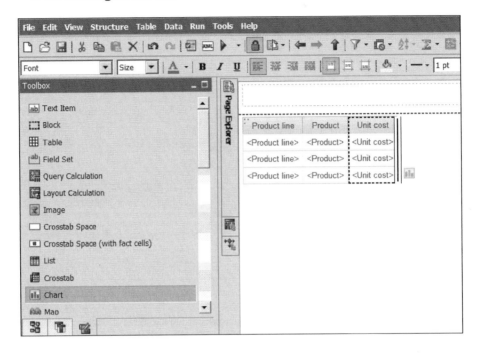

4. Choose an appropriate chart type. In this recipe, we will choose **Line with Markers**.

5. From the source pane, drag **Quantity** from **Sales fact** into the chart as the **Default measure (y-axis)**. Drag **Month key** from the **Time** dimension under **Categories (x-axis)** and **Product** from the **Products** dimension under **Series** as shown in the following screenshot:

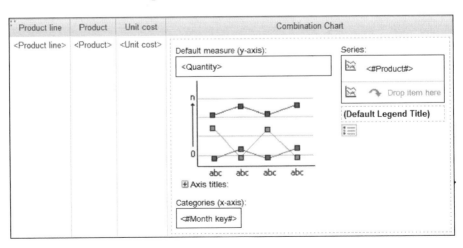

Please note that we are using the month key here in order to show the monthly figures in the correct order. Later on you can use a category label to show month names. Directly pulling the month name results in alphabetic sorting is an incorrect trend.

6. Now click anywhere on the chart and choose **Data / Master Detail Relationships** from the menu bar.

7. Create a new link and connect **Product** items from both the queries as shown in the following screenshot:

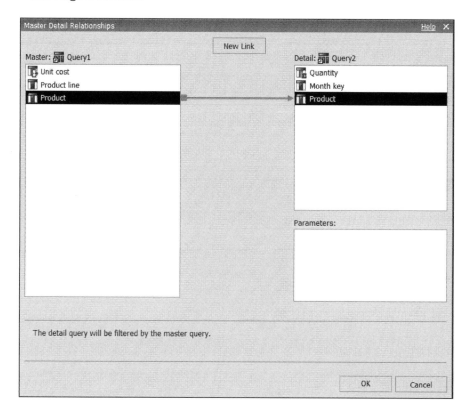

8. Click on the **OK** button to come back on the report page. Now select the **Y1 Axis** of the chart by clicking on it.

9. Change its **Use Same Range for All Instances** property to **No**.

10. Now click on the chart and click on the **Filter** button from the toolbar and then click on **Edit Filters**.

11. Define a detailed filter on **Year** from the **Time** dimension as required. In this recipe, we will hard code it to 2012. So, the filter is defined as `[Sales (query)].[Time].[Year] = 2012`.

    Though in practical cases, you would have to filter for year, rather than hard-coding.

12. Run the report to test it.

13. Update the chart properties (size, marker, color, and so on) for better presentation as shown in the following screenshot:

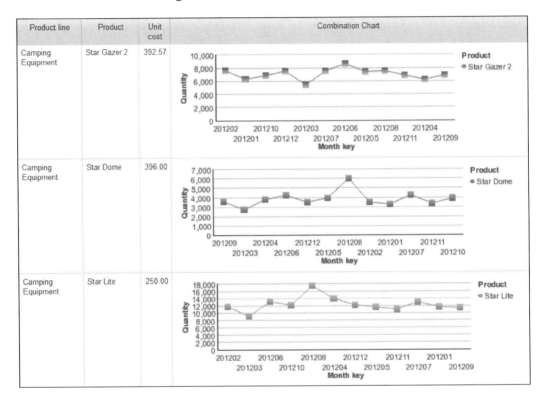

How it works...

Cognos Report Studio allows one report object to be nested within another list report. In the previous recipe, we saw that the Report Studio automatically creates nesting for us. In this recipe, we manually created nesting for finer control.

The master-detail relationship

We need to define this relationship in the following cases:

▸ When outer and inner report objects use different queries

▸ For any nesting other than a list within a list

In order to generate the report, Cognos first fires the master query on the database to retrieve the records. Then for each record, it fires the detail query with the filtering as defined in the master-detail relationship.

Hence, the detail query is executed multiple times, each time with different filtering.

As it has to retrieve very small amounts of information at a time, a page of output is returned very quickly. This is particularly useful when the report is accessed interactively.

In Report Studio, you can turn on an option from **VIEW Menu | Visual Aid | Show Master Detail Relationships**.

This will highlight the data containers that have master-detail relationships with an icon like this: 🖼. By double-clicking on the icon, you can quickly open the relationship for viewing and editing.

There's more...

By using separate queries for the outer and inner report object in nesting, we can have more control on what information is retrieved. In this example, we want to show a sales trend (chart) only for one year—we hard coded it to 2004. Hence, the chart query needs to be filtered on year.

However, the outer query (the list of product lines and products) does not need this filtering.

As you can see in the report output, there are some rows with no corresponding graph. For example, **Personal Accessories / Auto Pilot**. This means there was no selling of this product in the year 2004. If we had used the same query for the list and the chart, this row would have been filtered out resulting in loss of information (product and unit cost) to the users.

See also

We are going to explore more chart features later when we talk about the new charts in IBM Cognos 10 in *Chapter 11, Charts and New Chart Features*.

Writing back to the database

Writing back to the database is perhaps the most frequently requested functionality by business users—writing some notes or comments back to database, for a particular entry on the report. Though there is no direct functionality provided in Cognos Report Studio for this, it is still possible to achieve it by putting together multiple tools. This recipe will show you how to do that.

The business wants to see sales figures by products. They then want to write some comments for the products from the same interface. The comments need to be stored in the database for future retrieval and updating.

You will need access on the backend database and Framework Manager for this recipe.

As we are only concentrating on Report Studio in this book, we will not cover the Framework Manager options in depth. The power users and Report Studio developers need not be masters in Framework Modeling, but they are expected to have sufficient knowledge of how it works. There is often a Framework Manager Specialist or modeler in the team who controls the overall schema, implements the business rules, and defines hierarchies in the model.

Getting ready

Create a simple list report with **Product key**, **Product**, and **Sales Quantity** columns. Create appropriate sorting, aggregation, and prompts.

How to do it...

To complete this recipe, we will use a stored procedure to do the write back action to the database. This is illustrated in the following steps:

1. We will start by creating a table in the database to store the comments entered by users. For that, open your database client and create a table similar to the one shown later. In this recipe, we are using a simple table created in an MS SQL Server 2008 database using the SQL Server Management Studio. The table is defined as follows:

```
CREATE TABLE [dbo].[ProductComments](
[ProductID] [int] NOT NULL,
[Comment] [varchar](255) NULL,
```

```
CONSTRAINT [PK_ProductComments] PRIMARY KEY CLUSTERED
(
[ProductID] ASC
)WITH (PAD_INDEX  = OFF, STATISTICS_NORECOMPUTE  = OFF, IGNORE_
DUP_KEY = OFF, ALLOW_ROW_LOCKS  = ON, ALLOW_PAGE_LOCKS  = ON) ON
[PRIMARY]
) ON [PRIMARY]
```

2. After creating the table in step 1 in the backend, we will now write a stored procedure that will accept product key and comments. It will enter this information in the table and then return all the product keys and corresponding comments back as shown in the following code:

```
CREATE PROCEDURE [dbo].[InsertComment] @ProductID int, @Comments
VARCHAR(255)
AS
BEGIN
IF ((select count(*) from
[dbo].ProductComments
where ProductID = @ProductID) = 0)
INSERT INTO [dbo].ProductComments VALUES (@ProductID,@Comments)
ELSE
UPDATE [dbo].ProductComments
SET Comment = @Comments WHERE ProductID = @ProductID
END
Select ProductID,Comment from [dbo].ProductComments
GO
```

3. Please ensure that the user account used to access the database from Cognos has been given the EXECUTE permission on the stored procedure. On SQL Server, you can do that using the GRANT PERMISSION command.

4. Now open your Framework Model and import this stored procedure as a **Stored Procedure Query Subject**. You need to configure the input parameters as `Prompts`. This is shown in the following screenshot:

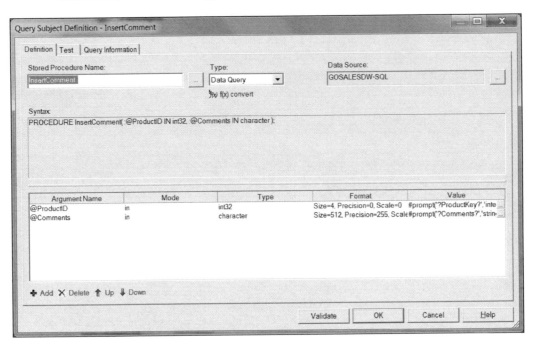

5. As you can see in the previous screenshot, **@ProductID** and **@Comments** are the stored procedure parameters. They have **in** mode which means they accept input. For the values we will be defining prompts so that we can use them inside the reports.

6. For the parameter **@ProductID**, click on the **Value** button. A new pop-up window will appear that will help you to set the value as you can see in the following screenshot:

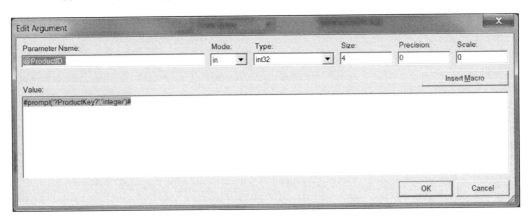

7. Click on **Insert Macro** and define the macro as `#prompt('?ProductKey?','integer')#`.

8. Repeat the same for the **@Comments** parameter and define another macro for the **?Comments?** parameter as well.

9. Verify the model and publish it.

10. Now, we will create a new report which users will use to insert the comments about the product. For that start with a new list report.

11. Use the **InsertComment** stored procedure query subject for this report. Drag **Product ID** and **Comment** columns on this report as shown in the following screenshot:

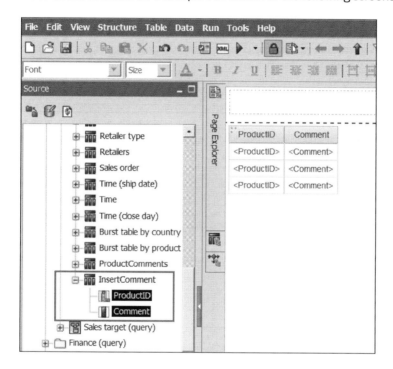

12. Create a prompt page for this report. Insert a **Text Value** type of prompt and connect it to the existing parameter called **Comment**.

13. Save this report as drill report. We will call it as `2.5 Writing Back to Database - Drill` in this recipe.

14. Now reopen the first report. Drag a **Text Item** as a new column on the report and define the text as **Insert Comment** as shown in the following screenshot:

Product key	Product	Quantity	Write Comment ..
<Product key>	<Product>	<Quantity>	Insert Comment ...
<Product key>	<Product>	<Quantity>	Insert Comment ...
<Product key>	<Product>	<Quantity>	Insert Comment ...

15. Create a drill-through from this text column by clicking on the **Drill-through** icon. Set **Writing Back to Database – Drill** as drill target. Check the option of **Open in New Window**.

16. Edit the parameter for this drill by clicking on the Edit button.

17. Map the **ProductKey** parameter to the **Product key** data item as shown in the following screenshot:

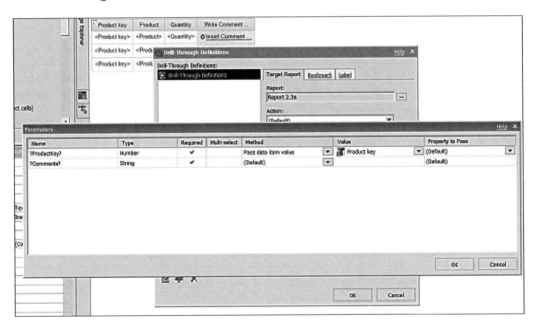

18. Run the report to test it.

How it works...

Cognos Report Studio on its own cannot perform data manipulation on a database. It cannot fire DML statements and hence can't write back to the database.

However, Cognos allows reports to execute the **Stored Procedure** and show the result output on the report page. For this, we need to import the **Stored Procedure** as query subject within Framework Manager. When a report that uses this query subject is run, Cognos executes the **Stored Procedure** on the database. We can use this opportunity to perform some DML operations, for example, inserting or updating rows in tables.

When we import a **Stored Procedure** into Framework Model, it allows us to define an expression for every input parameter. In step 3 of this recipe, we defined the parameter value to be prompts. The prompt parameters, namely **ProductKey** and **Comments** then become visible in the report.

Once we have imported the **Stored Procedure** in Framework Model, mapped the input parameter to prompts and published the package, we are ready to start with reports.

We created a report (drill report) to use the **Stored Procedure** and hence allow users to insert the comments. In this report, we created a text prompt and linked it to the **Comments** parameter. The Product Key is passed from the main report. This way we achieve the write-back to the database.

After inserting/updating the row, **Stored Procedure** returns all the records from the comments table. We show those records in a simple list report to users.

There's more...

This recipe is a very basic example to demonstrate the capability. You can build upon this idea and perform more sophisticated operations on the database.

Adding conditional formatting

The business wants to see company sales figure by years and quarters. They want to highlight the entries where sales are below 5,000,000.

We will assume that database provides us the **Quarter number** and we need to convert that to words. We will use conditional formatting for that. Also, where sales is below 5 million, the cell will be shown in red using another conditional variable.

Getting ready

Create a simple list report with **Year** and **Quarter (numeric)** columns from the **Sales / Time** query subject.

Drag **Quantity** from **Sales fact**.

Group by **Year** and sort by **Quarter**.

How to do it...

Conditional formatting is used to enhance the report visualization. Here is how we can define conditional formatting in the created report:

1. Go to **Condition Explorer** and click on **Variables** as shown in the following screenshot:

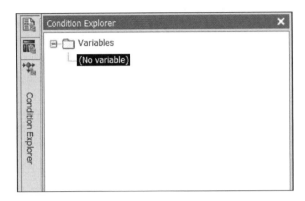

2. Drag a new string variable from the **Toolbox** pane. Define the expression as `[Query1].[Quarter (numeric)]`.

3. Change the name of the variable to `Convert_To_Words` as shown in the following screenshot:

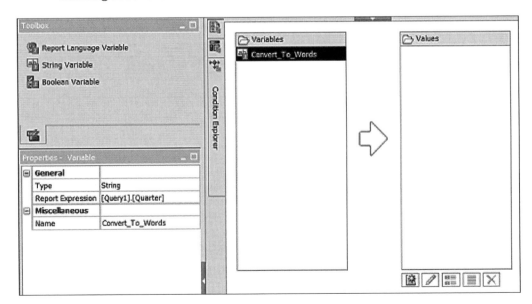

4. Add four values for the variable; the numbers 1 to 4.

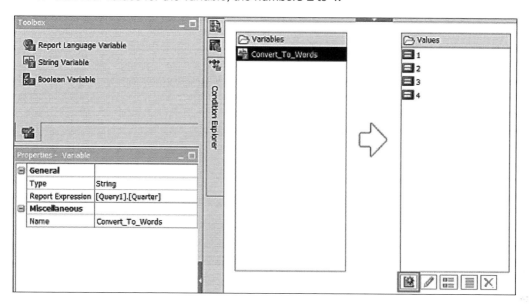

5. Now add a Boolean variable and define it as [Query1].[Quantity]< < 5000000.

6. Call this variable Show_Red as shown in the following screenshot:

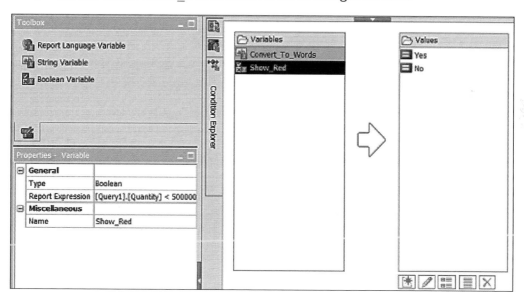

7. Go to the report page and select the **Quarter (numeric)** column. For the **Text Source Variable** property, select Convert_To_Words as the variable and then click on **OK**.

8. Select the **Quantity** column and attach Show_Red to the **Style Variable** property.

9. Now from **Conditional Explorer**, iterate through every condition for the different values of `Convert_To_Words` and set corresponding text for the **Quarter** column, that is, set **First Quarter** for value 1, and so on.

10. For `Show_Red` as yes, select the **Quantity** column and change the background color to red.

11. Run the report to test the output as shown in the following screenshot:

Year	Quarter (numeric)	Quantity
2004	First Quarter	4,877,058
	Second Quarter	5,105,718
	Third Quarter	5,110,315
	Fourth Quarter	5,081,639
2005	First Quarter	6,258,427
	Second Quarter	5,579,643
	Third Quarter	5,556,853
	Fourth Quarter	6,129,762
2006	First Quarter	6,094,787
	Second Quarter	6,783,135
	Third Quarter	6,467,989
	Fourth Quarter	6,595,879
2007	First Quarter	8,382,882
	Second Quarter	8,344,594
	Third Quarter	2,466,410

How it works...

Here we are defining conditional variables to trap the specific conditions and perform required actions on corresponding rows. There are three types of conditional variables: String, Boolean, and the report language variable.

The String variable

The String type of variable allows you to define different possible values that the expression can be evaluated into. You only need to define the values for which you need to define specific style or text. The rest are taken care of by the Other condition.

The Boolean variable

This variable is useful when the expression only evaluates into true or false and you need to format the entries accordingly.

The report language variable

This type of variable returns the language in which report is run by the user. You don't need to define any expression for this type of variable. You simply need to choose the languages for which you want to perform certain actions (like display titles in the corresponding language, or show the respective country flag in header).

Here, we have used one variable of String type and one of Boolean type.

There's more...

There are some other important style variables to check out.

The style variable property

By assigning a variable to this property, we can control the styling aspect of the object which includes font, colors, data format, visibility, and so on.

The text source variable property

By assigning a variable to this property, we can control the text/values being shown for that object. We can provide static text or a report expression. We can also choose to show value or label of another data item in the selected object.

In this example, we used this property to display the appropriate quarter name. Please note that it was possible to achieve the same result by putting a CASE statement in the data expression. However, the purpose here is to highlight the function of text source variable.

Formatting negative values

Business owners need to see the sales figures by month and their month-on-month difference.

If the difference is negative (fall in sales) then it needs to be shown in red and values need to be in brackets.

Getting ready

Create a simple list report with **Time / Year**, **Time / Month (numeric)**, and **Sales fact / Quantity** as columns.

Group **Year** and sort **Month (numeric)** in ascending order.

How to do it...

Showing negative values in red and between brackets is a familiar practice for analysts in tools like Excel. Here are the steps to create the exact same formatting in your reports:

1. Add a new query calculation to the list. Define the expression as `running-difference([Quantity])`. Call this item as **Running Difference**.

2. Open the **Data Format** properties for this calculation from the **Property** list.

3. Set the **Format type** as **Number** and the **Negative Sign Symbol** as brackets **()** as shown in the following screenshot:

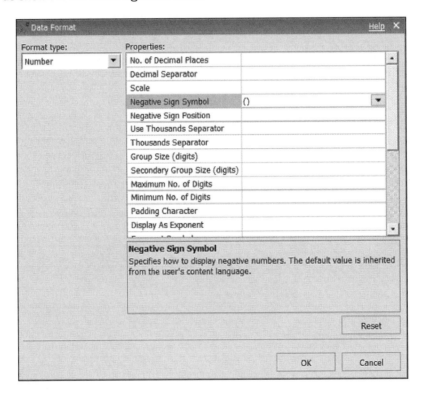

4. Now go to **Condition Explorer** and create a new condition variable of Boolean type. Define the condition as `[Query1].[Running Difference] < 0` as shown in the following screenshot:

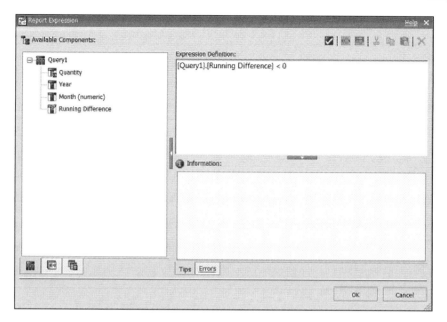

5. Call the variable as `Show_Red`.

6. Now go back to the report page and select the **Running Difference** column. Assign the `Show_Red` variable as **Style Variable** from the property list.

7. Choose the **Yes** condition for `Show_Red` from the conditional explorer. Select the **Running Difference** column from the list and open its **Font** properties.

8. Set the font foreground color to red as shown in the following screenshot:

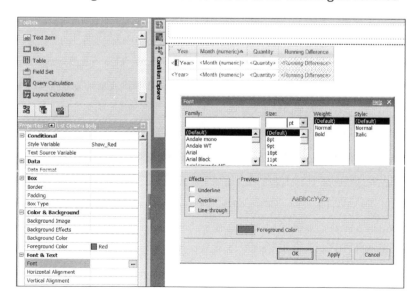

9. Click on the **OK** button. Double-click on the green bar to come out of condition. Run the report to test it as shown in the following screenshot:

Year	Month (numeric)	Quantity	Running Difference
2004	1	1,604,216	
	2	1,607,491	3,275
	3	1,665,351	57,860
	4	1,542,002	(123,349)
	5	1,704,903	162,901
	6	1,858,813	153,910
	7	1,750,683	(108,130)
	8	1,719,957	(30,726)
	9	1,639,675	(80,282)
	10	1,554,362	(85,313)
	11	1,689,478	135,116
	12	1,837,799	148,321
2005	1	2,047,167	209,368
	2	2,227,565	180,398
	3	1,983,695	(243,870)
	4	1,917,087	(66,608)
	5	1,800,216	(116,871)
	6	1,862,340	62,124
	7	1,763,284	(99,056)
	8	1,825,241	61,957

How it works...

One purpose of this recipe is to introduce you to the powerful aggregation functions provided by Cognos.

Running Difference

The **Running Difference** function returns difference between value in current row and previous row. You can also control the scope and level of aggregation.

In this example, we leave the scope and level of aggregation to default.

There are other such functions provided in Report Studio (for example, Running-Maximum, Running-Count, Running-Total, and so on) which are useful in real life scenarios.

Showing negative values in red and brackets

MS Excel has traditionally been the most popular and widely-used tool for information access. It is easy to use and gives enough power for the business users to do their analysis. It readily allows you to display negative numbers in red and brackets, which is a popular choice in the finance world.

However, under the **Data Format** options of Report Studio, you can only choose to display the negative numbers in brackets. You cannot specify to show them in different colors. Hence, we have to create a conditional variable here and define the foreground color accordingly.

Playing with conditional styles

Assume that the following report needs to be formatted such that quantities below 1.7 million will be highlighted with red background and those above 2 million should be green. Also, we need the negative values for **Running Difference** (month-on-month) to be shown in red and in brackets as shown in the following screenshot:

As shown in the previous recipe, this would have needed us to define two conditional variables. Then attach each to the corresponding column as **Style variable** to define the styles. With one more such numeric column, the author had to define one more variable and repeat the exercise. Let's see how the new conditional styling feature solves this problem.

Getting ready

Write a new report similar to the one shown in the previous screenshot.

How to do it...

In this recipe, we are going to examine more ways to enhance the reports look and feel. To do this:

1. Select the **Quantity** column on the report page.

2. Open the new **Conditional Styles** dialog box from the **Properties** pane. Alternatively, you can also click on the **Conditional Styles** button from the toolbar.

3. Create a new **Conditional Style** as shown in the following screenshot:

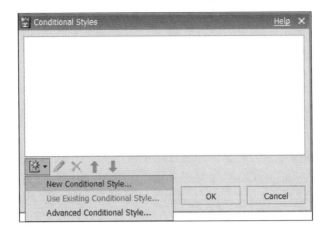

4. Choose **Quantity** to base the conditions on.

5. Define three values (0, 1.7 million, and 2 million) by hitting the new value button in the bottom-left corner. This will look like the following screenshot:

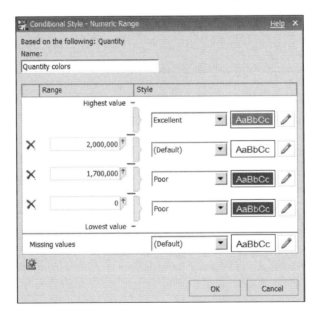

6. Also, choose corresponding styles for each range as shown in the previous screenshot. Give appropriate names, like `Quantity colors` in this case.

7. Similarly, define the negative values for the **Running Difference** column to be shown in red as shown in the following screenshot:

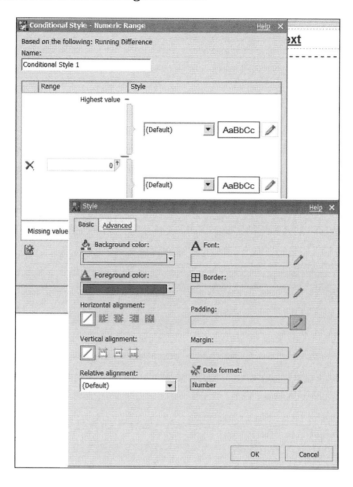

8. Run the report to test it as shown in the following diagram:

Year	Month (numeric)	Quantity	Running Difference
2004	1	1,604,216	
	2	1,607,491	3,275
	3	1,665,351	57,860
	4	1,542,002	(123,349)
	5	1,704,903	162,901
	6	1,858,813	153,910
	7	1,750,683	(108,130)
	8	1,719,957	(30,726)
	9	1,639,675	(80,282)
	10	1,554,362	(85,313)
	11	1,689,478	135,116
	12	1,837,799	148,321
2005	1	2,047,167	209,368
	2	2,227,565	180,398
	3	1,983,695	(243,870)
	4	1,917,087	(66,608)
	5	1,800,216	(116,871)
	6	1,862,340	62,124
	7	1,763,284	(99,056)
	8	1,825,241	61,957

How it works...

With this feature, we can now define styling for any column without explicitly defining the conditional variable. The styling can be based on the values on the column itself or some other column.

Also, defining actual formatting (font, color, border, and so on) for different conditions is now done within one dialog box. This is more author-friendly than traversing through the conditional variable pane and choosing each condition.

There's more...

The previous example defines very basic value-based range or classification.

You can also choose the **Advanced Conditional Style** option under this property, which allows you to define an expression and have better control over conditions than just classifying the values into ranges.

Using conditional blocks – many reports in one

The purpose of this recipe is to introduce you to a very useful and powerful control of Report Studio called **conditional blocks**.

Users want a report on sales figures. They want the facility to split the numbers by product lines, periods, or retailer region, any one at a time. For convenience purposes, they don't want three different reports, instead they are looking for one report with the facility to choose between the report types.

Getting ready

Create a report with three list objects. Define the list columns as follows:

▶ **List 1**: **Products / Product line** and **Sales fact / Quantity**

▶ **List 2**: **Time / Year**, **Time / Month**, and **Sales fact / Quantity**

▶ **List 3**: **Retailers / Region** and **Sales fact / Quantity**

Define appropriate grouping, sorting, and aggregation for all the list objects. Make sure that all objects use different queries as shown in the following screenshot:

How to do it...

Conditional blocks are very powerful tool that you can make your report very fixable. In this recipe, we will create three different reports, but using the conditional blocks we will be able to show them in the same report. The procedure to do this is as follows:

1. We will start by creating a prompt for the report type. Go to **Page Explorer** and add a prompt page.

2. Drag a new value prompt object on to the prompt page. Define parameter name as `paramReportType`. Do not define any filtering, use value, or display value in the prompt wizard.

3. Select the value prompt and open **Static Choices** from its properties.

4. Define three static choices as shown in the following screenshot:

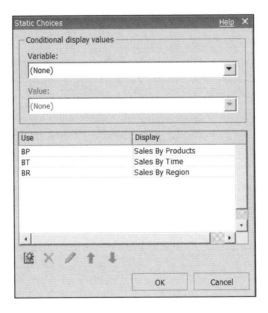

5. Now go to **Condition Explorer** and create a new `String` variable. Define it as `ParamValue('paramReportType')`.

6. Add three values for this variable as BP, BT, and BR. Change the name of the variable to `ReportType`.

7. Now go to the report page. Add a new **conditional block** from the **Toolbox** pane.

8. Select the conditional block and open the **Block Variable** dialog from the properties. Select the **ReportType** variable from the dropdown and then click on the **OK** button as shown in the following screenshot:

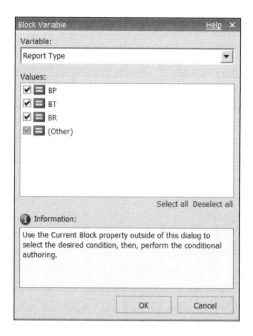

9. Now choose **BP** as the current block from properties. Select the first list object that shows sales quantity by products. Drag this list into the conditional block. Please note that you need to use the Ancestor button to select the whole list before dragging it in.

10. Change the current block property of the conditional block to **BT**. Drag the **Sales by Time** list into the block.

11. Repeat the same for **BR** and the last list object.

12. On the report page header, select the **Double click to edit text** item. Change its **Source type** property to **Report expression**.

13. Define the expression as `ParamDisplayValue('paramReportType')`.

14. Run the report to test it.

How it works...

We saw how to define conditional variables and use them as style variables in the *Adding conditional formatting* recipe. In this recipe, we are checking how conditional variables can be used with the conditional blocks.

A conditional block is a useful component that allows you to show certain objects in a certain condition. While condition styling and rendering are for finer control, conditional blocks are useful for coarse actions like showing/hiding whole object and switching between objects.

Here, all list objects use different queries. So, each query subject will have only the required columns. Depending on the prompt selection, only one of those queries will be fired and will bring back appropriate columns.

It was possible to have just one list object and one query subject with all columns, and hide/ show columns are required. This will be done using conditional styling that you have already learnt. However, the purpose of this recipe is to introduce you to conditional blocks. Now you can be creative and use the conditional blocks in real life scenarios. Please note that we checked for the use value in condition variable (`paramValue`) whereas we showed the display value (`paramDisplayValue`) in header. This topic was discussed in *Chapter 1, Report Authoring Basic Concepts*.

There's more...

It is good practice to define something to be displayed for the `Other` condition of the conditional variable. Do not keep the block empty for any condition, unless that is the requirement.

Conditional block finds its application in many scenarios. For example, showing certain warnings like **No records found** or displaying summary or detailed report depending on the user's choice.

Defining drill-through from crosstab intersection

We have a crosstab report that shows sales quantity by month and order method. We need to create drill-through links from months and sales values.

Getting ready

Create two target reports for the drill-throughs. One should take only **Month** as parameter. The other should take **Month** and **Order method type**. These reports will be referred to as Drill-1 and Drill-2 reports respectively.

Create a simple crosstab report to be used as main report. Pull **Time/Month** on rows, **Order method / Order method type** on columns, and **Sales fact / Quantity** as the measure.

How to do it...

In this recipe, you will see how to create a drill-through from a crosstab intersection to another report. To do this:

1. Select the **Month** item placed on crosstab rows. Click on the drill-through definition button from the toolbar.

2. This opens the drill-through definitions dialog. Create a new definition. Select Drill-1 as **Target Report**. Map the month parameter with the **Month** data item as shown in the following screenshot:

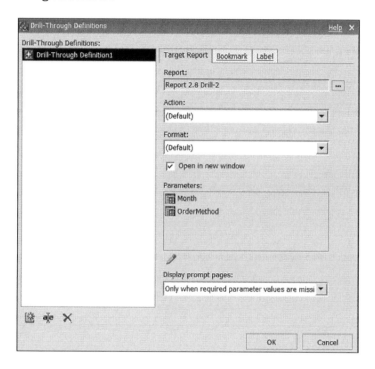

3. Now click on the unlock button from the toolbar to unlock the items.

4. Select the text item from the crosstab intersection. Hit the drill-through button again.

5. Create a drill link to Drill-2.

6. Run the report and test both the drill links.

How it works...

You will notice that when we created the drill-through from row titles (**Month**), we didn't have to unlock the items. Whereas, for the intersection, we had to unlock them.

Now try one thing. Lock the report objects again and select the crosstab intersection. Try to create drill-through now. You will see that the drill-through definition button is disabled.

For some unknown reason, Report Studio doesn't allow you to create drill-through from crosstab intersection. You need to select the **Fact cells** class or the **Text item** within the intersection. By unlocking the object, we select the text item within the intersection and create a link from there.

Another way is to right-click on the intersection and to choose **Select Fact cells**. This will enable the drill-through button and let you define one.

Overriding crosstab intersection drill-through definitions

Let us consider an extension of the last recipe. Let us say the users want to see a discontinuous crosstab as main report. Instead of just **Order method type** as a column, we need to display **Order method type** and **Product line** as columns.

The rows display **Month**. The measure is sales quantity.

The drill-through from the intersection has to go to the appropriate report depending on whether the column is **Product line** or **Order method type**.

Getting ready

Create a new drill-through target that accepts **Month** and **Product line** as parameters. We will call it Drill-3 from now on.

For the main report, we will use the same crosstab report as in the previous recipe.

How to do it...

In the previous recipe, we saw how to create a drill-through from a crosstab intersection to another report. In this recipe, we want to make it more complex. The drill-through line should be different based on the crosstab column. To complete this recipe perform the following steps:

1. We will start by creating the discontinuous crosstab on the main report. We already have the Order method on columns. Drag **Product line** also onto the crosstab, as a column. The report will look as shown in the following screenshot:

Quantity	<#Order method type#>	<#Product line#>
✿ <#Month key#>	✿ <#1234#>	✿ <#1234#>
✿ <#Month key#>	✿ <#1234#>	✿ <#1234#>

2. Now select the intersection cells under the **Product line** column.

3. From its **Properties**, set **Define contents** to **Yes**. This will make the intersection empty.

4. Unlock the report items. Drag **Quantity** from the **Data Items** pane again on the report in this empty crosstab intersection.

5. You will notice that there is no drill-through for this instance of **Quantity** as shown in the following screenshot:

Quantity	<#Order method type#>	<#Product line#>
✿ <#Month key#>	✿ <#1234#>	<Quantity>
✿ <#Month key#>	✿ <#1234#>	<Quantity>

6. Now select this instance of **Quantity** and define the drill-through definition in the same way as you did previously. The only difference will be that the target report is Drill-3, which accepts **Product line** and **Month**.

7. Run the report to test both the drill-throughs from intersections.

How it works...

In the last recipe, we saw that creating drill-through link from a crosstab intersection needs that we unlock the item and create it from the text item within.

In the case of a discontinuous report, we have different items on columns (**Product line** and **Order method type**). However, when you select the text item from intersection, Report Studio doesn't distinguish between them.

Hence, we need to select the intersection under one of the column items and set its **Define content** to **Yes**. This means we want to override the contents of this intersection and define the contents ourselves.

After changing the property, Report Studio makes that intersection empty. We can then unlock the items and drag any measure/calculation into it. We chose to drag **Quantity** again. Now Report Studio will distinguish between both the **Quantity** items (the one under **Product line** and the one under **Order method types**).

Finally, we defined drill-through to Drill-3 appropriately.

There's more...

You can also use the **Define content** option to override the information being displayed. For example, if you want to show **Revenue** under **Product lines** instead of showing **Quantity**.

This also gives you the opportunity to define styles differently and use conditional styling.

3
Using JavaScript Files – Tips and Tricks

In this chapter, we will cover the following:

- ▸ Defining dynamic default values for prompts
- ▸ Changing the title of the value prompt
- ▸ Validating textbox prompts
- ▸ Showing/hiding controls at runtime
- ▸ Selecting and submitting values automatically
- ▸ Manipulating the Date Time control
- ▸ Creating a variable width bar chart using JavaScript

Introduction

Report Studio is a web-based tool and the reports designed in Cognos Report Studio are accessed through a web browser. This allows us to do certain web page specific tasks, for example, embedding our own HTML code or JavaScript files.

Often, business users need certain functionality which is not naturally available in Cognos Report Studio. Hence, a new area has evolved in the Cognos Report Studio developer's world—"JavaScripting".

With JavaScript, we can do certain manipulations on the objects used for prompt pages. Please note that this was not officially introduced in the initial Cognos documentation. However, lately many such techniques were published on the IBM website itself.

In this chapter, we will look at some recipes that will teach you very useful and commonly required functionalities achieved using JavaScript files. All these recipes are valid for IBM Cognos 10. For Cognos 8, some code changes might be required. There are a lot of examples and reading material is available for prior versions on the Internet.

After trying these recipes, you can build upon the ideas to write more sophisticated scripts and do a lot more with your Cognos Reports. Please note that IBM doesn't directly support these techniques and does not guarantee any upward or backward compatibility. However, they are aware that developers are widely using them, and hence IBM will try to maintain most of the objects, properties, and events in the future.

The level of JavaScript that we will be using in this chapter is basic. However, if you have never used JavaScript before, I would recommend getting familiar with JavaScript basics using books or online tutorials. The website `http://www.w3schools.com/js` is a good source with a nice collection of samples and provides a quick tool to try your own scripts.

Please note that all the JavaScript-based recipes will need you to enable JavaScript in your web browser. Usually, it is enabled by default.

Defining dynamic default values for prompts

Suppose that we have a report which allows users to select a shipment month. In our data warehouse, the Time dimension (for shipment month) contains values up to the current month. However, the business owners frequently select the prior month, so they want the prompt to have the prior month selected by default.

Getting ready

Create a report that filters on the **Shipment Month Key**. Create a prompt page and add a value prompt for the **Shipment Month Key**.

How to do it...

To achieve the requirements of the business owner, we will write a JavaScript code that selects the second value from the top by default. In order to do this, perform the following steps:

1. Open the prompt page in the report and select the value prompt. Adjust the sorting property such that the **Shipment Month Keys** are populated in the descending order.

2. Let's start by adding an HTML item before the **Shipment Month** value prompt. The HTML should be `<span id = 'A1'>`.

3. Now add another HTML item after the **Shipment Month** value prompt. The HTML should be `</span>`, as shown in the following screenshot:

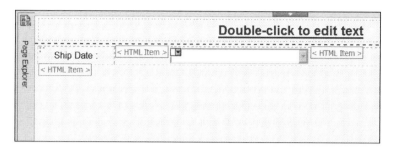

4. Now add another HTML item to the prompt page.

5. Define the item as shown in the following code:

```
<script>
var theSpan = document.getElementById("A1");
var a = theSpan.getElementsByTagName("select");   /* This stmt
return an array of all value prompts within span */
for( var i = a.length-1; i >= 0; i-- )   /* now loop through the
elements */
{ var prompts = a[i];
  if( prompts.id.match(/PRMT_SV_/))
    {prompts.selectedIndex = 3;  } /* This selects the second
  options from top */
  canSubmitPrompt();
}
</script>
```

6. Execute the report to test it.

How it works...

The logic used here is that we first sort the months in descending order and then select the second option from the top. As the values populated from the database are up to the latest month, the second value from the top will be the previous month.

As mentioned at the beginning of the chapter, Report Studio prompt pages are similar to any other HTML pages with most of the controls being standard web controls. The HTML item in Report Studio is a powerful component which allows us to embed our own code within the page generated by IBM Cognos.

When we put a JavaScript within an HTML item, it is automatically executed when the page loads.

Span

With IBM Cognos 8.3, the report viewer architecture has been majorly changed. Before IBM Cognos 8.3, it was common practice to define a NAME or ID for the prompt controls and use that to manipulate controls at runtime through JavaScript.

However, from Version 8.3 onwards, the IDs of the controls are generated randomly and are not fixed. So, it is a little difficult to get hold of a control. For this reason, we have defined a span around the control that we want to manipulate.

By wrapping the control within the span tags, we will reduce the scope of our search in JavaScript.

GetElementsByTagName

As we want to capture the value prompt within the span, we search for elements with the `select` tag within the span A1.

If we want to perform the same operation on multiple value prompts, we can put them all within the same span. The `GetElementsByTagName` function returns an array of elements with the specified tag.

SelectedIndex

Once a value prompt object is captured in a variable, we can set its `SelectedIndex` property to set the selection to the required value.

CanSubmitPrompt

In prior versions of Cognos, we used the `CheckData()` function to submit the prompt value. This means Report Studio will accept the value and the adornments will disappear. However, from Version 8.3 onwards, we can use a global `CanSubmitPrompt()` function for the same purpose.

There's more...

A more suitable example of dynamic selection is iterating through the value prompt options and selecting one based on a condition.

You can use the JavaScript functions to capture the system date and accordingly work out the prior month. Then, traverse through all the values and select an appropriate one. Similarly, you can iterate through all the prompt values and select the required entry based on value instead of hard-coding `selectedIndex` to 3.

Changing the title of the value prompt

In the previous example, the first line of the value prompt shows the data item name, that is, **Month key (ship date)** as shown in the following screenshot:

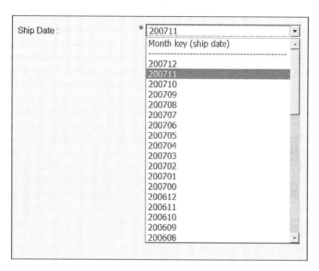

The business owners want to change this to a more generic and user-friendly text.

Getting ready

We will use the report generated in the previous recipe.

How to do it...

We need to add a line to the JavaScript from the previous recipe to change the text of first option (index 0). To do this perform the following steps:

1. Open the prompt page of the report created in the previous recipe.

2. Double-click on the HTML item that contains the JavaScript.

3. Replace the code with the following:

```
<script>
var theSpan = document.getElementById("A1");
var a = theSpan.getElementsByTagName("select");
for( var i = a.length-1; i >= 0; i-- )
  { var prompts = a[i];
  if( prompts.id.match(/PRMT_SV_/))
  { prompts.selectedIndex = 3;
```

```
        prompts.options[0].text = 'Choose Shipment Month'; /*
        This is the new line added to script */
    }
    canSubmitPrompt();
}
</script>
```

4. Run the report to test it as shown in the following screenshot:

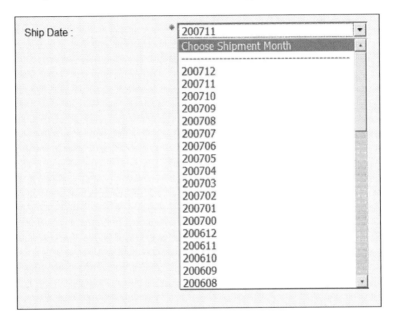

How it works...

By default, the first line of a value prompt is the name of the data item. If you define the data item expression within brackets, that is, (`[Sales (query)].[Time (ship date)].[Month key (ship date)]`) in this example, then the first line of the value prompt is populated by the parameter name.

However, there is no property within Report Studio that would allow us to put a custom title. Hence, we are using JavaScript. We already know how to capture the prompt control using the `GetElementsbyTagName` function. Once it is captured, we can manipulate the values. We change the text property of the `options[0]` element to update the first line of the prompt.

There's more...

You can also use the REMOVE() function to remove particular lines of a value prompt. It is often useful to remove the first two lines (title and separator) using the following statements:

```
Prompts.remove(0);
Prompts.remove(1);
Prompts.removeAttribute("hasLabel");
```

Validating textbox prompts

Let's say there is a report with a textbox prompt. Users are expected to enter a phone number in *(nnn) nnn-nnnn* format in that prompt.

In this recipe, we will write a code to validate the value entered by the user and submit the report only if the value entered is in the specified format.

Getting ready

Pick any report and add a textbox prompt to it. We will add a JavaScript to validate that textbox.

How to do it...

We want to make sure that the user will write the phone number in the right format. So, we will validate the number entered by the user using JavaScripts, and in case the number is not following the required format, a warning message will appear to the user with the correct format. To do this, perform the following steps:

1. Wrap the textbox prompt within a span in the same way as we did in prior recipes.

2. Add the following script to the page footer:

```
<script>
function ValidatePage()
{
   var theSpan = document.getElementById("A1");
   var a = theSpan.getElementsByTagName("input"); /* this
captures the textbox */
   for( var i = a.length-1; i >= 0; i-- )
   {
     var link = a[i];
     if( link.id.match(/PRMT_TB_/))
        {phoneRegex = /^\(\d{3}\) \d{3}-\d{4}$/; /* This is
        regular expression to allow only the strings in (nnn)
        nnn-nnnn format */
```

```
        if( !link.value.match( phoneRegex ) ) {
            alert( 'Please enter phone number in (nnn) nnn-nnnn
            format' );
            link.focus();
            link.select();
            return; }

        else {promptButtonFinish();}
        }
    }
}

/* Following is standard code to get FormWarpRequest*/
var fW = (typeof getFormWarpRequest == "function"
?getFormWarpRequest() : document.forms["formWarpRequest"]);
if ( !fW || fW == undefined) { fW = ( formWarpRequest_THIS_
?formWarpRequest_THIS_ : formWarpRequest_NS_ );}

/* This returns all elements of Button tag */var buttons = fW.getE
lementsByTagName("BUTTON");
for (var i=0; i<buttons.length; i++)
{
   if (buttons[i].id.match(/finish/)) // Capture the finish
button
   {
      if (buttons[i].onclick.toString().indexOf('finish') >
0)
      { buttons[i].onclick = ValidatePage;} /* This
overrides the FINISH button and attaches it to our function */
   }
}
</script>
```

How it works...

We first define a function called `ValidatePage()` that captures the textbox value and
checks whether it follows the required format. We are using the `match` function of JavaScript
which allows us to parse the textbox string against our regular expression. The regular
expression $\wedge\backslash(\backslash d\{3\}\backslash)$ $\backslash d\{3\}-\backslash d\{4\}\$$ allows only the string in *(nnn) nnn-nnnn* format.
Please note that there is a space in the phone number string format. If you forget this
space while trying the prompt, the number will not be considered as a correct entry.
You can read more about regular expressions and also try some on this website:
`http://www.regular-expressions.info/javascriptexample.html`.

If the textbox value matches with our regular expression, we call the `promptButtonFinish()` function to submit the prompt page. Otherwise, we show an error message and set the focus back to the textbox.

Finally, this `ValidatePage()` function is attached to the **Finish** button by the second part of the script. We capture the **Finish** button by its `TagName` (`buttons`) and ID match (`/finish/`) and then override its `OnClick` event.

Showing/hiding prompt controls at runtime

Let's say a report shows sales quantity by product line and order method type. Users need to filter on either product line or order method type, any one at a time.

They would like a facility to select which prompt they would want to filter on, and depending on the selection, the prompt should appear.

Getting ready

Create a list report that shows product lines, order method types, and sales quantity. Create two options filters—one on product lines and the other on order methods.

How to do it...

In this recipe, we will use JavaScript to control showing or hiding a prompt based on the selection of another prompt. To do this, perform the following steps:

1. We will start by creating prompts for both the filters. For that, add a prompt page and add two value prompts. Use the prompt wizard to connect them to the parameters (product line and order method).

2. Set the **Hide Adornment** property of both the prompts to **Yes**.

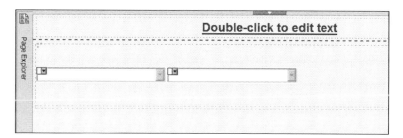

3. Now drag an HTML item just before the product line prompt. Define it as follows:

```
<Input type = radio Name = r1 title= "Click me to select
Product Line..." Value = "PL" onclick=
"radioSelect(this)">Product Line
      
<Input type = radio Name = r1 title= "Click me to select
Order Method..." Value = "OM" onclick=
"radioSelect(this)">Order Method
      
<span id = 'ProductSpan'>
```

4. Now add another HTML item between the product line prompt and order method prompt. Define it as `</span> <span id = 'OrderSpan'>`.

5. Finally, add a third HTML item after the order method prompt. Define it as follows:

```
</span>
<script>
var fW = (typeof getFormWarpRequest == "function"
?getFormWarpRequest() : document.forms["formWarpRequest"]);
if ( !fW || fW == undefined) { fW = ( formWarpRequest_THIS_
?formWarpRequest_THIS_ : formWarpRequest_NS_ );}
var theSpan = document.getElementById("ProductSpan");
var a = theSpan.getElementsByTagName('select');
for( var i = a.length-1; i >= 0; i-- )
{ var ProductBox = a[i];
  ProductBox.style.display = 'none'; }
theSpan = document.getElementById("OrderSpan");
a = theSpan.getElementsByTagName('select');
for( var i = a.length-1; i >= 0; i-- )
{ var OrderBox = a[i];
  OrderBox.style.display = 'none'; }

function radioSelect(rad)
{ if (rad.value == "PL")   /* Hide OrderBox and show
ProductBox */
  { ProductBox.style.display = '';
  OrderBox.style.display = 'none';
}
else if (rad.value == "OM") /* Hide ProductBox and show OrderBox
*/
{ ProductBox.style.display = 'none';
  OrderBox.style.display = '';
}
else /* Hide both controls */
{ ProductBox.style.display = 'none';
  OrderBox.style.display = 'none'; }
}
</script>
```

Now your prompt page will look like the following screenshot in Report Studio:

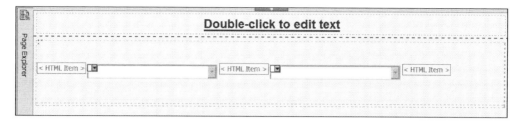

6. Run the report to test it. You will see two radio buttons. Depending on which one you select, one of the prompts will be visible as shown in the following screenshot:

How it works...

This recipe works in three parts. First, we defined the radio buttons in the HTML item. This is our own code, so we can control what happens when users select any of the radio buttons.

> Before explaining how this recipe works, I would like the readers to know that it is possible to achieve the required functionality using conditional blocks instead of JavaScript. You would use the auto-submit functionality of the radio button prompt, which will then cause the conditional block to show the appropriate prompt.

Then, we wrapped both the prompts into spans so that we can capture them in the JavaScript and manipulate the properties.

Finally, we wrote the JavaScript to toggle the display of prompts depending on the radio button selection.

There's more...

When the prompt is hidden through the `style.display` property, the adornments aren't hidden. That is why we set the adornments to off in step 2.

When the visibility of a control is turned off, the control is still present on the form and the selected value (if any) is also submitted in the query when the user clicks on the **Finish** button.

Hence, it is preferred that we reset the selection to `index(0)` when a prompt is hidden. For information on how to select a value through JavaScript, please refer to the *Defining dynamic default values for prompts* recipe of this chapter.

Selecting and submitting values automatically

A business report has numerous prompts on the prompt page. Often, users want to run a report for the latest month in the database, **Camping Equipment** product and **E-mail** as an order method.

They want a facility to either manually select values for these prompts or alternatively run the report for the previous selections on a single button click.

Getting ready

Create a list report with **Product line**, **Order method**, and **Sales Quantity** as columns.

Create optional filters on **Product line**, **Order method**, and the shipment month, that is, **Month Key (shipment date)**.

Create a prompt page with three value prompts for these filters.

How to do it...

In this recipe, we will add a custom button on the prompt page that will allow users to quickly run the report for frequently used selections. To do this, perform the following steps:

1. We will start by wrapping the prompts within a span so that they can be captured easily in JavaScript. Add one HTML tag before and one after each prompt to define the spans. Define the spans as **PL**, **OM**, and **SM** for **Product Line**, **Order Method**, and **Shipment Month** respectively. This is similar to the wrapping we have done in most of the prior recipes.

2. Add one more HTML item on the prompt page after all the prompts and define it as follows:

```
<script>
function defaultSelect()
{
  var a = document.getElementById("PL");
  var PL = a.getElementsByTagName("select");
```

```
  for( var i = PL.length-1; i >= 0; i-- ) /* Captures
Product Line prompt */
  {
    var PLBox = PL[i];
  }


  a = document.getElementById("OM");
  var OM = a.getElementsByTagName("select");
  for( var i = OM.length-1; i >= 0; i-- ) /* Captures Order
Method prompt */
  {
    var OMBox = OM[i];
  }


  a = document.getElementById("SM");
  var SM = a.getElementsByTagName("select");
  for( var i = SM.length-1; i >= 0; i-- ) /* Captures
Shipment Month prompt */
  {
    var SMBox = SM[i];
  }
  PLBox.selectedIndex = 2;
  OMBox.selectedIndex = 2;
  SMBox.selectedIndex = 4;
  canSubmitPrompt();
  promptButtonFinish();
}
</script>
<button type="button" onclick="defaultSelect()" class="bt"
style="font-size:8pt">Run for Defaults</button>
```

Now your prompt will look similar to the following screenshot in Report Studio:

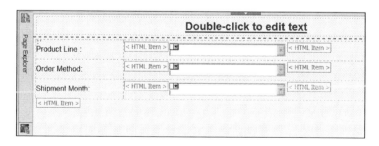

3. Run the report to test it. You should see a button that you did not see in Report Studio. When you click on the button, it will automatically select the prompt values and run the report as shown in the following screenshot:

How it works...

In this recipe, we are mixing two techniques learnt from previous recipes. In the *Defining dynamic default values for prompts* recipe, we learnt how to capture a value prompt and change its selection.

So, we are using the same technique here but instead of calling on `Page Load`, we are calling the routine when users click on the button.

Then, we are also using a function, `promptButtonFinish()`, that we used in the *Validating textbox prompts* recipe to submit the prompt.

The custom button is defined using the `<button>` tag, and as it is our own object, we can easily make it call our JavaScript function for the `on click` event.

As mentioned in the *Defining dynamic default values for prompts* recipe, you will not hardcode the `selectedIndex` in your script. Instead, you should traverse through all the prompt selection options and choose one based on the value. For example, look for **Camping Equipment** so that its order in the list won't matter.

Please refer to one such example on the IBM website at this URL: `http://www-01.ibm.com/support/docview.wss?uid=swg21343424`.

There's more...

This technique is very useful in real-life scenarios. You can define multiple buttons for different frequently used selections. It saves time for users and makes the reports convenient to use, especially when there are more than five prompts.

Manipulating the Date Time control

There is a report that allows users to filter on **Shipment Date Time** using the **Date Time** control. By default, Cognos selects the current date and midnight as the date and time.

Report Studio allows you to override this with another static default value. However, a business will usually run the report for the end of the previous business day (5 pm).

In this recipe, we will learn how to change the default date and time for a Date Time control to the end of the previous business day.

Getting ready

Create a dummy report that shows sales quantity by shipment day. Define a filter on shipment day.

How to do it...

In this recipe, we want to change the default date and time for a Date Time control to the end of the previous business day using JavaScript. To do this, perform the following steps:

1. We will start by adding a Date Time control to the report. For that, add a new prompt page.
2. From **Toolbox**, drag **Date & Time Prompt** onto the prompt page. Connect it to the **Shipment Day** filter using an appropriate parameter in the prompt wizard.
3. Now select the prompt and set its **Name** property to **ShipmentDate** as shown in the following screenshot:

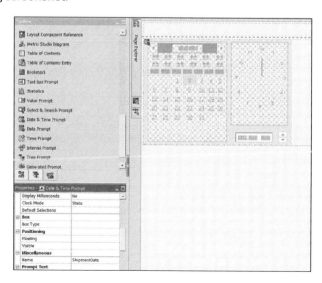

4. Now add an HTML item to the prompt footer after the **Finish** button. Define it as follows:

```
<script>
function subtractDay ()
{ var dtToday = new Date();
   var dtYesterday = new Date( dtToday - 86400000 );
   // NOTE 86400000 = 24 hours * 60 (minutes per hour) * 60
(seconds per minute) * 1000 milliseconds per second)
   var strYesterday = [dtYesterday.getUTCFullYear(),    dtYesterday.
getMonth()+1, dtYesterday.getDate()].join("-");
   return strYesterday;
}
function subtractTime ()
{ var Time = "17:00:00.000"; return Time;
}
pickerControlShipmentDate.setValue( subtractDay() );
timePickerShipmentDate.setValue( subtractTime() );
</script>
```

5. Run the report to test it. You will see that the value of the Date Time control is set to the previous day, which is 5 pm by default.

How it works...

Here we use standard JavaScript functions to work out the date of the previous day. Please note that this date is computed based on the system date on the user's machine.

Then, we apply this date to the **Date Time control** using a `pickerControl<name>` object. Also, we set the time to 5 pm using the `setValue` function of the `timePicker<name>` object.

You can similarly do more date and string manipulations to find `First of Month`, `Last of Month`, and so on. I found the following script on the Internet for generating commonly used dates:

```
<script language="JavaScript" runat="SERVER">
var today = new Date();
var thisYear = today.getYear();
var thisMonth = today.getMonth();
var thisDay = today.getDate();

function rw(s1, s2)
{
   Response.Write("<tr><td>"+s1+"</td><td>"+s2+"</td></tr>");
}
Response.Write("<table border='1'>");
rw("Today:", today.toDateString());
```

```
//Years
var fdly = new Date(thisYear - 1, 0, 1);
rw("First day of last year:", fdly.toDateString());

var ldly = new Date(thisYear, 0, 0);
rw("Last day of last year:", ldly.toDateString());

var fdty = new Date(thisYear, 0, 1);
rw("First day of this year:", fdty.toDateString());

var ldty = new Date(thisYear + 1, 0, 0);
rw("Last day of this year:", ldty.toDateString());
var fdny = new Date(thisYear + 1, 0 ,1);
rw("First day of next year:", fdny.toDateString());

var ldny = new Date(thisYear + 2, 0, 0);
rw("Last day of next year:", ldny.toDateString());

//Months
var fdlm = new Date(thisYear, thisMonth - 1 ,1);
rw("First day of last month:", fdlm.toDateString());

var ldlm = new Date(thisYear, thisMonth, 0);
rw("Last day of last month:", ldlm.toDateString());

rw("Number of days in last month:", ldlm.getDate());

var fdtm = new Date(thisYear, thisMonth, 1);
rw("First day of this month:", fdtm.toDateString());

var ldtm = new Date(thisYear, thisMonth + 1, 0);
rw("Last day of this month:", ldtm.toDateString());

rw("Number of days in this month:", ldtm.getDate())

var fdnm = new Date(thisYear, thisMonth + 1, 1);
rw("First day of next month:", fdnm.toDateString());

var ldnm = new Date(thisYear, thisMonth + 2, 0);
rw("Last day of next month:", ldnm.toDateString());

rw("Number of days in next month:", ldnm.getDate());

Response.Write("</table>");

</script>
```

There's more...

You can write more sophisticated functions to work out the previous working day instead of just the previous day.

You can mix this technique with other recipes in this chapter to tie the selection event with the button click or radio buttons; that is, a particular date/time can be selected when a user clicks on the button or selects a radio button.

Creating a variable width bar chart using JavaScript

A report shows the **Unit cost** and **Unit price** of all products. It also works out the **Profit Margin** from these two.

Business owners are naturally more interested in products with a high profit margin as well as a high unit price.

Getting ready

Create a simple list report with **Product**, **Unit cost**, and **Unit price** as columns.

Also, add a calculated item called Margin to the list to compute the profit margin and define it as follows:

```
([Unit price]-[Unit cost])/[Unit cost]
```

How to do it...

In this recipe, we will create a variable width bar chart using JavaScript that shows a bar for every product. The length of bar will indicate the profit margin, whereas the width will indicate the unit price. To do this, perform the following steps:

1. Drag a new HTML item onto the list report as a new column.

2. Unlock the report objects using the unlock button. Add four more HTML items in the column where you added the HTML item in the previous step. The report should look like the following screenshot:

Product	Unit cost	Unit price	Margin	HTML Item				
<Product>	<Unit cost>	<Unit price>	<Margin>	< HTML Item >	< HTML Item >	< HTML Item >	< HTML Item >	< HTML Item >
<Product>	<Unit cost>	<Unit price>	<Margin>	< HTML Item >	< HTML Item >	< HTML Item >	< HTML Item >	< HTML Item >
<Product>	<Unit cost>	<Unit price>	<Margin>	< HTML Item >	< HTML Item >	< HTML Item >	< HTML Item >	< HTML Item >

3. Now define the first HTML item as:

```
<script>
var barlen=100*((
```

4. For the second HTML item, set the **Source Type** to **Data Item Value** and select **Margin** as **Data Item** as shown in the following screenshot:

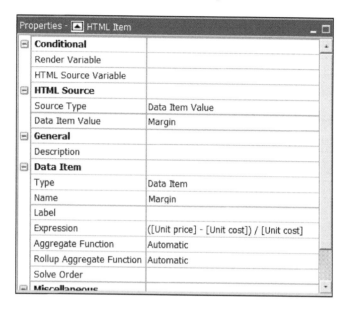

5. Define the third HTML item as:

```
));
var barheight=((
```

6. For the fourth HTML item, again set the **Source Type** to **Data Item Value**. Select **Unit price** as **Data Item**.

7. Define the fifth and last HTML item as:

```
)/10) ;
var myBar='<div style="background-color:blue; width:' +barlen+';
height:' + barheight +'"></div>' ;
document.write(myBar) ;
</script>
```

8. Run the report to see the output. It will look like the following screenshot:

Product	Unit cost	Unit price	Margin	HTML Item
Aloe Relief	1.92	5.23	1.72	
Astro Pilot	108.55	173.08	0.59	
Auto Pilot	152.98	235.00	0.54	
Bear Edge	23.53	40.52	0.72	
Bear Survival Edge	45.70	92.29	1.02	
Bella	37.17	68.22	0.84	
Blue Steel Max Putter	89.41	180.63	1.02	
Blue Steel Putter	41.20	90.95	1.21	
BugShield Extreme	2.42	7.00	1.89	
BugShield Lotion	2.33	7.00	2.00	
BugShield Lotion Lite	1.88	7.00	2.72	
BugShield Natural	1.86	6.00	2.23	
BugShield Spray	1.83	6.01	2.28	
Calamine Relief	2.83	6.00	1.12	
Canyon Mule Carryall	41.18	73.50	0.78	
Canyon Mule Climber Backpack	52.50	76.86	0.46	
Canyon Mule Cooler	15.27	32.69	1.14	
Canyon Mule Extreme Backpack	238.88	460.52	0.93	
Canyon Mule Journey Backpack	213.33	370.86	0.74	
Canyon Mule Weekender Backpack	165.91	285.89	0.72	

As you can see, **Bugshield Lotion Lite** has a huge profit margin. **Canyon Mule Extreme Backpack** might have a relatively low profit margin, but its unit price is high, and hence it is also an important product for the business.

In short, the area of the bar (width X height) indicates the importance of a product to the business.

How it works...

Report Studio has in-built chart objects which allow you to create sophisticated and detailed charts. However, in this case, we don't have any complex charting requirements.

We just want to highlight the products with high profitability. The JavaScript used in this recipe has the following structure:

```
<script>
var barlen=100*((length_driver)) ;
var barheight=((width_driver)/10) ;
var myBar='<div style="background-color:blue; width:' +barlen+';
height:' + barheight +'"></div>' ;
document.write(myBar) ;
</script>
```

We have split it into five HTML items so that the `length_driver` and `width_driver` can be replaced with any data item from the query. We have used the **Margin** and **Unit price**, but any other data item or calculation can be used as per the business requirement.

The multiplier (100) and divisor (10) are scaling factors as we need to scale the actual values to pixels. We know that **Margin** is in percentage and the value range is approximately 0.5 to 30. Hence, we multiply it by 100 to get the bars in the range of 50 to 300 pixels long. Similarly, **Unit price** is scaled down by 10 to get a bar width in the range of 5 to 50 pixels.

You can change the scaling to appropriate values in order to achieve nice looking bars.

There's more...

JavaScripts are executed on the client side within the web browser; hence there is no load on the server to produce these charts.

However, please note that this technique is useful only when users are interactively using the report in a web browser. Also, users must have JavaScripts enabled in their browser. It doesn't work for PDFs, Excel sheets, or any output format other than HTML.

4
The Report Page – Tips and Tricks

In this chapter, we will cover the following:

- ► Showing images dynamically (traffic light report)
- ► Handling the missing image issue
- ► Dynamic links to an external website (a Google Maps example)
- ► Alternating drill links
- ► Showing tooltips on reports
- ► Merged cells in Excel output
- ► Worksheet name in Excel output
- ► Conditional column titles

Introduction

In this chapter, we will look at some tricks that I have learned over the period. As mentioned before in this book, Cognos Report Studio does have a flexible structure which allows us to implement all types of complex reports and charts. Here we will see some techniques that will help us to build better and more complex reports.

Showing images dynamically (traffic light report)

In *Chapter 2, Advanced Report Authoring*, we created a report in the *Formatting negative values* recipe. This report shows the *month-on-month* difference in sales quantity.

Business wants to give this report a "dashboard" look by putting traffic light images (red, yellow, and green) in each row based on whether there is a rise in sales or a fall.

Getting ready

We will use the report based on the *Formatting negative values* recipe in *Chapter 2, Advanced Report Authoring* for this recipe.

Open that report in Cognos Report Studio and save a copy with a new name.

> Please note that you will need administrator rights on the Cognos server to complete this recipe. If the server is installed on your personal machine, you will have these rights by default.

How to do it...

In this recipe, we will use three images (red, yellow, and green) as performance indicators in the report. To do this, perform the following steps:

1. First we need to create three icons or images for red, yellow, and green. They should be already available on the Cognos server in the `{Cognos Installation}\ webcontent\samples\images` folder. If not, then create them using any image editor software or use the images supplied with this book.

2. Once you have the three images which you need to conditionally show on the report, place them on the Cognos server in the `{Cognos Installation}\webcontent\ samples\images` folder. If the folder is not there, create one.

3. Now open the report that shows the month-on-month Running Differences as shown in the following screenshot:

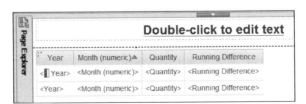

4. Insert a new image from the **Toolbox** pane on the list report as a new column.

5. Now go to **Condition Explorer** and create a new string variable. Define the expression as follows:

```
if ([Query1].[Running Difference] > 0)
then ('green')
else if ([Query1].[Running Difference] < 0)
then ('red')
else ('yellow')
```

6. Call this variable `Traffic` and define three possible values for it (red, yellow, and green).

7. Now go back to the report page. Select the image. Open its **URL Source Variable** dialog box. Choose the variable **Traffic** and click on **OK** as shown in the following screenshot:

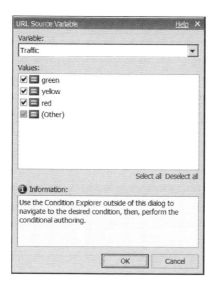

8. From **Condition Explorer**, choose the **red** condition. Now click on the image again. It will allow you to define the image URL for this condition.

9. Set the URL to `../samples/images/Red.jpg` as shown in the following screenshot:

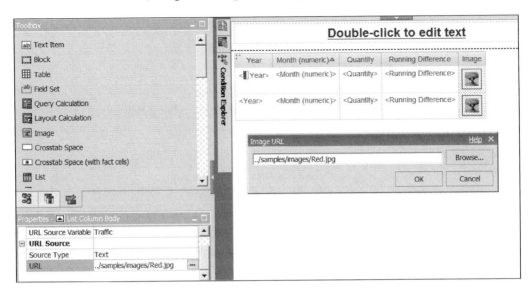

10. Similarly, define the URL for **yellow** and **green** conditions as `../samples/images/yellow.jpg` and `../samples/images/green.jpg` respectively.

11. Run the report to test it as shown in the following screenshot:

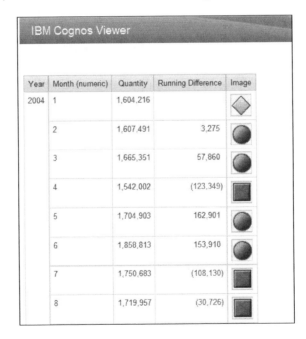

How it works...

Cognos Report Studio allows you to put the images in the report by specifying the URL of the image. The images can be anywhere on the intranet or Internet. They will be displayed properly as long as the URL is accessible from Cognos application server and gateway. You might also need to check the IIS security and allow Anonymous Read and Browse accesses if you have a problem loading the pictures saved on your local server.

In this recipe, we are using a report which already calculates the Running Difference. Hence, we just had to define a conditional variable to trap different possible conditions. The **Image** component allows us to define the URL for different conditions by attaching it to the **Traffic** variable in step 7.

There's more...

In this case, though the URL of the image changes dynamically, it is not truly 100 percent dynamic. There are three static URLs already defined in the report, and one is picked up depending on the condition.

We can also use a data item or report expression as a source of the URL value. In that case, it will be totally dynamic and based on the values coming from the database; Cognos will work out the URL of the image and display it correctly.

This is useful when the image filenames and locations are stored in the database. For example, Product Catalog kind of reports.

Please note that this recipe works fine in HTML, PDF, and Excel formats. Also, we have used relative URLs for the images, so that the report can be easily deployed to other environments where Cognos installation might be in a different location. However, we need to ensure that the images are copied in all environments in the folder mentioned in step 2.

Handling the missing image issue

In the previous recipe, we saw how to add images to the report. You will be using that technique in many cases, some involving hundreds of images (for example, Product Catalog).

There will often be a case in which the database has a URL or image name, whereas the corresponding image is either missing or inaccessible. In such a case, the web browser shows an error symbol. This looks quite ugly and needs to be handled properly.

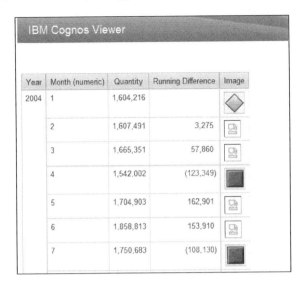

In this recipe, we will see how to handle this problem gracefully.

Getting ready

We will use the report prepared in the previous recipe. We need to delete the Green.jpg file (or rename it to something else) from the server in order to create the missing image scenario.

How to do it...

In this recipe, we will first delete the green indicator image to test the problem of a missing image then we will see how to handle it. To do this, perform the following steps:

1. In the previous recipe, we added an image object and defined its conditional URLs. We need to replace that image with an **HTML Item**. For that, unlock the report objects and delete the image component. Add an **HTML Item** in the same column as shown in the following screenshot:

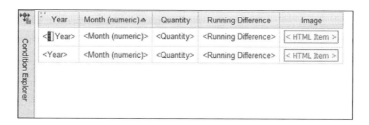

2. Select this **HTML Item** and from the **Properties** pane, set its **HTML Source Variable** to **Traffic** (please note that we already have this conditional variable in the previous recipe).

3. Now define the HTML for different conditions. Start with **red**. Choose **red** from **Conditional Explorer** and define the HTML as `<img src="../samples/images/red.jpg" alt="downsell" onError="img2txt(this)"/>`.

4. For **yellow**, define the HTML as `<img src="../samples/images/yellow.jpg" alt="No Change" onError="img2txt(this)"/>`.

5. For **green**, define HTML as `<img src="../samples/images/green.jpg" alt="Upsell" onError="img2txt(this)"/>`.

6. Now go back to the **No Variable** state by double-clicking on the green bar, and add another HTML item on the report. Put it just before the list.

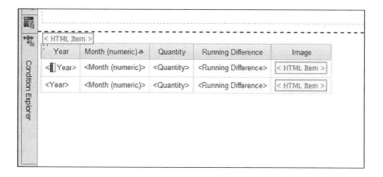

7. Define this HTML as follows:

```
<script>
function img2txt(img) {
txt = img.alt;
img.parentNode.innerHTML=txt;}
</script>
```

8. Now run the report to test it as shown in the following screenshot:

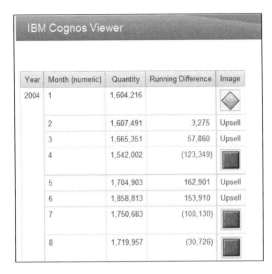

As you can see, if the image is missing, the report will now handle it gracefully and show some text instead of an error image.

How it works...

Here we are using our custom code to display the image instead of using Cognos Report Studio's in-built **Image** component.

We have pulled an HTML item onto the report and defined it to display different images depending on the condition using the `<img>` tag. This tag allows us to define an alternative text and `onError` event as well. We are using the `onError` event to call our custom made JavaScript function called `img2txt`.

This function replaces the HTML item with text which was originally defined as alternative text. Hence, if `green.jpg` is missing, this function will replace it with the text Upsell.

There's more...

As we are using HTML code and JavaScript in this technique, it works in HTML format only. This technique will be useful for a lot of graphical reports (dashboards, scorecards, online product catalogs, and so on).

Dynamic links to an external website (a Google Maps example)

In this recipe, we will introduce you to the Hyperlink component.

Let's say that a report shows retailer information by products. It shows various fields like **Retailer name**, **Contact information**, **City**, and **Postal zone**. Business wants to have a link to Google Maps that will show a retailer's place on the map using the **Postal zone** information.

As the addresses might change in the backend, the technique needs to be dynamic to pick up the latest postal zone.

Getting ready

Create a simple list report that shows retailer information by **Product lines** as shown in the following screenshot:

How to do it...

In this recipe, we will add a hyperlink to the report that will open a Google map once you have clicked on it. To do this, perform the following steps:

1. From the **Toolbox**, drag a hyperlink object onto the report as a new column as shown in the following screenshot:

2. Change its **Text** property to **Map**. Set the **URL Source Type** to **Report Expression** and define the report expression as `http://maps.google.com/maps?q=' +` `[Query1].[City (multiscript)]` as shown in the following screenshot:

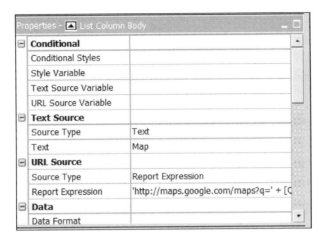

3. Run the report to test it as shown in the following screenshot:

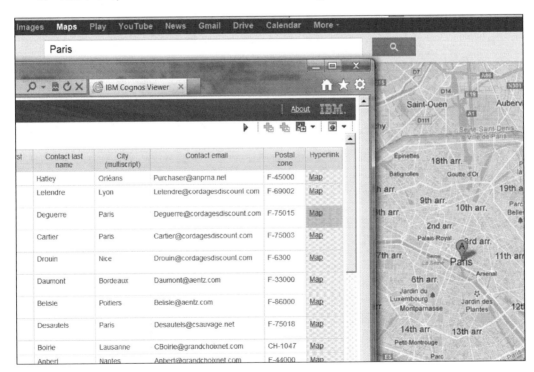

As you can see, there is a link for each retailer record. If you press *Shift* and click on the link, it will open Google Maps for the corresponding postal zone in a new window.

How it works...

Here we are using the **Hyperlink** component of Cognos Report Studio. We can define the URL as any static link.

However, for our requirements, we have defined a report expression. This allows us to provide a dynamic link which picks up the latest postal zone from the database. We are passing the postal zone to Google Maps as part of a URL.

The **Hyperlink** component works in HTML as well as Excel and PDF report formats. This object currently does not have the property to define whether the link target should open in a new window or the same window. Just clicking on the link opens the target in the same window, whereas pressing *Shift* and then clicking on the link opens the target in a new window.

There's more...

You can use this technique to call any external website that accepts parameters within a URL. You can pass multiple parameters too.

Alternating drill links

In this recipe, we will learn about a limitation of drill links and how to overcome it using Render Variable.

Let's say there is a crosstab report which shows sales quantity by month and order method. We need to provide a drill-through facility from the intersection. However, the drill-through target needs to be different depending on the order method.

If the order method is e-mail, the drill-through from the intersection should go to a report called Alternating Drill Link—Drill Report 2. For all other order methods, it should go to Alternating Drill Link—Drill Report 1.

Getting ready

Create a crosstab report to serve as the main report. Drag **Month key (ship date)** on rows, **Order method type** on columns and **Quantity** on the intersection.

Create two list reports to serve as drill reports. In the sample provided with this book, we have used two list reports for this. One accepts the **Order method** and **Month**. The other accepts only **Month** and is designed to work for the order method **E-mail**.

How to do it...

In this recipe, we will create two different drill-through links in the crosstab intersection based on the order method. To do this we will start by performing the following steps:

1. As already learnt in *Chapter 2, Advanced Report Authoring*, create a drill-through to first drill the report from the crosstab intersection as shown in the following screenshot:

Quantity	<#Order method type#>	<#Order method type#>
<#Month key (ship date)#>	✪<#1234#>	✪<#1234#>
<#Month key (ship date)#>	✪<#1234#>	✪<#1234#>

2. Now make sure that the report objects are unlocked. Select the intersection text item (which now looks like a hyperlink as there is already a drill-through defined). Hold the *Ctrl* key and drag the text to the right within a cell.

3. This should create a copy of the text item within that cell and it will look like the following screenshot:

Quantity	<#Order method type#>	<#Order method type#>
<#Month key (ship date)#>	✪<#1234#>✪<#1234#>	✪<#1234#>✪<#1234#>
<#Month key (ship date)#>	✪<#1234#>✪<#1234#>	✪<#1234#>✪<#1234#>

4. Now select this copy of the text item. Hit the drill-through button to open definitions. Delete the existing drill-through to the first report. Create a new drill to a second report. So, now we have two text items in the cell, each going to different drill reports.

5. Create a string type of **Conditional Variable**. Define it as follows:

```
if ([Query1].[Order method] = 'E-mail') then ('E-mail')
else ('Other')
```

Call it **OrderMethod** and define the two values to be **E-mail** and **Other**.

6. Now go back to the report page. Select the first text item from the intersection. Open its **Render Variable** property. Choose the **OrderMethod** variable and select to render for **Other** as shown in the following screenshot:

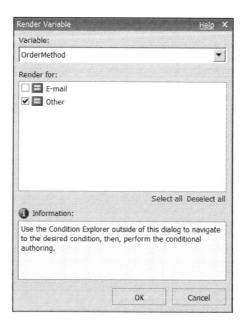

7. Similarly, define the Render Variable for the second text item, but choose to render for **E-mail**.

8. Run the report to test it. You will see that clicking on the intersection numbers opens the first drill report for any order method other than **E-mail**, whereas for the numbers under **E-mail**, the second drill report opens.

How it works...

First, let me explain the limitation here. CRS allows us to define multiple drill targets for an item. However, there is no facility to define a conditional target. So, if we define two targets, Cognos will ask users to select one at runtime.

In our scenario, we want Cognos to go straight to one of the two targets depending on the order method condition. For that, we are using the Render Variable property.

Render Variable

This property allows us to attach a conditional variable to the report object and define the conditions for which the object will be rendered.

This works best with String variables. For a Boolean type of conditional variable, rendering is possible only for 'Yes'.

Instead of defining two targets on the same text item, we are creating two text items and controlling their rendering.

There's more...

Even with a String type of conditional variable, rendering cannot be defined for the default (Other) condition. Hence, we had to define our own Other condition.

Showing tooltips on reports

A report shows all-time sales quantity by product names. As this report is used online (HTML format in a browser), the business owners think it will be handy to show **Product description** as a tooltip on the product names. When the users hover their mouse pointer over a **Product** name, a tooltip should appear describing the product.

Getting ready

Create a simple list report with **Product name**, **Product description**, and **Sales Quantity** as columns.

How to do it...

We don't want to show the **Product description** as column, but want to use the data item in further steps. To do this, perform the following steps:

1. Select the **Product description** column body. Use the **Select Ancestor** and go up one level by selecting **List Column**. In the properties you will find a property **Render**, use **No**. This will ensure that the column will not appear/render at runtime as shown in the following screenshot:

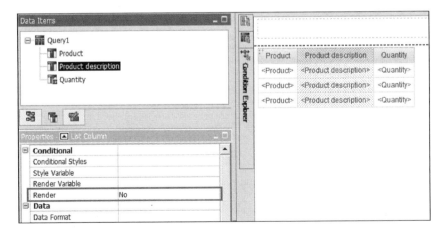

2. On the report page, unlock the report objects by hitting the unlock button.

3. Insert an **HTML Item** in the **Product** column just before the text item. Insert another **HTML Item** after the text item. This will look like the following screenshot:

4. Make the first **HTML Item** a **Report Expression** and define it as `<span title="' +` `[Query1].[Product description] + '">`.

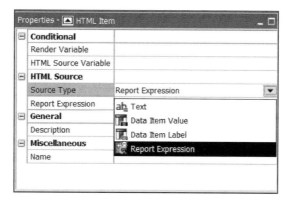

5. Make the second **HTML Item** a **Text** and define it as `</span>`.

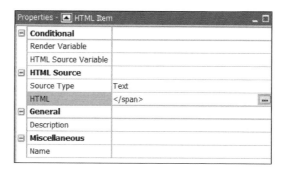

6. Run the report to test it as shown in the following screenshot:

How it works...

Here we are using our familiar and very useful HTML tag called `<span>`. We used it earlier for applying JavaScript for prompt manipulation. In this recipe, we are wrapping the product name within a span and defining its **Title** to be **Product description**.

When the report is run in a web browser, the title is shown as a **tooltip**.

There's more...

Once you define the span, you can do much more to the item. For example, overriding the mouse events. Please refer to HTML guides for this.

See also

▸ The *Defining dynamic default values for prompts* recipe in *Chapter 3, Using JavaScript Files – Tips and Tricks*

Merged cells in Excel output

Let's say there is a list report with many columns. The report shows the title in the page header. Users mostly access this report in Excel format.

When the output is generated, Cognos puts the output in the first cell (A1). This stretches the **A** column as shown in the following screenshot:

	A	B	C	D	E
1	**Merged Cells in Excel ...**				
2					
3	Product line	Product	Order method type	Quantity	Gross profit
4	Camping Equipment	Star Peg	E-mail	110,414	107,393.72
5	Personal Accessories	Polar Extreme	Sales visit	3,500	245,420.93
6	Personal Accessories	Seeker Extreme	Telephone	9,668	730,651.1
7	Camping Equipment	Canyon Mule Extreme Backpack	Sales visit	17,552	3,424,423.78
8	Personal Accessories	Edge Extreme	E-mail	12,415	402,640.85
9	Camping Equipment	TrailChef Double Flame	Special	2,529	143,686.52
10	Golf Equipment	Hailstorm Titanium Woods Set	Web	73,867	41,366,732.8
11	Personal Accessories	Seeker 35	Telephone	22,992	630,723.6
12	Camping Equipment	Hibernator Camp Cot	Sales visit	34,213	1,098,834.73
13	Outdoor Protection	Calamine Relief	Sales visit	16,586	52,577.62
14	Personal Accessories	Glacier Deluxe	Fax	2,832	96,432.44
15	Personal Accessories	Inferno	Fax	7,937	210,399.43
16	Personal Accessories	Venue	Special	1,550	46,758.04
17	Mountaineering Equipment	Firefly Charger	E-mail	8,400	247,746.17
18	Mountaineering Equipment	Husky Rope 100	Mail	1,301	129,200.86
19	Mountaineering Equipment	Husky Harness Extreme	Mail	2,515	125,203.55
20	Personal Accessories	Venue	Fax	8,518	257,094.66
21	Personal Accessories	Astro Pilot	E-mail	1,839	108,289.74

In this recipe, we will see how to get Cognos to generate merged cells so that the columns are not stretched.

Getting ready

Create a simple list report. Put a report title in the page header as shown in the following screenshot:

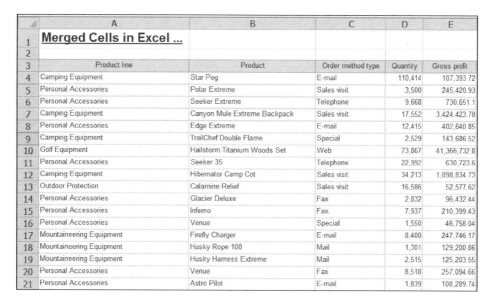

How to do it...

We can merge cells in Excel in the same way we merge columns in a table in Cognos. In fact, this is what we are going to do:

1. Insert a **Table** from the **Toolbox** pane into the report header.

2. Set the **Number of columns** to 4. Keep **Number of rows** at 1. Click on **OK** as shown in the following screenshot:

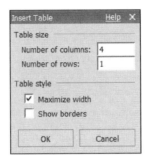

3. Now select the first cell of the table. Hold down the *Shift* key and select the last cell of the table. This should select all the cells.

4. From the menu, select **Table / Merge Cells**. This will merge four cells into one.

5. Now unlock the report objects. Select the report title and drag it inside the table.

6. Change the text font and size appropriately.

7. Run the report in Excel to test it. As you can see in the following screenshot, the title will now be shown in merged cells and hence the first column won't be stretched:

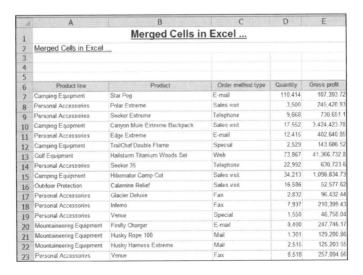

How it works...

When we merge the cells of a table, this is remembered in the report specification in the form of a column span. In our example, the report spec says `<tableCell colSpan="4">`. When the report runs in Excel form, this is properly translated into merged cells.

Not many developers know about this feature, but it is a very useful one. After reading this, you will use it in many real-life scenarios.

Worksheet name in Excel output

A report has three list report objects (Sales by products, Sales by region, and Sales by order method). Users prefer to access it in Excel format.

They want the three reports to be populated on three different sheets and each sheet should be named appropriately.

Getting ready

Create a report with three list report objects and pull appropriate columns in each.

How to do it...

To generate different names for the sheets in Excel, we will create different pages in the report and give each page a meaningful name.

1. Open **Page Explorer** and add two new **Page** objects as shown in the following screenshot:

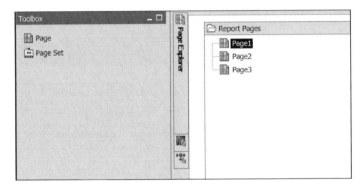

2. Select each of them and change their names in properties to the names shown in the following screenshot:

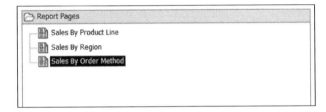

3. Now cut the list objects from the first page and paste in the appropriate report page.

4. Run the report in Excel to test it as shown in the following screenshot:

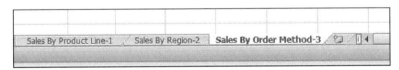

As you can see, Cognos produces three sheets with the names the same as what we defined for **Page name** (with an auto-incrementing number appended). Each sheet will show the list object we placed in the corresponding page.

How it works...

When we generate the report in Excel format, the name of the worksheet matches the name of the page in Report Studio. A number is appended to make sure that names are unique. This is useful for long reports where one page will span multiple sheets.

There's more...

There is a lot of demand for dynamic sheet names. For example, if we create a page set for products so that Cognos will create one sheet per product, then we can expect to name the sheets by products.

However, there is currently no facility to define such dynamic names (data item or expression). Some users have requested this enhancement to IBM and this feature might be added in a future version of CRS.

Conditional column titles

This recipe is meant to introduce you to the Text Source Variable property.

Let's say there is a crosstab report that shows sales quantity by order method (rows) and months (columns). We need to conditionally show full month names or short names depending on the user's selection on the prompt page.

Getting ready

Create a crosstab report with **Order method / Order method type** on rows, **Time (ship Date) / Month (ship date)** on columns and **Sales fact / Quantity** in the intersection.

Create a value prompt on the prompt page with the following specification:

- **Static choices**: Full name, short name
- **Parameter name**: Choice
- **User Interface (UI)**: Radio button group

How to do it...

To conditionally show full month names or short names depending on the user's selection on the prompt page, we will use the Text Source Variable property.

1. Go to **Conditional Explorer** and create a Boolean variable. Call it **Is_FullName** and define it as `ParamDisplayValue('choice')` = `'Full Name'` as shown in the following screenshot:

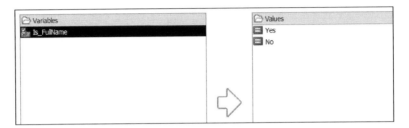

2. Now go to the report page and select **<#Month (ship date)#>** from the column titles. Set its Text Source Variable to **Is_FullName** as shown in the following screenshot:

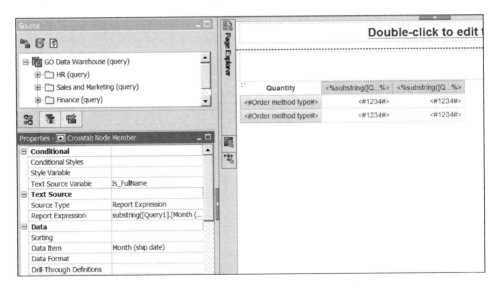

3. From **Conditional Explorer**, choose the **Yes** condition for the variable. This will allow you to define the text for columns. Set the **Source Type** to **Data Item Value**. Choose **Month (ship date)** as **Data Item Value** as shown in the following screenshot:

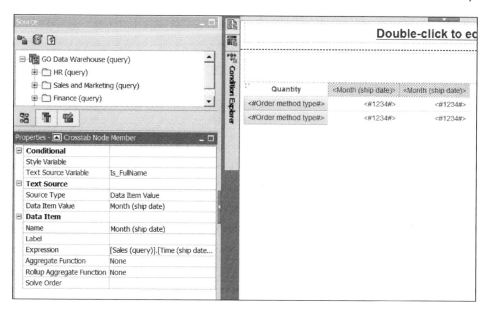

4. Now choose the **No** condition for the Boolean variable. Set the **Source Type** for the **<Month (ship date)>** column to report expression. Define the expression as `substring([Query1].[Month (ship date)], 1, 3)`.

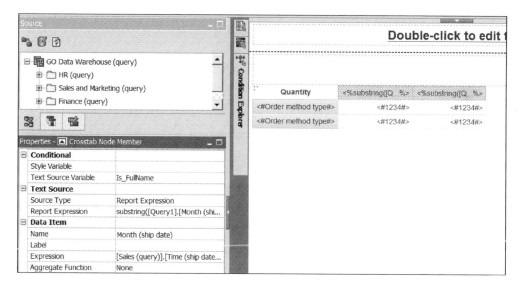

5. Run the report to test it as shown in the following screenshot:

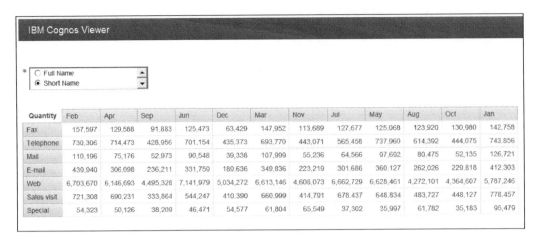

How it works...

Here we are using the Text Source Variable property to link the text being shown in column titles to the conditional variable.

Once the variable is defined for each condition, we can define a static text, a data item value, or a report expression to be shown in the column title. This way we can conditionally change the column titles. The same can be applied to row titles as well.

5
Working with XML

In this chapter, we will cover the following:

- ▶ Changing drill links quickly
- ▶ Copying and pasting drill links
- ▶ Removing references to old packages or items
- ▶ A hidden gem in XML – row level formatting

Introduction

This chapter will show some advanced techniques that involve changing the XML specification of a report outside of Report Studio. This is a common practice among experienced report writers. It often saves a lot of time and also provides some functionality that is not available in Report Studio.

You should preferably have an XML editor application for this. I have used Visual Studio. The advantages of using an XML editor are visual aids to help XML editing, automatic tag completion, tree like expand-collapse functionality, and easy search and replace. However, if you don't have one, you can also use any generic text editor for these recipes, for example, Textpad or Notepad.

If you don't know anything about XML, it would be worth reading about it on the Internet. There are websites like `www.xmlfiles.com` and `www.w3schools.com/xml` that are good for basic understanding and practice. After reading about XML and following the recipes step-by-step, you will not only be able to perform the actions covered in this chapter, but you will also have the confidence to do more XML editing of reports on your own.

It is advisable to make a backup of the original report before replacing it with an XML-modified one outside Report Studio.

Changing drill targets quickly

While the project is in the development stage, many things can change. Files are moved, folders are renamed, and sometimes requirements change. This often results in reworking.

Assume that a crosstab report has been designed to drill to a target report from an intersection. The drill target report accepts many parameters and their mapping is already done. However, because of some changes in business requirements, the drill from intersection now needs to go to another report that is already designed to accept the same parameters; we only need to change the target in the main report.

In this recipe, we will see how to quickly change the target report for a drill-through definition without the need to map the parameters again.

Getting ready

Create a crosstab report and save it as `Report 5.1 -Drill from crosstab intersection` as shown in the following screenshot:

Quantity	<#Order method type#>	<#Order method type#>
<#Month (ship date)#>	✿ <#1234#>	✿ <#1234#>
<#Month (ship date)#>	✿ <#1234#>	✿ <#1234#>

Create a drill-through link from the crosstab intersection to a list report and pass multiple values. Save this report as `Report 5.1 - Drill from crosstab intersection Drill 2` as shown in the following screenshot:

Month (ship date)	Order method type	Product line	Quantity	Unit price
<Month (ship date)>	<Order method type>	<Product line>	<Quantity>	<Unit price>
<Month (ship date)>	<Order method type>	<Product line>	<Quantity>	<Unit price>
<Month (ship date)>	<Order method type>	<Product line>	<Quantity>	<Unit price>

Create one more copy of the previous report and save it as `Report 5.1 - Drill from crosstab intersection Drill 1`.

So, now we have the folder structure.

The main report (`Report 5.1 -Drill from crosstab intersection`) has been designed to call `Report 5.1 - Drill from crosstab intersection Drill 2`. We will change it to call `Report 5.1 - Drill from crosstab intersection Drill 1` instead by editing the XML. This way we will not have to define the parameter mapping again and it will save the developer time.

How to do it...

In this recipe, we will see how to quickly change the target report for a drill-through definition without the need to map the parameters again by modifying the XML specification of the report as seen in the following steps:

1. Open the main report in Report Studio.

2. Unlock the report objects and select the crosstab intersection. Click on the **Drill-through Definition1** button on the toolbar and examine the drill-target as shown in the following screenshot:

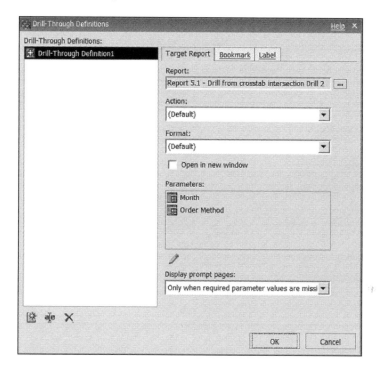

Notice that the drill-through has been designed to go to `Report 5.1 - Drill from crosstab intersection Drill 2` and pass two parameters called `Month` and `Order Method`. In real life, you will usually have many parameters passed.

3. Now close the dialog box. Navigate to the **Tools | CopyReporttoClipboard** option from the menu. This will copy the XML specification of the report on to the clipboard as shown in the following screenshot:

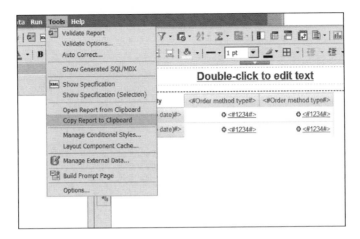

4. A pop-up screen will appear with the report XML specifications. Copy it.

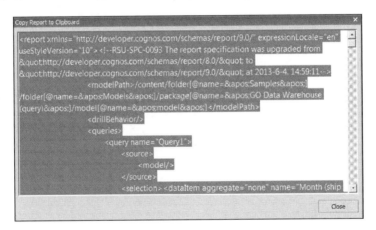

5. Note that the previous screen will appear only if you are using Firefox to open Report Studio. If you are using Internet Explorer, the XML specifications will be copied directly to the clipboard.

6. Open any text editor or XML editor and paste the XML specifications.

7. Now go to **Cognos Connection**. For the `Report 5.1 - Drill from Crosstab intersection Drill 1` report, click on the Set Properties Report 5.1 button as shown in the following screenshot:

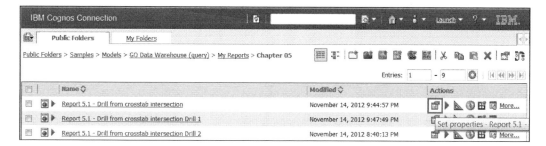

8. Click on the **View search path** link as shown in the following screenshot:

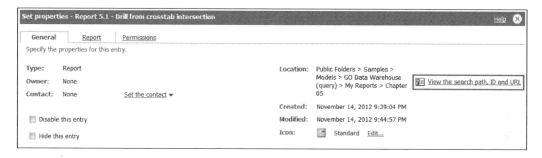

9. A dialog box will pop up with the following information. Select the content in **Search path** and copy it as shown in the following screenshot:

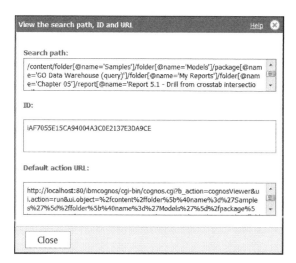

10. Go back to the XML specification pasted into the text or XML editor. Replace all the report paths referring to `Drill 2` with that of `Drill 1`. In our recipe, we will search for all instances of:

```
/content/folder[@name='Samples']/folder[@name='Models']/
package[@name='GO Data Warehouse (query)']/folder[@name='My
Reports']/folder[@name='Chapter 5']/report[@name='Report 5.1 -
Drill from crosstab intersection Drill 2']
```

And replace them with:

```
/content/folder[@name='Samples']/folder[@name='Models']/
package[@name='GO Data Warehouse (query)']/folder[@name='My
Reports']/folder[@name='Chapter 5']/report[@name='Report 5.1 -
Drill from crosstab intersection Drill 1']
```

11. Now copy the whole XML specification (the modified one) onto the clipboard.

12. Go back to Report Studio and choose the **Tools | OpenReportfromClipboard** option as shown in the following screenshot:

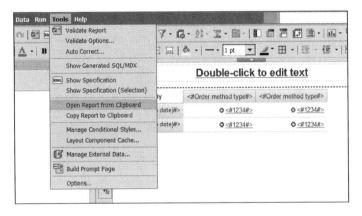

13. A pop-up screen will appear. Paste the copied report XML specifications and then click on **OK** as shown in the following screenshot:

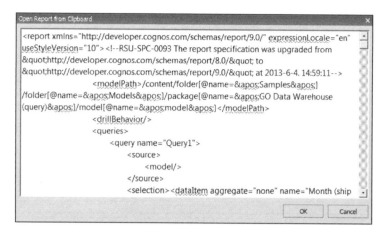

14. Check the drill-through target again. It should have changed to Drill 1 with all the parameters still mapped correctly.

15. Save the report as the main report.

How it works...

In Report Studio if you change the target report for an existing drill-through definition, then you will have to redefine the parameter mapping. Here we are achieving that without the need to redefine the mapping.

For that we are directly modifying the XML specification of the report. When we copy a report to the clipboard, its XML specification is copied. We then edit it in an editor and replace all the references to the Drill 2 report with references to the Drill 1 report.

Finally, we copy the modified XML back into Report Studio and find that the drill target is successfully changed.

There's more...

It is advisable to use an XML editor rather than a normal text editor as it allows you to understand the tags better and hence reduces the chances of errors.

You can explore the `<reportDrills>` tag more and try changing different properties/ members within that.

Copying and pasting drill links

Let's say that a crosstab report shows **Sales Quantity** by quarter (rows), **Product line** (columns), and **Order method** (columns). The report has several filters.

There is a drill-through report which is to be called from the report columns, that is, **Product line** and **Order method**. When called, all the filter values are to be passed.

In this recipe, we will see how to define the drill-through and parameter mapping once and then copy and paste it for other drills, thereby reducing the development time.

Getting ready

Create a crosstab report to be used as the main report in the following format:

Quantity	<#Product line#>	<#Order method type#>
<#Quarter#>	<#1234#>	<#1234#>
<#Quarter#>	<#1234#>	<#1234#>

Define all the prompts and filters on the main report.

Now create a drill report that will accept all these parameters and additional information like **Product line** and **Order method type**. This is shown as follows:

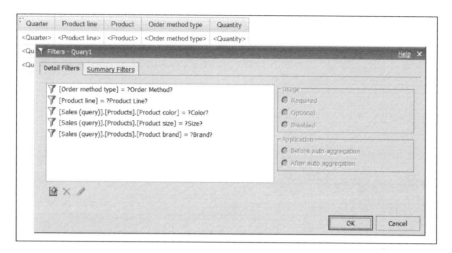

Here we will see how to define the drill-through and parameter mapping once and then copy and paste it for other drills by modifying the XML specifications. Perform the following steps:

1. We will start by defining the drill-through from the **Product line** columns. Do it manually from Report Studio in a conventional way. Map all the parameters appropriately as shown in the following screenshot:

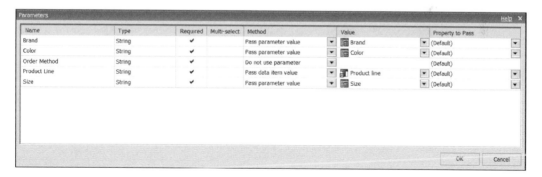

2. Now select the **Order method** column title. Create a drill-through link and select the target report. Don't do the parameter mapping. We are not doing the mapping here as we will copy and paste it in later steps to reduce development time.

3. Select **Copyreporttoclipboard** from the menu and paste it in a new file in the XML editor. I used Visual Studio for this.

4. Look for the `<drillTargetContext>` tag. This will help you find the correct drill from **Product line** (which has all the mapping done) as shown in the following screenshot:

```
<reportDrills>
    <reportDrill name="Drill-Through Definition1">
        <drillLabel>
            <dataSource>
                <staticValue/>
            </dataSource>
        </drillLabel>
        <drillTarget showInNewWindow="true">
            <reportPath path="/content/package[@name='GO Data Warehouse
                <XMLAttributes>
                    <XMLAttribute name="ReportName" value="Drill - Copy
                    <XMLAttribute name="class" value="report" output="r
                </XMLAttributes>
            </reportPath>
            <drillLinks>
                <drillLink>
                    <drillTargetContext>
                        <parameterContext parameter="Brand"/>
                    </drillTargetContext>
```

5. Copy the whole `<reportDrill>` element (that is, everything from the `<reportDrill>` tag to the `</reportDrill>` tag).

6. Now look for the `<reportDrills>` tag and search for the one that relates to order method. This one doesn't have the mapping defined.

```
<crosstabNode>
    <crosstabNodeMembers>
        <crosstabNodeMember refDataItem="Order method" edgeLocation="e2">
            <style>...</style>
            <contents>
                <textItem>
                    <dataSource>...</dataSource>
                    <reportDrills>
                        <reportDrill name="Drill-Through Definition1">
                            <drillLabel>
                                <dataSource>
                                    <staticValue/>
                                </dataSource>
                            </drillLabel>
                            <drillTarget>
                                <reportPath path="/content/package[@name='GO Da
                                    <XMLAttributes>
                                        <XMLAttribute name="ReportName" value="
                                        <XMLAttribute name="class" value="repor
                                    </XMLAttributes>
                                </reportPath>
                            </drillTarget>
                        </reportDrill>
                    </reportDrills>
```

7. Replace the existing `<reportDrill>` element with the one copied in step 5.

8. Copy the whole XML specification back onto the clipboard and open it in Report Studio. Examine the drill-through from the **Order method type** column titles.

9. You will see that the mapping is now successfully copied. Make appropriate changes to it if required. Here, we will pass **Order method** instead of **Product line** as shown in the following screenshot:

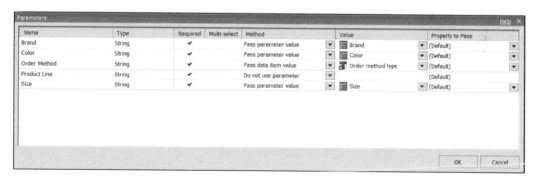

Name	Type	Required	Multi-select	Method	Value	Property to Pass
Brand	String	✔		Pass parameter value	Brand	(Default)
Color	String	✔		Pass parameter value	Color	(Default)
Order Method	String	✔		Pass data item value	Order method type	(Default)
Product Line	String	✔		Do not use parameter		(Default)
Size	String	✔		Pass parameter value	Size	(Default)

10. Run the report to test it.

How it works...

This recipe is extremely useful when a report has many drill links and lots of parameters to be passed in each drill.

We define the parameter mapping for one drill link which gets saved in the corresponding `<reportDrill>` element. Then, we define other drill links without doing the parameter mapping. Finally, we copy the XML elements in the editor which in turn copies the parameter mapping across.

There's more...

This recipe might look tedious at first glance, but once you practice it, you will realize that it is useful in big reports with loads of drill links. Also, once you examine the `<reportDrills>` element carefully from the XML, you will understand how Cognos Report Studio stores the drilling information. This will be useful in writing your own utilities to parse or modify the report specification.

Removing references to old packages or items

As a part of development, a framework model might need changes. Often, the package names, namespaces names, and query subject names are changed. Sometimes, when the report is moved to another environment, such differences are encountered. This results in errors and needs every data item to be redefined.

In this recipe, we will see how to quickly change all the references without redefining all the data items.

Getting ready

Take any report that is working fine and verify that it is without any errors. We will take one report based on the `GO Data Warehouse (query)` package.

How to do it...

The idea here is to remove these references from the XML specifications of the report. To do this, perform the following steps:

1. Open the framework model for the **GO Data Warehouse (query)** package. Change the name of the namespace being used by the report. Here we will change the **Sales(query)** namespace to **Sales Renamed**.

2. Rename the package `GO Data Warehouse (query)` to `GO Data Warehouse Renamed` and publish it.

3. Now open the report and change its package connection to `GO Data Warehouse Renamed`. This will start the report validation and will return with errors as shown in the following screenshot:

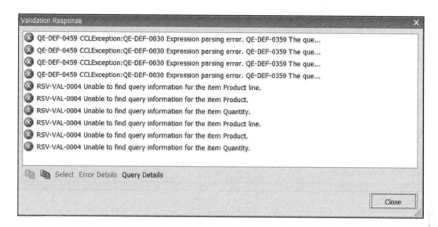

4. Examine the error detail and you will notice that it has a reference to the namespace that is now renamed as shown in the following screenshot:

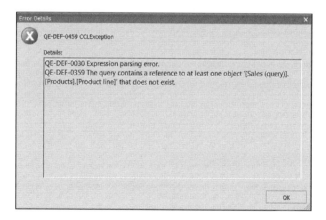

5. Now copy the report to the clipboard and paste it into your XML editor.

6. Replace all instances of `[Sales (query)]` with `[Sales Renamed]` as shown in the following screenshot:

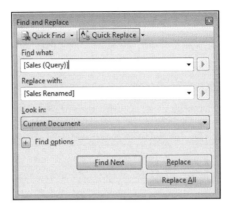

Copy the report back into the clipboard and open it in Report Studio.

7. Verify the report. It should validate with no errors.

How it works...

The data items are stored in the report specification in the following format:

```
[Namespace Name].[Query Subject].[Query Item]
```

The folder names are not stored. Hence, if the folder names are changed in the framework model, the reports can function fine without any change. However, if the namespace, query subject, or query item is renamed, the report needs to be updated.

Here, namespace is renamed. This is referenced many times in the report (in every data item). Manually changing it in Report Studio is a tedious job. Hence, we are opening the report specification in the XML editor and doing a simple search and replace operation to change all the references.

A hidden gem in XML – row level formatting

As you now know, a Cognos report is an XML definition. When you create or update a report in Report Studio, the corresponding XML tags are added to or modified in the report specification. However, it is possible to directly add or modify XML tags that are not visible from the Studio as an object or property.

In this recipe, we will see how to define crosstab row level formatting in the XML to reduce development and maintenance time.

Assume that there is a crosstab report with many measures on columns. The business wants to highlight the rows that belong to costly products (>25 units). Instead of defining conditional formatting for every column, we will modify the XML here to directly define row level formatting.

Getting ready

Create a report with product name on rows and various measures on columns, shown as follows:

	<#Quantity#>	<#Unit cost#>	<#Unit price#>	<#Unit sale price#>	<#Revenue#>	<#Gross profit#>	<#Product cost#>
<#Product#>	<#1234#>	<#1234#>	<#1234#>	<#1234#>	<#1234#>	<#1234#>	<#1234#>
<#Product#>	<#1234#>	<#1234#>	<#1234#>	<#1234#>	<#1234#>	<#1234#>	<#1234#>

How to do it...

In this recipe, we will see how to define crosstab row level formatting in the XML, which can save a lot of time during the development and maintenance of reports.

1. Define a conditional variable of Boolean type to identify costly products (which are to be highlighted in the report) as shown in the following screenshot:

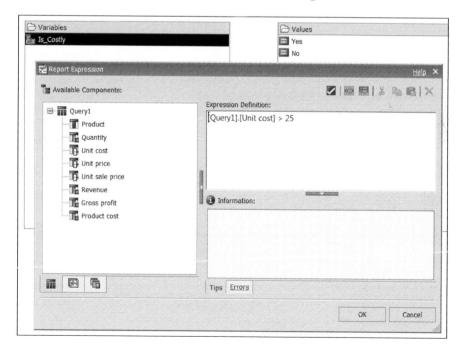

Call this variable Is_Costly.

2. Now select the first column **Quantity**. Attach the conditional variable `Is_Costly` to it as **Style variable**. Define the appropriate formatting for this column for both the conditions (**Yes** and **No**). We have already talked about defining conditional styles in prior chapters.

3. Now copy the report to the clipboard and paste in a new file in an XML editor. I have used Visual Studio for this purpose.

4. Run a search for the `<conditionalStyles>` tag. You will find this element under the **Quantity** data item.

5. Copy the whole element, that is, from `<conditionalStyles>` to `</conditionalStyles>`. This should be something as shown in the following code:

```
<conditionalStyles>
  <conditionalStyleCases refVariable="Is_Costly">
    <conditionalStyle refVariableValue="1">
      <CSS value="background-color:lime"/>
    </conditionalStyle>
  </conditionalStyleCases>
  <conditionalStyleDefault>
    <CSS value="background-color:yellow"/>
  </conditionalStyleDefault>
</conditionalStyles>
```

6. Now locate the `<crosstabRows>` element. You will see that it has a `<crosstabNodeMember>` defined for **Product**.

7. Under the **Product** crosstab node, you will find another tag called `<crosstabFactCell>`, which contains two nodes, `<contents>` and `<style>`, as shown in the following code:

```
<crosstabFactCell>
  <contents>
  <textItem><dataSource><cellValue/></dataSource></textItem>
  </contents>
  <style>
    <defaultStyles><defaultStyle refStyle="mv"/></defaultStyles>
  </style>
</crosstabFactCell>
```

8. Now replace the `<style>` tag with the `<conditionalStyles>` tag copied in step 5. The code will now look like the following:

```
<crosstabFactCell>
  <contents>
  <textItem><dataSource><cellValue/></dataSource></textItem>
  </contents>
  <conditionalStyles>
    <conditionalStyleCases refVariable="Is_Costly">
```

```
      <conditionalStyle refVariableValue="1">
        <CSS value="background-color:lime"/>
      </conditionalStyle>
    </conditionalStyleCases>
    <conditionalStyleDefault>
      <CSS value="background-color:yellow"/>
    </conditionalStyleDefault>
  </conditionalStyles>
</crosstabFactCell>
```

9. Copy the whole XML back onto the clipboard and open it in Report Studio.

10. Run the report to test it.

	Quantity	Unit cost	Unit price	Unit sale price	Revenue	Gross profit	Product cost
Mountain Man Digital	111,905	20.00	41.61	40.11	4,459,781.51	2,221,681.51	2,238,100.00
Polar Sports	229,591	58.88	122.70	118.52	26,893,295.4	13,374,977.32	13,518,318.08
Star Lite	477,692	250.00	370.13	353.20	168,191,550.48	48,768,550.48	119,423,000.00
EverGlow Kerosene	315,202	20.00	31.55	30.76	9,659,101.43	3,355,061.43	6,304,040.00
TX	596,594	103.86	190.46	190.46	112,878,735.7	51,250,678.64	61,628,057.06
Trendi	899,925	30.15	50.08	50.07	44,986,931	17,879,003.92	27,107,927.08
Trail Scout	56,575	152.90	238.00	236.88	13,068,175	4,432,506.95	8,635,668.05
Edge Extreme	315,175	80.00	119.69	112.73	35,565,705.25	10,351,705.25	25,214,000.00
Hibernator Lite	646,970	60.00	90.09	84.85	54,974,184.56	16,155,984.56	38,818,200.00
Husky Rope 50	143,333	100.91	160.00	151.38	21,727,836.8	7,264,103.77	14,463,733.03
BugShield Lotion	773,324	2.33	7.00	6.88	5,247,006.31	3,445,161.39	1,801,844.92
Single Edge	3,754,893	8.56	12.78	12.06	45,261,289.11	13,119,405.03	32,141,884.08
EverGlow Butane	117,948	40.63	67.73	64.49	7,558,900.7	2,766,673.46	4,792,227.24
Hailstorm Titanium Irons	110,668	466.57	928.53	860.58	94,940,604.6	43,780,613.33	51,159,991.27
Auto Pilot	25,369	152.98	235.00	235.00	5,961,715	2,081,421.45	3,880,293.55
Compact Relief Kit	188,018	9.03	23.00	21.98	4,054,976.36	2,352,820.06	1,702,156.30
Star Gazer 3	123,717	438.62	707.29	666.43	83,014,109.49	28,538,827.49	54,475,282.00
Canyon Mule Cooler	940,802	15.27	32.69	30.93	27,873,971.62	13,970,120.62	13,903,851.00
Husky Rope 200	64,819	370.35	574.98	544.26	35,314,312.37	11,308,595.72	24,005,716.65
Course Pro Golf and Tee Set	910,687	2.88	10.64	8.38	9,033,712.92	6,353,920.52	2,679,792.40

As you can see, the whole row is formatted based on the condition.

How it works...

In Report Studio, there is no option to select and modify the whole row in a crosstab. Hence, if we want to do any row level formatting, we need to do it for each column.

However, if you examine the XML report, you will notice that it has an element for fact cells under crosstab rows. Here, we are overriding this element and defining our own style to be applied for every fact cell within that row.

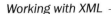

Instead of manually writing the whole conditional style code, we have first applied conditional styling on one column (**Quantity**) and then copied the same under **Crosstab rows** so that it is applied on all the columns.

There's more...

This recipe will save your development time as you don't have to define the conditional styling for every column. Also, in the future if styling needs to be changed, it can be changed from just one place rather than doing so for every column. Hence, it will save maintenance time as well.

You can also experiment with the `<crosstabColumns>` tag to style the whole column when there are multiple members on rows.

See also

► The *Formatting data – dates, numbers, and percentages* recipe in *Chapter 1, Report Authoring Basic Concepts*

6
Writing Printable Reports

In this chapter, we will cover the following:

- ▶ Controlling the container size and rows per page
- ▶ Eliminating orphan rows
- ▶ Defining page orientation and size (and overriding them for one page)
- ▶ Avoiding page title repetition
- ▶ Horizontal pagination
- ▶ Page numbering with horizontal pagination
- ▶ Choosing the output format from a prompt
- ▶ Choosing the right colors
- ▶ Defining page sets
- ▶ Cautions about HTML items and JavaScript files
- ▶ Displaying the report name in a footer

Introduction

Let's assume that the business' reports need to be printed or exported in PDF for sharing and printing purposes. This part is often ignored while defining the technical specification and the actual development of reports. This chapter will give you some tips and will show you the options within the Studio that you should use during development to make your reports more printable.

Controlling the container size and rows per page

In this recipe, we will examine the various options regarding the data container size and rows per page.

Getting ready

Create a simple list report with product attributes and sales quantity as columns:

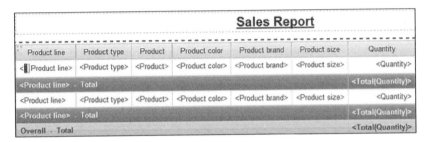

Define grouping and aggregation as shown previously.

How to do it...

To control the size of the list table and the number of rows per page, change the properties of the report. To do this, perform the following steps:

1. On the report page, click on any column from the list.

2. Using the **Ancestor** button, select **Whole List** from the **Properties** tab.

3. Set **Rows Per Page** to **50** as shown in the following screenshot:

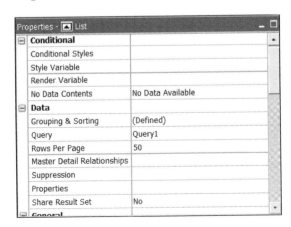

4. Now open the **Size & Overflow** property. Set the width of the list to **100%** as shown in the following screenshot:

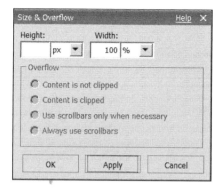

5. Run the report in HTML and PDF formats to test it as shown in the following screenshot:

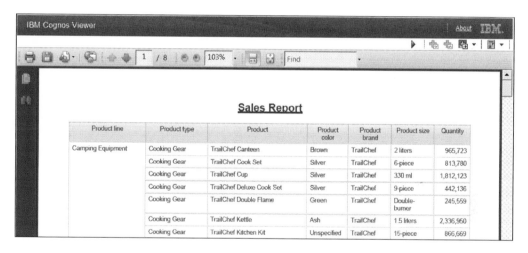

6. Save the report for use in the next recipe.

How it works...

You will notice in the output that the HTML report shows 50 rows per page. There is a scrollbar on the right for browsing the report page, whereas in PDF it only shows a full page of rows per page.

In practice, the two most frequently used output formats by users are HTML and PDF. HTML is great for interactivity and speed, whereas PDF is useful for printing.

When reports are run in the HTML format, by default, they show 20 rows per page. Users can then click on the **Next Page** link to go to the next page. This can sometimes be tedious as it is easier to see more information on one page and scroll down than it is to click on the **Next Page** link every time. Here, we achieve that by setting the **Rows Per Page** property of the list container. This ensures there are less user-clicks required to browse the whole data.

The beauty of this feature is that it doesn't affect the PDF output. The PDF generated will still show only the appropriate number of rows to be filled on each page. Hence, the text is still readable and the report is printable.

The **Size & Overflow** property of the list is also very useful to make it presentable. Here, we are setting the width to 100 percent so that the list is stretched to cover the page width. The columns are appropriately distributed across the page width. This is commonly used in business reporting, though some companies prefer non-stretched, center-aligned lists.

Please note that this feature is not particularly useful if users would prefer the report output in the Excel format because this will spread the report over multiple sheets, each having only the specified number of rows.

There's more...

Please take some time to explore other **Size & Overflow** properties. The following screenshot shows a piece of information which is found in the Cognos Help and gives you something to experiment with:

Option	Description
Height	Sets the height of the object.
Width	Sets the width of the object.
Content is not clipped	If the contents of the block exceed the height or width of the block, the block automatically resizes to fit the contents.
Content is clipped	If the contents of the block exceed the height or width of the block, the content is clipped. **Note:** The clipped content still exists. It is just not visible in the block.
Use scrollbars only when necessary	If the contents of the block exceed the height or width of the block, scrollbars are added to the block.
Always use scrollbars	Scrollbars are added to the block.

Eliminating orphan rows

When a grouped report with a header or footer is generated with equal number of rows per page, it might create some orphan rows. Please refer the following screenshot:

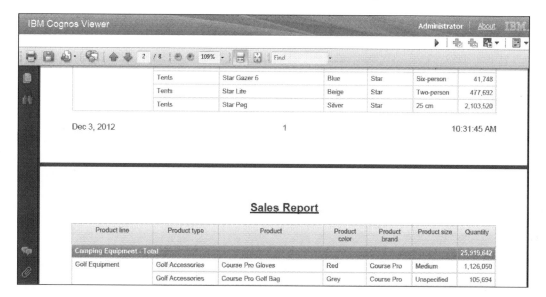

As you can see, the totals row for **Camping Equipment** has moved on to the next page and looks like an orphan. In this recipe, we will show you how to solve such issues of orphan rows.

Getting ready

We will use the report that we created in the previous recipe.

How to do it...

To complete this recipe, we have to specify in the list properties the number of rows to keep with the footer. To do this, perform the following steps:

1. Open the report from the location where you saved it in the previous recipe. In Cognos Report Studio, open the report page. Select any column in the list.

2. Using the **Ancestor** button, select the **List** object.

3. Open the **Pagination** property and set **Keep with footer** to 5 as shown in the following screenshot:

4. Run the report to test it as shown in the following screenshot:

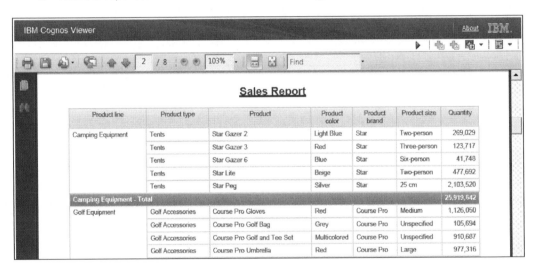

How it works...

As you can see in the previous screenshot, Cognos moved five rows on to the next page to connect to the **Camping Equipment - Total** row.

The property **Keep with footer** specifies how many rows need to be with the footer so that it doesn't stand out as an orphan. This setting will take precedence over the **Rows Per Page**.

There's more...

If there is a group header, you can also use the **Keep with header** property to make sure that the header row is not left as an orphan.

Defining page orientation and size (and overriding them for one page)

In this recipe, we will see how to specify page orientation and size to achieve better printouts. We will also see how to override these settings for certain pages.

Getting ready

Use the report created in the previous recipe.

Add a new report page called **Title** and use it to define the title page at the beginning of the report.

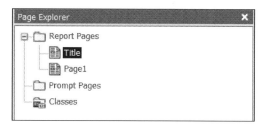

How to do it...

It is a common request for printable reports to control the report orientation. Here is how to do this:

1. Open the report in Report Studio. From the menu, choose **File | PDF Page Setup** as shown in the following screenshot:

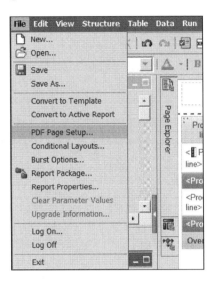

2. Define the **Orientation** as **Landscape** and **Paper Size** as **Letter** as shown in the following screenshot:

3. Now open **Page Explorer** and open the **Title** page.

4. Select any object on the page. Using the **Ancestor** button from **Properties**, choose the **Page** object.

5. Open its **PDF Page Setup** property.

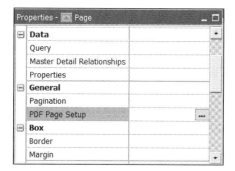

6. Select the **Override the page setup for this page** option and set the **Orientation** to **Portrait** and size to **A4** as shown in the following screenshot:

7. Run the report in PDF format and check the output.

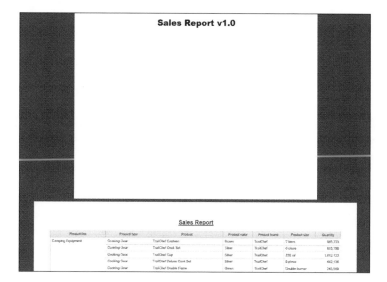

How it works...

This is quite a self-explanatory and menu-driven functionality. With Cognos 8.3 onwards, it is called **PDF Page Setup**. In earlier versions, it was just called **Page Setup**.

The sizes and orientations that I have mentioned in the recipe are for example purposes. You should choose the ones that are standard in your organization.

Avoiding page title repetition

The report title defined in the page header is repeated on every page. Let's say that the business owners want it to appear only on the first page. This recipe will show you how to achieve this.

Getting ready

We will use the report created in the previous recipe.

How to do it...

The business owners want the title of the report to appear only on the first page. To do this, perform the following steps:

1. We will start by deleting the title from the page header, as this object repeats on every page.

2. Now select the **List** object and open the **List Headers & Footers...** dialog from the toolbar or menu as shown in the following screenshot:

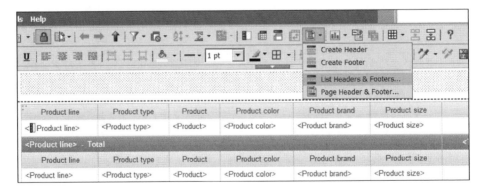

3. Check the option of **Overall header** and click on the **OK** button as shown in the following screenshot:

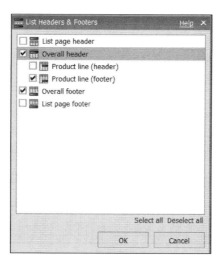

4. From the properties of the list, define **Column Titles** as **At start of details** as shown in the following screenshot:

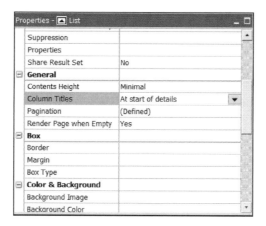

5. Now select the newly added header row from the start of the list. Add the required title to it and define formatting (font size, alignment, and so on) as shown in the following screenshot:

6. Run the report to test it.

How it works...

Anything we add to the page header and page footer is repeated on every page. This consumes space and ink on the PDF output used for printing.

Hence, we use the **Overall header** option for the list which is shown only once—at the beginning of the list header.

There's more...

The **Summary** or **Grand Total** shown for the quantity itself is the **Overall list footer** here. Hence, if there are any objects that you would like to show at the end of the report, you need to add one more footer line.

This can be done by selecting **Insert List Row Cells Below...** as shown in the following screenshot:

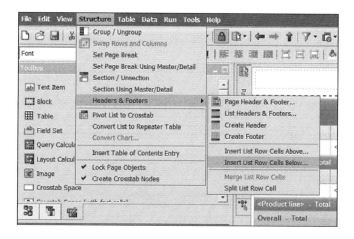

Horizontal pagination

The horizontal pagination feature is made available only from IBM Cognos Version 8.4. It is very useful for printing a very wide report and hence this recipe will show you how to use it.

Earlier versions of Cognos used to fit all report columns in one report width. Hence, in spite of selecting the **Landscape** orientation, some very wide reports had to be sized down, leaving them difficult to read. Now, we can choose to span the columns across the pages and hence keep the size intact and readable.

Getting ready

We will use the report created in the previous recipe. In order to mimic the idea that the report can't fit in one page width, we will change the **PDF Page Setup** as shown in the following screenshot:

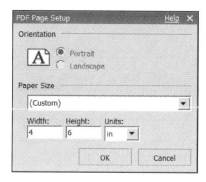

How to do it...

Our report will not fit on one page. To solve this we can change the properties of the list report. To do this, perform the following steps:

1. Open the report in Report Studio.

2. Select the **List** object using the **Ancestor** button.

3. From the **Properties** window, open the **Pagination** dialog box.

4. Ensure that the **Allow horizontal pagination** option is checked as shown in the following screenshot:

5. Run the report in PDF format to test it as shown in the following screenshot:

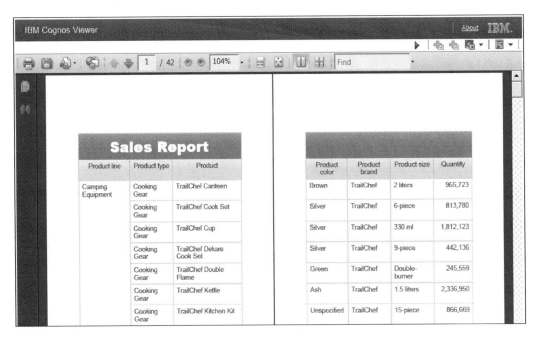

How it works...

This is again a straightforward and menu-driven feature. When a report can't fit in one page width, and if the **Allow horizontal pagination** option is checked, Cognos will span the columns across multiple pages.

They can then be printed and easily referred to side-by-side, which is much better than sizing the contents down and making them unreadable!

There's more...

You can choose a column and define its **Pagination** to **Repeat every page**. That column will then repeat on every page when a report spans many pages horizontally. Columns like **Serial Number** or **Order Number** can be set to this, which will make reading the printouts (side-by-side) easier.

Page numbering with horizontal pagination

Let's assume that there is a report that is very wide as well as long. It is decided that horizontal pagination will be used so that the report is printed over multiple A4 sheets with big readable fonts. However, when this report is printed, it is very difficult for the users to understand how they stitch together horizontally, and when actually a new page starts. Let's see how to solve this issue using appropriate page numbering.

Getting ready

Open the **Sales** report with horizontal pagination prepared in the previous recipe.

How to do it...

We want to modify the report that we created in the previous recipe to include page numbers so that it can be easier for users to work with the report. We can do this by changing the properties of the report page as we will see in the following steps:

1. Click anywhere on the report page and choose **PAGE** from the **Select Ancestor Properties** pane.

2. Open the **Pagination** property and check the **Enable horizontal page numbering** option as shown in the following screenshot:

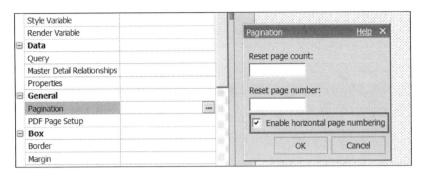

3. By default, there will be a **Page Number** object in **Page Footer**. If you can't find it, you can insert a new **Page Number** object from the toolbox.

4. Select this **Page Number** object and from its **Properties**, choose **Number Style** as **1-a** as shown in the following screenshot:

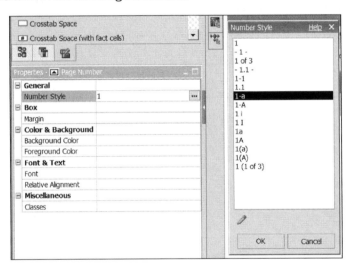

5. Now run the report to see how page numbers appear in the footer. Notice that for the first page split over multiple sheets, the footer displays 1-a, 1-b, 1-c, and so on. When the next report page starts, the numbering changes to 2-a, 2-b, 2-c, and so on.

How it works...

By enabling horizontal page numbering, we are making sure that Cognos generates appropriate page numbers with subsections to clearly show how pages are split over multiple sheets horizontally.

Choosing the output format from a prompt

After all of the previous recipes, you must have understood by now that reports need to be generated in the PDF format for printing purposes.

The default output format is HTML, which is good for interactive reports with drill-downs and drill-throughs. However, it is not printer friendly. They would see one page of output at a time with navigation links at the bottom of the screen, and hence printing the whole report is not straightforward. For printing, users need to run the report in PDF format. Clicking on the PDF icon resubmits the report query and users have to wait for the execution to finish.

It will be handy to control the report output from a prompt page. In this recipe, we will add a prompt control which asks users to specify the output format. This way, users can think of the application beforehand (interactive, printing, analysis, and so on) and decide whether the output should be HTML, PDF, Excel, or something else.

Getting ready

We will use the list report that we created in the previous recipe.

How to do it...

In this recipe, we will use JavaScript to create the required prompt as we can see in the following steps:

1. Open the report in Report Studio.
2. Add a new prompt page to the report from **Page Explorer**.
3. Open the prompt page and insert a new HTML item in the page body.
4. Define the HTML item as follows:

```
<html>
<head>
<script language="javascript">
function gotoUrl()
{var obj=document.all['OutputFormat'];
/* Below function passed the selected output format to the server
*/
window.onload(gCognosViewer.getRV().viewReport(obj.options[obj.
selectedIndex].value));
}
  </script>
</head>
<body>
<!-- Below will create a dropdown with choices -->
```

```
    <select name="OutputFormat" OnBlur="javascript:gotoUrl()">
<option value="HTML">HTML</option>
<option value="PDF">PDF</option>
<option value="singleXLS">Excel 2000 Single Sheet</option>
<option value="spreadsheetML">Excel 2007</option>
<option value="XLWA">Excel 2002</option>
<option value="XLS">Excel 2000</option>
<option value="CSV">Delimited text (CSV)</option>
<option value="XML">XML</option>
</select>
</body>
</html>
```

5.   Run the report to test it as shown in the following screenshot:

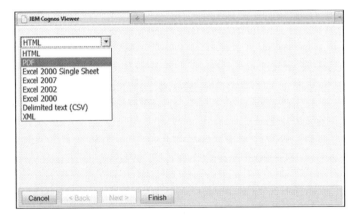

How it works...

This script displayed various output format options in a dropdown. Whatever is selected by the user is passed to the viewer application. This way, we can control the output format from a prompt page.

There's more...

Instead of giving all the formats as options, you can narrow it down to only HTML, PDF, and Excel. Alternatively, you can also put a checkbox for **Printable**, and if the user selects it, pass the value as PDF or otherwise HTML.

Choosing the right colors

Let's say that most of the business' reports are printed on a grayscale printer. This recipe will highlight the importance of choosing the right colors when reports are meant for printing.

Getting ready

We will use the report used in all the previous recipes for this recipe.

How to do it...

We want to examine the effect of the colors used on the printable reports. To do this, perform the following steps:

1. Open the report in Report Studio. Select the list column titles.

2. From **Properties**, open the **Background Color** dialog. Go to the **Web Safe Colors** tab.

3. Select the #CC99FF color (sixth column, tenth row).

4. Now select the product line footer (sub total) row and set its background color to #CCFF33 (thirteenth column, tenth row).

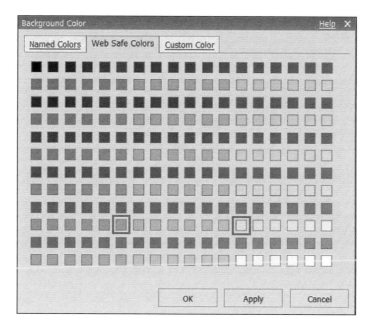

5. Run the report and examine colors. Now print the report and examine colors. You will notice that though both the colors are very different (one is a shade of green and the other is purple), they look almost the same on the grayscale printout.

6. Now change the list column titles to any color from the ninth or eleventh row. Print the output and you will see that the colors are distinguishable.

How it works...

If you print the whole palette on a grayscale printer, you will notice that rows have alternating light and dark shades. Hence, any two cells from the same row will have very similar output, but those from neighboring rows will have distinguishable shades as shown in the following screenshot:

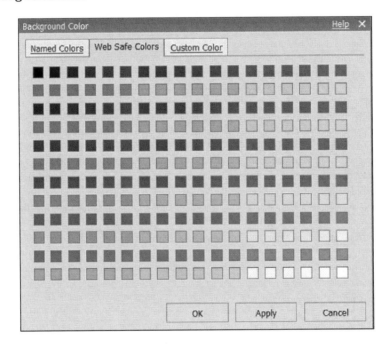

Hence you should always choose one color from an odd numbered row and the other color from an even numbered row.

There's more...

It is good practice to choose a color from a palette rather than defining a custom RGB color. This ensures that the colors can be correctly shown to most output formats.

Defining page sets

In a grouped report, it might be sensible to start a new group at a new page. In this recipe, we will see how to achieve this for the product line grouping.

Getting ready

We will use the report generated in the previous recipe for this recipe.

How to do it...

In this recipe, we want to start each new group on a new page. To do this perform the following steps:

1. Open the report in Report Studio and go to **Page Explorer**.

2. From **Toolbox**, drag a new **Page Set**.

3. Move the existing report page under this new **Page Set** (within **Detail Pages**) as shown in the following screenshot:

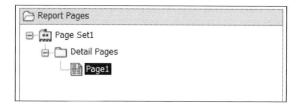

4. Now select the **Page Set**, and from its **Properties**, set the **Query** to the one being used from the report list (that is, **Query1**) as shown in the following screenshot:

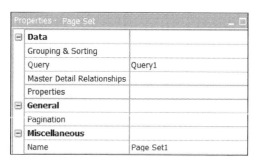

5. Open the **Grouping & Sorting** dialog and drag the **Product line** under **Groups** as shown in the following screenshot:

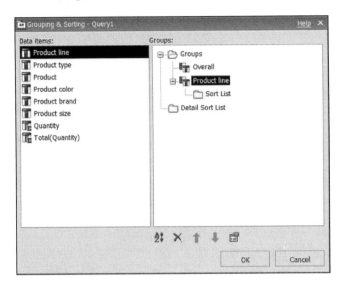

6. Now run the report to test it.

How it works...

When we create **Page Set**, Cognos generates the report output as a bunch of pages rather than one continuous report. The pages are driven by the query and grouping that we defined in the **Page Set** properties.

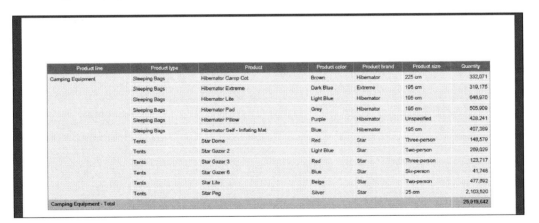

Here, it will create a new page for every **Product line**. Hence, a new group will start from a new page. This applies to HTML as well as PDF. In Excel, this will create multiple sheets.

Cautions about HTML items and JavaScript files

This recipe shows you that the HTML items and JavaScript files used on the report page are not executed when a report runs in PDF or Excel.

Getting ready

Open the report that we created in the *Creating a variable width bar chart using JavaScript* recipe in *Chapter 3, Using JavaScript Files – Tips and Tricks*.

How to do it...

Here, we will run the report in both HTML and PDF format as described in the following steps:

1. Run the report in HTML format. Ensure that the bar charts are generated fine.

2. Now re-run the report in PDF format.

3. Notice that bar charts are absent from the PDF output.

How it works...

When users run the report in any format other than HTML, the prompt page generated is still a web page. Therefore, any scripts put on the prompt page (for example, default selections) work fine. However, when the actual report is generated, it will execute the scripts only in HTML format. Therefore, the script actions fail in case of PDF, Excel, or any other non-HTML output.

Displaying the report name in a footer

When you have many reports (tens or hundreds) on Cognos Portal and a user sends you one output with some query, the first step to identify which report it is from, becomes difficult.

Hence it is good practice to print the report name and path in the footer of all pages. This allows quick reference to which report's output it is from when discussing over the printed reports.

Instead of manually typing the report name and path in each report, we will use a calculation here to avoid maintenance.

Getting ready

We will use the report generated in the previous recipe.

How to do it...

Here we can use a Layout calculation to return the report name. To do this, perform the following steps:

1. Open the report in Report Studio.

2. From the toolbox, drag **Layout Calculation** into the page footer at the appropriate place.

3. Define the calculation as follows:

   ```
   ReportPath () + ' : ' + ReportName ()
   ```

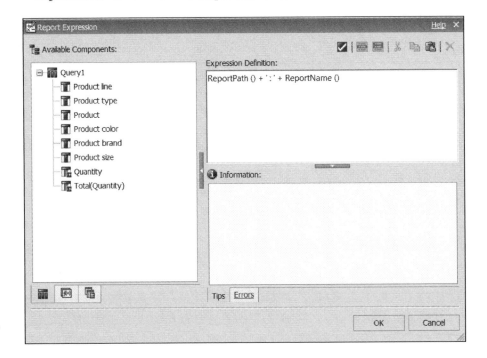

4. Click on **OK** and change the format of this calculation to a more suitable format (generally a small print like 7pt and gray color).

5. Run the report to check that the report path and name are displayed properly.

How it works...

By using functions to return **Report Path** and **Report Name**, we not only avoid the need to manually type those in, but we also avoid maintenance. In future, if a report is renamed or moved to another folder, it automatically reflects in the footer. This proves very handy when discussing the output in printed form (for any change or issue), as it's clear which Cognos report it is from. It also clearly shows if the output is from a user's own MY FOLDER, which you cannot directly access.

7
Working with Dimensional Models

In this chapter we will cover the following:

- List report or crosstab report
- Filtering rows or columns
- Filtering a whole report
- Adding a prompt into Slicer and its limitations
- Achieving zero suppression
- Aggregation versus preaggregated values
- Using the roleValue() function
- Swapping dimensions using MUN manipulation

Introduction

This chapter will discuss some concepts that you should know when developing reports against dimensional or **DMR (Dimensionally Modeled Relational)** sources. We will use two packages in this chapter. The **GO Data Warehouse (analysis)** package is of DMR type, whereas **Sales and Marketing (cube)** is a Cognos PowerCube-based package which is purely dimensional in nature. Both packages come as a standard sample within the **IBM Cognos Samples** installation.

List report or crosstab report

This recipe shows that most of the time it is possible to use a crosstab report instead of a list report and then discusses the pros and cons of each.

Getting ready

We will use the **GO Data Warehouse (analysis)** package for this recipe.

How to do it...

In this recipe we will start by creating a list report, and then we will create a crosstab report to see the difference:

1. Create a new list type of report based on this package.

2. Drag columns onto the list report as follows. Create grouping and sorting for **Product line** and **Product**:

3. Run the report to test it.

4. Now save this report and create a new report of crosstab type.

5. Drag items onto the crosstab report as follows. Define sorting on **Product line** and **Product**:

6. Run the report to test it.

How it works...

You will see that both the reports bring back the same data. As a rule, everything you can do with list can be done with crosstab. It is general practice to use lists for relational models whereas crosstabs are used for dimensional models. I believe this practice comes from the fact that multidimensional databases (cubes) are accessed using **Multidimensional Expressions** (**MDX**) that naturally return the data in two axes.

However, the biggest factors that drive the choice as per my opinion are:

- Dynamicity of columns
- Number-oriented or text-oriented
- Report access method (HTML or not)

When the number of columns and column members are dynamic in nature and driven by values from a dimension or query subject, you need to use crosstab.

Crosstab reports can show only numbers in the intersections. The textual fields need to be on rows or columns. Therefore, if you need to show more textual information, you should use a list report rather than pulling them all as nested rows on a crosstab report which will deteriorate the performance.

List reports are better for interactive (HTML) output. As soon as Cognos receives the top 20 (or whatever the setting is) rows, the first page is displayed to the users. Therefore, it reduces the wait time. With a crosstab report, more often than not, Cognos waits for full data before showing even the first page.

Another point is that if you can get your report working in crosstab, then you can plot it on a graph/chart, as it works exactly like a crosstab. Therefore, not just the data source type, but all these factors should be considered before making your decision.

Filtering rows or columns

This recipe will show you how to filter row or column members in a crosstab report.

Getting ready

This report will be based on the dimensional source. Therefore, please use the **Sales and Marketing (cube)** package for this recipe.

How to do it...

In this recipe we will see how to filter the report by hiding the empty rows as follows:

1. Create a new crosstab report.

2. Drag **Year** and **Month** onto columns and **Retailer name** onto rows. Drag the **Revenue** measure onto the intersection:

Revenue	<#Year#>		<#Year#>	
	<#Month#>	<#Month#>	<#Month#>	<#Month#>
<#Retailer name#>	<#1234#>	<#1234#>	<#1234#>	<#1234#>
<#Retailer name#>	<#1234#>	<#1234#>	<#1234#>	<#1234#>

3. Run the report to test it. The report will look as follows:

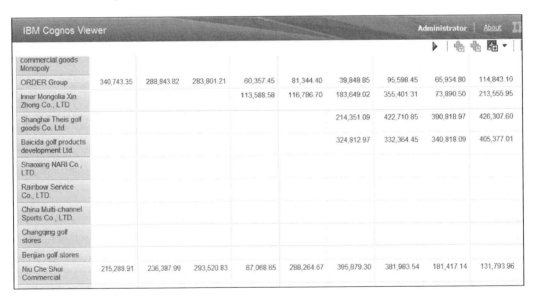

4. Now we will try to filter the rows so that only retailers that have data are displayed. For that, delete **Retailer name** from rows.

5. Drag a new **Query Calculation** tool onto rows:

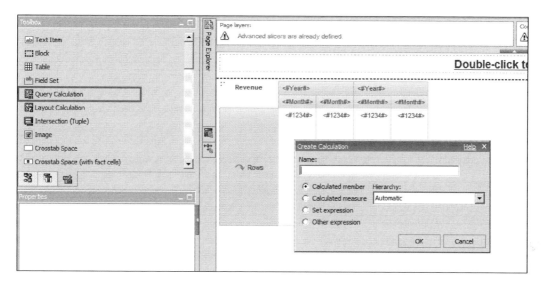

6. Name this set `Filtered Ret` and base it on the **Retailers** dimension. Select the calculation type as **Set expression**:

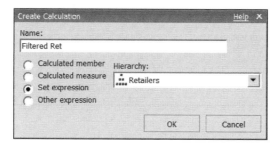

7. Define the set expression as:

```
filter ([sales_and_marketing].[Retailers].
    [Retailers].[Retailer name], [Revenue] is not null)
```

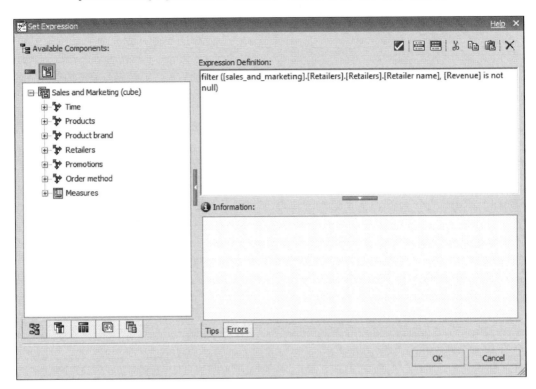

8. Now run the report to test it:

How it works...

The **Report Studio** filters (summary and detail) are useful mainly with relational data sources and list reports. With cube-based reports, you can achieve better performance by filtering the row and column members beforehand in the expression that pulls the members.

Here we use the `filter` function, which allows us to define the criteria. The criteria can be based on the member properties or measures. We used it for zero rows suppression; hence, we filtered on the required measure. However, you can also filter on member properties, caption, keys, and so on. It is common practice to have certain flags or categories as member properties which can then be used for filtering depending on the user selection.

There's more...

Another way to achieve the same result is to use the already available functionality to suppress the zero rows and columns. Please refer to the *Achieving zero suppression* recipe for details.

This recipe teaches you a general concept of filtering out the members on rows and columns which you can use for many criteria in addition to zero suppression.

Filtering a whole report

This recipe will show you how to filter the values of a whole report based on a data item that does not appear on the report. We will filter the report created in the previous recipe to show the values for a selected **Product line**.

Getting ready

We will use the report created in the previous recipe for this recipe.

How to do it...

In this recipe, we will filter the report based on a member which is not used in the report itself, as follows:

1. Open the report in the **Report Studio**.
2. Go to **Query Explorer** and open the query used by the crosstab on the report page.
3. From the **Source** pane of **Insertable Objects**, browse for the cube for the required member. Here we will search for **Golf Equipment** from the **Product line** hierarchy.

4. After locating the member, drag it onto the query under **Slicer**:

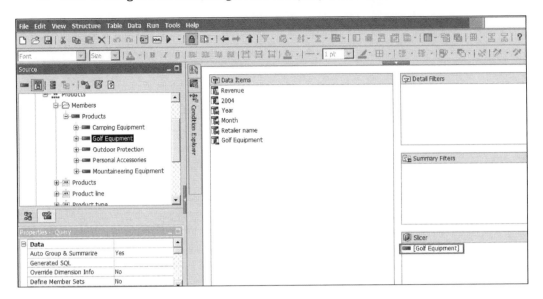

5. Run the report to test it.

How it works...

When you want to define a context for the values or filter the values based on a dimension which does not appear on the report, you can use **Slicer**.

You can drag a member or set of members under **Slicer**. This defines the overall context for the query and all the numbers in the crosstab are filtered for that member or set of members. Again, use of **Slicer** goes naturally with the way multi-dimensional databases are accessed. Using a summary or a detailed filter instead of **Slicer** is possible, but not advisable.

There's more...

You can make the **Slicer** member/member set dynamic, so that users can select a value for it from the prompt. This is covered in the next recipe.

Adding a prompt into Slicer and its limitations

In the previous recipe, we saw that we can filter the whole report by a member or member set using **Slicer**. This recipe will show you how to add a prompt into **Slicer** to make it dynamic.

Getting ready

We will use the report that we created in the previous recipe for this recipe. We will need to remove **Golf Equipment** used in the previous recipe from **Slicer**.

How to do it...

In this recipe we will see how to add a prompt into **Slicer**, as follows:

1. Open the **Query Explorer** and explore the query being used by crosstab. Remove the **Golf Equipment** filter from the **Slicer** section.

2. From the **Toolbox** pane, drag a new **Slicer Member Set** under **Slicer**.

3. Define the set as:

   ```
   [sales_and_marketing].[Products].[Products].[Product line]
       ->?pProductLine?
   ```

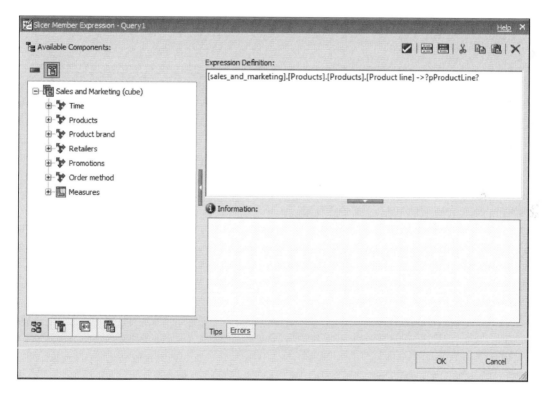

4. Run the report to test it.

How it works...

When you run the report, you will set Cognos to automatically prompt you to select a **Product line** value. When you select one, the report runs and pulls data for the selected **Product line** value.

Here, we are using **Slicer** for the same application as in the previous recipe. However, instead of hard-coding a particular member, we are making it prompt-driven. The first part of the expression (before the pointer (**->**)) defines the hierarchy. The second part is the parameter name which is dynamically replaced by **Member Unique Name** (**MUN**) based on your selection.

There's more...

You will notice that you can select only one value for **Product line**. This is because the expression expects only one member. However, it is possible to make it multi-select. For that, put the expression within the Set () function.

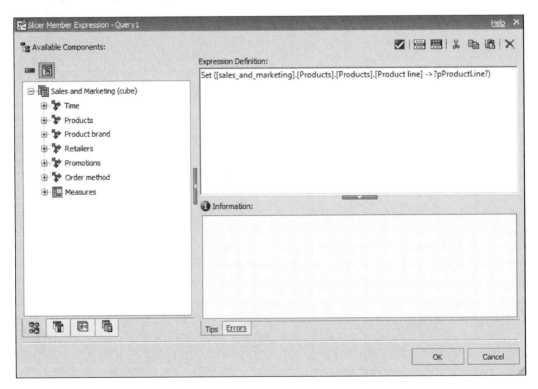

Now when you run the report, you will be prompted for **Product line** and you will be able to select more than one value.

It's good practice to define your own prompt on the prompt page instead of letting Cognos generate the prompt at runtime. That way, you can have control on the appearance, ordering, and performance of the prompt page.

More Info

The biggest issue with **Slicer** is that you cannot make it optional. It works like a mandatory filter. There is a workaround to this which involves using the **Prompt Macro** functions. However, that adds complexity to the code. Instead, you can add a **TREE PROMPT** object to display the prompt values and users can select the **Root members** or **All members** option, which effectively means no filtering for that dimension. In our example, if we run the report for **ALL PRODUCTS** from the **Products** dimension, we are effectively seeing data for **Product line** without any filter.

Achieving zero suppression

We have already seen one way of suppressing zero rows in the *Filtering rows or columns* recipe. This recipe will show other possible ways to achieve zero suppression.

Getting ready

We will use the same report used in the *Filtering rows or columns* recipe, for this recipe.

How to do it...

In this recipe we will use the **Crosstab** properties to suppress zeros from the report as follows:

1. Open the report and remove the **Expression Definition** created in the original recipe and add **Retailer name**.

2. Now, select anything on the crosstab, and using the **Ancestor** button from the **Properties** tab, select the crosstab.

3. Open its **Suppression** property:

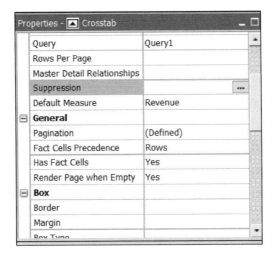

4. Select the **Rows only** option for **Suppression** and keep the appropriate checkboxes checked:

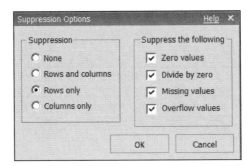

5. Run the report to test it.

How it works...

When you run the report, you will see that only those Retailers which have some data appear on the rows. This effect is the same as the filtering we had achieved by using the calculated member set.

I would say this is one of the most useful features you can choose to suppress only rows, only columns, both, or none. Also, you can choose whether you want to suppress zeros or divide by zero, missing values, or overflow values.

There's more...

If there is only one data container on the report, you can set the suppression options from the menu also. For that, go to **Data | Suppress** and choose the appropriate option:

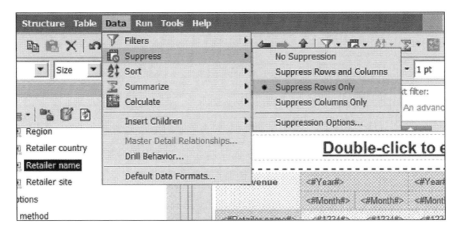

You can also use the **Suppress** icon from the toolbar:

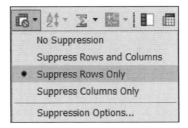

Aggregation versus preaggregated values

The biggest advantage of using a cube as a data source is their capability to pre-aggregate values. This recipe will show you how to exploit this feature of cubes in your Cognos reports.

Getting ready

Create a simple crosstab report using the **Sales and Marketing (cube)** package. Drag **Retailer name** and **Retailer site** onto rows and **Year** onto columns. Drag **Revenue** onto the intersection.

How to do it...

In this recipe we will start by creating the aggregation using the **Aggregate** button as follows:

1. First, we will create aggregation using the standard method. For that, select the **Retailer site** row.

2. From the toolbar, click on the **Aggregate** button and choose **Automatic Summary**:

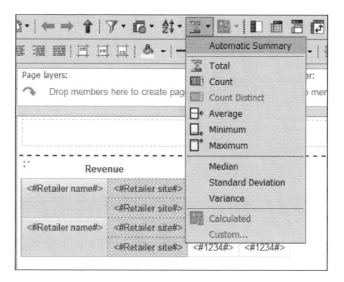

3. Run the report to test it:

Revenue		2004	2005	2006	2007
Consumer Club	San Diego	3,846,273.07	3,000,924.19	613,775.38	320,621.53
	Denver	3,704,775.33	3,969,586.24	4,033,096.12	2,033,583.90
	Atlanta	1,601,618.31	1,076,509.10	10,431.50	248.00
	Miami		525,735.58	84,379.58	107,371.14
	Los Angeles		996,455.65	3,205,220.72	2,140,545.58
	Washington			2,444.00	198.40
	Total	**9,152,666.71**	**9,569,210.76**	**7,949,347.30**	**4,602,568.55**
Mega-Outlet	Duluth	983,343.98	430,438.55	25,750.85	
	Chicago	721,897.81	651,648.88	21,075.85	
	Indianapolis	1,816,015.50	1,535,430.46	35,356.45	
	Detroit	1,358,376.00	1,018,820.89	41,268.20	
	Rapid City	9,411.00	16,661.75	18,289.85	
	Boise		467,214.83	556,269.17	353,436.58
	Total	**4,889,044.29**	**4,120,215.36**	**698,010.37**	**353,436.58**
Sporting Goods Direct	Montgomery	1,307,201.40	151,081.72	67,712.50	5,475.45
	Total	**1,307,201.40**	**151,081.72**	**67,712.50**	**5,475.45**
Extreme Outdoors	Houston	2,643,241.63	3,257,237.09	3,143,003.30	1,465,388.38

4. Now go back to the **Report Studio**. Delete the new row created for **Aggregation**.

5. Go to the second tab (**Data Item**) of **Insertable Objects**. Drag **Retailer name** again onto the report and drop it under **Retailer site** and format this row to be bold; shown as follows:

Revenue		<#Year#>	<#Year#>
<#Retailer name#>	<#Retailer site#>	<#1234#>	<#1234#>
	<#Retailer name#>	<#1234#>	<#1234#>
<#Retailer name#>	<#Retailer site#>	<#1234#>	<#1234#>
	<#Retailer name#>	<#1234#>	<#1234#>

6. Now run the report to test it:

Revenue		2004	2005	2006	2007
Consumer Club	San Diego	3,846,273.07	3,000,924.19	613,775.38	320,621.53
	Denver	3,704,775.33	3,969,586.24	4,033,096.12	2,033,583.90
	Atlanta	1,601,618.31	1,076,509.10	10,431.50	248.00
	Miami		525,735.58	84,379.58	107,371.14
	Los Angeles		996,455.65	3,205,220.72	2,140,545.58
	Washington			2,444.00	198.40
	Consumer Club	**9,152,666.71**	**9,569,210.76**	**7,949,347.30**	**4,602,568.55**
Mega-Outlet	Duluth	983,343.98	430,438.55	25,750.85	
	Chicago	721,897.81	651,648.88	21,075.85	
	Indianapolis	1,816,015.50	1,535,430.46	35,356.45	
	Detroit	1,358,376.00	1,018,820.89	41,268.20	
	Rapid City	9,411.00	16,661.75	18,289.85	
	Boise		467,214.83	556,269.17	353,436.58
	Mega-Outlet	**4,889,044.29**	**4,120,215.36**	**698,010.37**	**353,436.58**
Sporting Goods Direct	Montgomery	1,307,201.40	151,081.72	67,712.50	5,475.45
	Sporting Goods Direct	**1,307,201.40**	**151,081.72**	**67,712.50**	**5,475.45**
Extreme Outdoors	Houston	2,643,241.63	3,257,237.09	3,143,003.30	1,465,388.38

7. Notice that the aggregated values are the same.

How it works...

The first method that we used to create aggregation rows, utilizes Cognos' aggregation feature, which is the standard way of representing the relational data sources. However, Cognos won't use the pre-aggregated values from the cube in this case. Instead, it will calculate the aggregations at runtime either locally or at the database.

In order to utilize the pre-aggregation feature of the cube, we then dragged the item **Retailer name** under **Retailer site**. That way, we make **Report Studio** ask for the pre-aggregated values from the cube.

We can test that the values coming into the report from both approaches are the same and correct. The latter approach is good practice when writing a report against cubes. It dramatically improves the performance of the report.

There's more...

In the first approach, the aggregation row title is a static text, whereas in the second approach, the aggregation row titles change dynamically to show the **Retailer name**. Either way, you can control this by editing the **Source Type** property of the row title.

The roleValue() function

This recipe will show you a useful function which you will often need while working with dimensional and DMR models. As the purpose of this recipe is only to examine this function, we won't consider any specific business case here.

Getting ready

Create a new list report based on the **Sales and Marketing (cube)** package.

How to do it...

In this recipe we will see how the roleValue() function works and how you can use it in your reports, as follows:

1.   In **Source** under **Insertable Objects**, locate **Retailer name**:

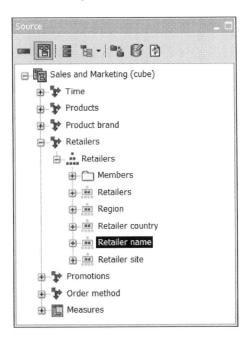

2. Drag it onto the list as a new column.

3. Now, add a new data item to the list. Define it as:

   `roleValue('_businessKey', [Retailer name]).`

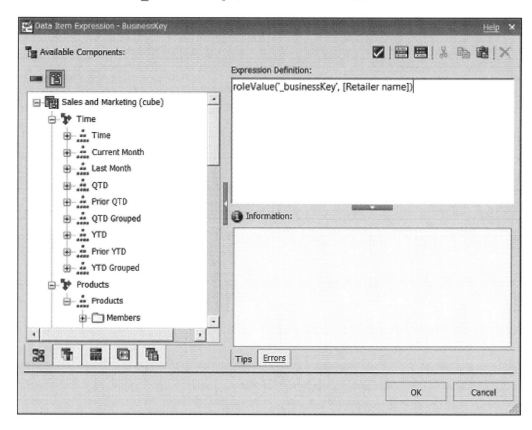

4. Add two more data items and define them as follows:

   `roleValue('_memberCaption', [Retailer name])`

   `roleValue('_memberUniqueName', [Retailer name])`

5. Run the report to test it:

Retailer name	BusinessKey	Caption	MUN
Consumer Club	6815	Consumer Club	[sales_and_marketing].[Retailers].[Retailers].[Retailer name]->[PC].[@MEMBER].[6815]
Mega-Outlet	6819	Mega-Outlet	[sales_and_marketing].[Retailers].[Retailers].[Retailer name]->[PC].[@MEMBER].[6819]
Sporting Goods Direct	6990	Sporting Goods Direct	[sales_and_marketing].[Retailers].[Retailers].[Retailer name]->[PC].[@MEMBER].[6990]
Extreme Outdoors	6804	Extreme Outdoors	[sales_and_marketing].[Retailers].[Retailers].[Retailer name]->[PC].[@MEMBER].[6804]
Husky Outfitters	7001	Husky Outfitters	[sales_and_marketing].[Retailers].[Retailers].[Retailer name]->[PC].[@MEMBER].[7001]
The Sports Factory	7045	The Sports Factory	[sales_and_marketing].[Retailers].[Retailers].[Retailer name]->[PC].[@MEMBER].[7045]
The Marketplace	6801	The Marketplace	[sales_and_marketing].[Retailers].[Retailers].[Retailer name]->[PC].[@MEMBER].[6801]
Hartman's	6818	Hartman's	[sales_and_marketing].[Retailers].[Retailers].[Retailer name]->[PC].[@MEMBER].[6818]
Sport Basement	7330	Sport Basement	[sales_and_marketing].[Retailers].[Retailers].[Retailer name]->[PC].[@MEMBER].[7330]
Weston Outfitters	6824	Weston Outfitters	[sales_and_marketing].[Retailers].[Retailers].[Retailer name]->[PC].[@MEMBER].[6824]
Game On! Sports	7012	Game On! Sports	[sales_and_marketing].[Retailers].[Retailers].[Retailer name]->[PC].[@MEMBER].[7012]
Odds and Ends Fishing Tackle	6994	Odds and Ends Fishing Tackle	[sales_and_marketing].[Retailers].[Retailers].[Retailer name]->[PC].[@MEMBER].[6994]
Donovan's Sports	6806	Donovan's Sports	[sales_and_marketing].[Retailers].[Retailers].[Retailer name]->[PC].[@MEMBER].[6806]
Jackson Sporting Goods	7246	Jackson Sporting Goods	[sales_and_marketing].[Retailers].[Retailers].[Retailer name]->[PC].[@MEMBER].[7246]
New Vision	7352	New Vision	[sales_and_marketing].[Retailers].[Retailers].[Retailer name]->[PC].[@MEMBER].[7352]

How it works...

When defining a DMR model in the **Framework Manager**, the modeler can define various columns as attributes. This `roleValue()` function allows you to access these attributes. This function takes two arguments: Role and Member/Set.

There's more...

We have seen the `Set()`, `Filter()`, and `roleValue()` functions so far. These are **OLAP** functions available for use in **Report Studio** when building a report against a dimensional data source. You can find a full list of OLAP functions under **DIMENSIONAL FUNCTIONS** on the **Functions** tab when editing any data item or creating a new calculated item. Please take the time to go through each dimensional function, including their usage and syntax.

Swapping dimensions using MUN manipulation

When a prompt is based on a dimension, the selected value is passed as a full qualifier (MUN), not just the key. This results in a limitation of the prompt's use. We cannot use the prompt to filter any other dimension. In this recipe, we will see how to override this limitation by performing the string manipulation of MUN.

Consider a business case where a cube has two time dimensions (say **Billing date** and **Transaction date**). Users want a choice on the prompt page to select which time dimension to filter on. Also, they will select a **Date** (**Year** or **Month**) on the prompt page, so we need to filter the appropriate time dimension.

Getting ready

Here we will use the **GO Data Warehouse (analysis)** package where we have two time dimensions that we can use in this recipe: the regular **Time** dimension and the **Time (ship date)** dimension.

How to do it...

In this recipe we will use a value prompt to select the required dimension that will be used in our report, as follows:

1. Firstly, we will add a value prompt (radio button) on the prompt page with **Static Choices** for **DimTime** and **DimTimeShip**:

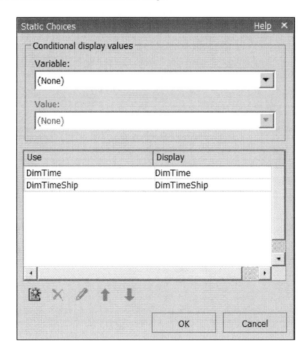

2. Now, add a new conditional variable to link to this radio button prompt:

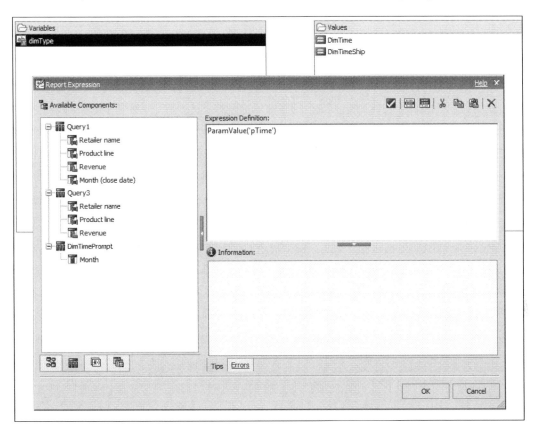

3. On the report page, add a conditional block and link it to the **dimType** variable defined in the previous step as Block Variable.

4. Set **Current Block** to **DimTime** and add a crosstab to the block. Drag valid members onto the crosstab as shown. Also, add text saying **Sliced By DimTime Dimension...**:

Sliced By DimTime Dimension ...		
Revenue	<#Product line#>	<#Product line#>
<#Retailer name#>	<#1234#>	<#1234#>
<#Retailer name#>	<#1234#>	<#1234#>

5. Now, set **Current Block** to **DimTimeShip** and add a new crosstab to the block. Drag the appropriate members onto the crosstab and add text saying **SlicedByDimTimeShip Dimension...**.

Sliced By DimTimeShip Dimension ...		
Revenue	<#Product line#>	<#Product line#>
<#Retailer name#>	<#1234#>	<#1234#>
<#Retailer name#>	<#1234#>	<#1234#>

6. By now we have achieved a report that will show one of the two crosstabs depending on the choice selected by the user on the radio button prompt. Now we will add the Time Dimension prompt.

7. For that, go to the prompt page and add a tree prompt based on **Time** dimension. Call the parameter **DimTime**.

8. Now go to the query that drives the **DimTime** crosstab. Add a slicer as:

```
[Sales].[Time].[Time].[Month] -> ?DimTime?
```

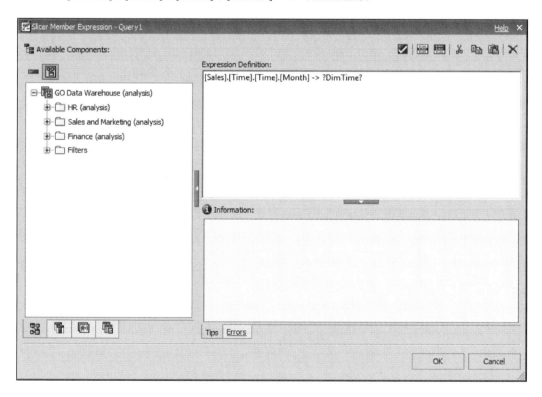

9. Finally, go to the query that drives the **DimTimeShip** crosstab. Add a slicer as:

```
#substitute( 'Month]' , 'Month (ship date)]', substitute(
    'Time]' , 'Time (ship date)]', substitute( 'Time]' ,
      'Time (ship date)]'  , '[Sales].[Time].[Time].
        [Month]')))#
```

10. Now run the report to test it. You will see that the report shows the appropriate crosstab depending on the selection, and both crosstabs filter data on different dimensions—though the prompt is based only on one dimension.

How it works...

The Substitute() function is a macro function to do literal replacements. It looks for the first occurrence of the mentioned string, 'Month]' for example, and replaces it with the substitution string – 'Month (ship date)]'. As we need to replace multiple occurrences, we need to use the Substitute() macro three times. Therefore, we successfully changed the MUN of the selected **Month** member to refer to the same member in the **Month (ship date)** hierarchy.

Though this recipe is very lengthy, the basic principle it shows here is the manipulation of the MUN using macros. We are using the Substitute() function to do the appropriate string replacements to achieve the desired MUN. We retain the KEY of the member and just change the preceding qualifier.

You can build upon this idea to achieve many sophisticated functionalities in the reports.

See also

To learn more about slicers and adding prompts to slicers, please refer to the earlier recipes of this chapter. Macros will be discussed in more detail in the next chapter.

8
Working with Macros

In this chapter we will cover the following:

- ▶ Adding data-level security using the CSVIdentityMap macro
- ▶ Using the Prompt macro in native SQL
- ▶ Making prompts optional
- ▶ Adding a token using macros
- ▶ Using the prompt() and promptmany() macros in query subjects
- ▶ Showing the prompt values in a report based on security
- ▶ String operations to get it right
- ▶ Showing a username in the footer

Introduction

This chapter will introduce you to an interesting and useful tool in IBM Cognos BI called **Macros**. They can be used in the **Framework Manager** as well as the **Report Studio**. In this book, we are not covering the **Framework Manager**; therefore, I will restrict myself to the use of macros in the **Report Studio**.

Generally, macros are thought to be a way to add programming and to automate tasks in most applications; for example, in Excel macros. However, in Cognos reporting, a macro is a way to make some key changes in the report specification at runtime based on prompt values, user security, and so on.

The Cognos engine understands the presence of a macro as it is written within a pair of hashes (#). It executes the macros first and puts the result back into the report specification like a literal string replacement. We can use this to alter data items, filters, and slicers at runtime.

In previous versions, it was difficult to find any information about **Macro Functions** within the **Report Studio**. With Version 10, IBM has put a new table in the data item editor to list all macro functions and their syntax. It can be seen as the last tab when you edit a data item or create a new calculation:

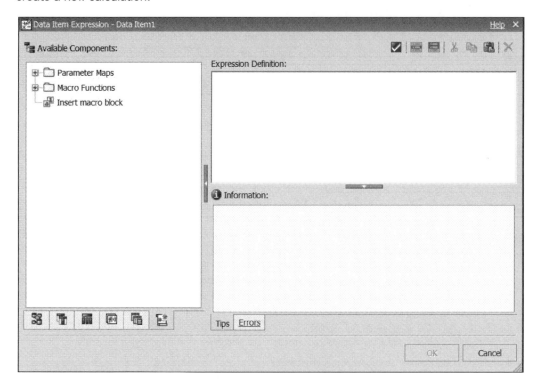

We have already seen one example of macros in the *Swapping dimensions using MUN manipulation* recipe in *Chapter 7, Working with Dimensional Models*. In this chapter, I will show you more examples and introduce you to more functions which you can later build upon to achieve sophisticated functionalities.

We will be writing some SQL against the GO Data Warehouse data source. Also, we will use the **GO Data Warehouse (query)** package for some recipes.

Adding data-level security using the CSVIdentityMap macro

Let's say that a report shows the employee names by region and country. We need to implement data security in this report so that a user can see the records only for the country they belong to. There are **User Groups** already defined on the Cognos server (in the directory) and users are made members of appropriate groups. For this recipe, I have added my user account to a user group called Spain.

Getting ready

Open a new list report with **GO Data Warehouse (query)** as the package.

How to do it...

In this recipe, we will start by creating a new list report using the following steps:

1. Drag the appropriate columns (**Country**, **City**, and **Employee name**) onto the report from the **Employee by Region** query subject:

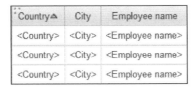

Country▲	City	Employee name
<Country>	<City>	<Employee name>
<Country>	<City>	<Employee name>
<Country>	<City>	<Employee name>

2. Go to **Query Explorer** and drag over a new detail filter.
3. Define the filter as:

```
[Country] in (#CSVIdentityNameList(',')#)
```

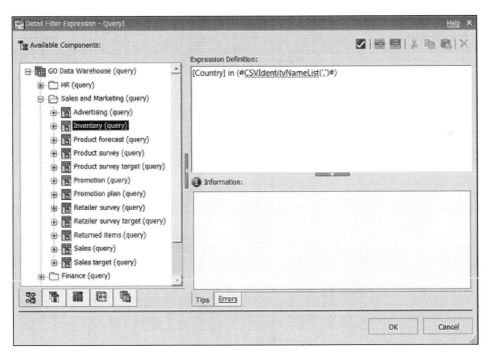

4. Run the report to test it. You will notice that a user can see only the rows of the country/countries of which he/she is a member.

How it works...

Here we are using a macro function called `CSVIdentityNameList`. This function returns a list of groups and roles that the user belongs to along with the user's account name. Therefore, when I run the report, one of the values returned will be **Spain** and I will see the data for **Spain**.

The function accepts a string parameter which is used as a separator in the result. Here, we are passing a comma (,) as the separator. If a user belongs to multiple country groups, he/she will see data for all the countries listed in the result of a macro.

There's more...

This solution, conspicuously, has its limitations. None of the user accounts or roles should be the same as a country name, because that will wrongly show data for a country the user does not belong to. For example, for a user called **Paris**, it will show data for the **Paris** region. So, there need to be certain restrictions. However, you can build upon the knowledge of this macro function and use it in many practical business scenarios.

Using the Prompt macro in native SQL

In this recipe, we will write an SQL statement to be fired on the data source. We will use the **Prompt** macro to dynamically change the filter condition.

We will write a report that shows a list of employees by region and country. We will use the Prompt macro to ask the users to enter a country name. Then, the SQL statement will search for the employee belonging to that country.

Getting ready

Create a new blank list report with the **GO Data Warehouse (query)** package.

How to do it...

In this recipe we will see how to use macros to pass a parameter to an SQL statement, as follows:

1. Go to **Query Explorer** and drag an **SQL** object onto the query subject that is linked to the list (**Query1** in most cases):

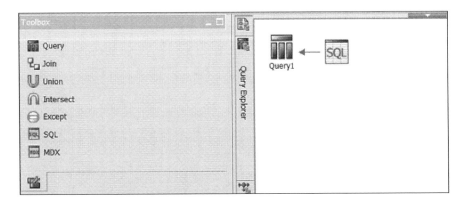

2. Select the **SQL** object and ensure that **great_outdoor_warehouse** is selected as the data source.

3. Open the SQL property and add the following statement:

```
SELECT DISTINCT "BRANCH_REGION_DIMENSION"."REGION_EN"
    "REGION" , "BRANCH_REGION_DIMENSION"."COUNTRY_EN"
        "COUNTRY" , "EMP_EMPLOYEE_DIM"."EMPLOYEE_NAME"
            "EMPLOYEE_NAME"

FROM "GOSALESDW"."GO_REGION_DIM" "BRANCH_REGION_DIMENSION",
    "GOSALESDW"."EMP_EMPLOYEE_DIM" "EMP_EMPLOYEE_DIM",
        "GOSALESDW"."GO_BRANCH_DIM" "GO_BRANCH_DIM"

WHERE ("BRANCH_REGION_DIMENSION"."COUNTRY_EN" IN (
    #PROMPT('REGION')#))

AND "BRANCH_REGION_DIMENSION"."COUNTRY_CODE" =
    "GO_BRANCH_DIM"."COUNTRY_CODE" AND "EMP_EMPLOYEE_DIM".
        "BRANCH_CODE" = "GO_BRANCH_DIM"."BRANCH_CODE"
```

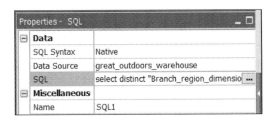

4. Hit the **OK** button. This will validate the query and will close the dialog box. You will see that three data items (`Region`, `Country`, and `Employee_Name`) are added to **Query1**.

5. Now go to the report page. Drag these data items onto the list and run the report to test it.

How it works...

Here we are using the Prompt macro in a native SQL statement. Native SQL allows us to directly fire a query on the data source and use the result on the report. This is useful in certain scenarios where we don't need to define any Framework Model. If you examine the SQL statement, you will notice that it is a very simple one that joins three tables and returns the appropriate columns. We have added a filter condition on country name which is supposed to dynamically change depending on the value entered by the user.

The macro function that we have used here is PROMPT (). As the name suggests, it is used to generate a prompt and returns the parameter value back to be used in an SQL statement.

The PROMPT () function takes five arguments. The first argument is the parameter name, and this is mandatory. It allows us to link a prompt page object (value prompt, date prompt, and so on) to the PROMPT () function. The rest of the four arguments are optional and we are not using them here. You will read about them in the next recipe.

Please note that we also have the option of adding a detail filter in the query subject instead of using the Prompt macro within the query. However, sometimes you would want to filter a table before joining it with other tables. In that case, using the Prompt macro within the query helps.

There's more...

Similar to the PROMPT () function, there is a PROMPTMANY () macro function. This works in exactly the same way and allows users to enter multiple values for the parameter. Those values are returned as a comma-separated list.

Making prompts optional

The previous recipe showed you how to generate a prompt through a macro. In this recipe, we will see how to make them optional using other arguments of the function.

We will generate two simple list reports, both based on a native SQL. These lists will show product details for a selected product line. However, the product line prompt will be made optional using two different approaches.

Getting ready

Create a report with two simple list objects based on native SQL. For that, create the query subjects in the same way as we did in the previous recipe. Use the following query in the SQL objects:

```
SELECT DISTINCT "SLS_PRODUCT_LINE_LOOKUP"."PRODUCT_LINE_EN"
"PRODUCT_LINE" , "SLS_PRODUCT_LOOKUP"."PRODUCT_NAME"
"PRODUCT_NAME" , "SLS_PRODUCT_COLOR_LOOKUP"."PRODUCT_COLOR_EN"
"PRODUCT_COLOR" , "SLS_PRODUCT_SIZE_LOOKUP"."PRODUCT_SIZE_EN"
"PRODUCT_SIZE"

 FROM "GOSALESDW"."SLS_PRODUCT_DIM" "SLS_PRODUCT_DIM",
"GOSALESDW"."SLS_PRODUCT_LINE_LOOKUP" "SLS_PRODUCT_LINE_LOOKUP",
"GOSALESDW"."SLS_PRODUCT_TYPE_LOOKUP" "SLS_PRODUCT_TYPE_LOOKUP",
"GOSALESDW"."SLS_PRODUCT_LOOKUP" "SLS_PRODUCT_LOOKUP",
"GOSALESDW"."SLS_PRODUCT_COLOR_LOOKUP" "SLS_PRODUCT_COLOR_LOOKUP",
"GOSALESDW"."SLS_PRODUCT_SIZE_LOOKUP" "SLS_PRODUCT_SIZE_LOOKUP",
"GOSALESDW"."SLS_PRODUCT_BRAND_LOOKUP" "SLS_PRODUCT_BRAND_LOOKUP"

 WHERE "SLS_PRODUCT_LOOKUP"."PRODUCT_LANGUAGE" = N'EN' AND
"SLS_PRODUCT_DIM"."PRODUCT_LINE_CODE" =
"SLS_PRODUCT_LINE_LOOKUP"."PRODUCT_LINE_CODE" AND
"SLS_PRODUCT_DIM"."PRODUCT_NUMBER" =
"SLS_PRODUCT_LOOKUP"."PRODUCT_NUMBER" AND
"SLS_PRODUCT_DIM"."PRODUCT_SIZE_CODE" =
"SLS_PRODUCT_SIZE_LOOKUP"."PRODUCT_SIZE_CODE" AND
"SLS_PRODUCT_DIM"."PRODUCT_TYPE_CODE" =
"SLS_PRODUCT_TYPE_LOOKUP"."PRODUCT_TYPE_CODE" AND
"SLS_PRODUCT_DIM"."PRODUCT_COLOR_CODE" =
"SLS_PRODUCT_COLOR_LOOKUP"."PRODUCT_COLOR_CODE" AND
"SLS_PRODUCT_BRAND_LOOKUP"."PRODUCT_BRAND_CODE" =
"SLS_PRODUCT_DIM"."PRODUCT_BRAND_CODE"
```

This is a simple query that joins product-related tables and retrieves the required columns.

How to do it...

Now, we will modify the SQL scripts that we just created for this recipe so that in one of them we will adjust the parameter to be optional and in the second we will make the parameter optional also, but with a default value:

1. We have created two list reports based on two SQL query subjects. Both the SQL objects use the same query as mentioned earlier. Now, we will start by altering them. For that, open **Query Explorer**. Rename the first query subject **Optional_defaultValue** and the second one **Pure_Optional**:

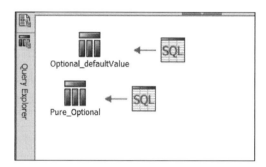

2. In the **Optional_defaultValue** SQL object, amend the query with the following lines:

    ```
    AND "SLS_PRODUCT_LINE_LOOKUP"."PRODUCT_LINE_EN" = #SQ(PROMPT
    ('PRODUCT LINE','STRING','GOLF EQUIPMENT'))#
    ```

3. Similarly, amend the **Pure_Optional** SQL object query with the following line:

    ```
    #PROMPT ('PRODUCT LINE','STRING','AND 1=1', ' AND "SLS_PRODUCT_
    LINE_LOOKUP"."PRODUCT_LINE_EN" = ')#
    ```

4. Now run the report. You will be prompted to enter a product line. Don't enter any value and just click on the **OK** button. Notice that the report runs (which means the prompt is optional). The first list object returns rows for **Golf Equipment**. The second list is populated by all the **Products**.

How it works...

Fundamentally, this report works the same as the one in the previous recipe. We are firing the SQL statements straight onto the data source. The filter condition in the WHERE clause is using the Prompt macro.

Optional_defaultValue

In this query, we are using the second and third arguments of the PROMPT() function. The second argument defines the data type of the value, which is String in our case. The third argument defines the default value of the prompt. When the user doesn't enter any value for the prompt, this default value is used. This is what makes the prompt optional. As we have defined Golf Equipment as the default value, the first list object shows data for **Golf Equipment** when the prompt is left unfilled.

Pure_Optional

In this query, we are using the fourth argument of the PROMPT() function. This argument is of string type. If the user provides any value for the prompt, the prompt value is concatenated to this string argument and the result is returned.

In our case, the fourth argument is the left part of the filtering condition; that is:

```
and "SLS_PRODUCT_LINE_LOOKUP"."PRODUCT_LINE_EN" = .
```

So, if the user enters the value as XYZ, the macro is replaced by the following filter:

```
and "SLS_PRODUCT_LINE_LOOKUP"."PRODUCT_LINE_EN" = 'XYZ'.
```

Interestingly, if the user doesn't provide any prompt value, then the fourth argument is simply ignored. The macro is then replaced by the third argument, which in our case is:

```
and 1=1.
```

Therefore, the second list returns all the rows when the user doesn't provide any value for the prompt. This way, it makes the PRODUCT_LINE_EN filter purely optional.

There's more...

The Prompt macro accepts two more arguments (fifth and sixth). Please check the help documents or Internet sources to find more information and examples about them.

Adding a token using macros

In this recipe, we will see how to dynamically change the field on which a filter is being applied to using a macro. We will use the prompt macro to generate one of the possible tokens and then use it in the query.

Getting ready

Create a list report based on native SQL similar to the previous recipe. We will use the same query that works on the product tables, but the filtering will be different. For that, define the SQL as follows:

```
SELECT DISTINCT "SLS_PRODUCT_LINE_LOOKUP"."PRODUCT_LINE_EN"
"PRODUCT_LINE" , "SLS_PRODUCT_LOOKUP"."PRODUCT_NAME" "PRODUCT_NAME" ,
"SLS_PRODUCT_COLOR_LOOKUP"."PRODUCT_COLOR_EN" "PRODUCT_COLOR" ,
"SLS_PRODUCT_SIZE_LOOKUP"."PRODUCT_SIZE_EN" "PRODUCT_SIZE"

FROM "GOSALESDW"."SLS_PRODUCT_DIM" "SLS_PRODUCT_DIM", "GOSALESDW"."SLS_
PRODUCT_LINE_LOOKUP" "SLS_PRODUCT_LINE_LOOKUP", "GOSALESDW"."SLS_PRODUCT_
TYPE_LOOKUP" "SLS_PRODUCT_TYPE_LOOKUP", "GOSALESDW"."SLS_PRODUCT_
LOOKUP" "SLS_PRODUCT_LOOKUP", "GOSALESDW"."SLS_PRODUCT_COLOR_LOOKUP"
"SLS_PRODUCT_COLOR_LOOKUP", "GOSALESDW"."SLS_PRODUCT_SIZE_LOOKUP"
"SLS_PRODUCT_SIZE_LOOKUP", "GOSALESDW"."SLS_PRODUCT_BRAND_LOOKUP" "SLS_
PRODUCT_BRAND_LOOKUP"

WHERE "SLS_PRODUCT_LOOKUP"."PRODUCT_LANGUAGE" = N'EN' AND
"SLS_PRODUCT_DIM"."PRODUCT_LINE_CODE" =
"SLS_PRODUCT_LINE_LOOKUP"."PRODUCT_LINE_CODE" AND
"SLS_PRODUCT_DIM"."PRODUCT_NUMBER" =
"SLS_PRODUCT_LOOKUP"."PRODUCT_NUMBER" AND
"SLS_PRODUCT_DIM"."PRODUCT_SIZE_CODE" =
"SLS_PRODUCT_SIZE_LOOKUP"."PRODUCT_SIZE_CODE" AND
"SLS_PRODUCT_DIM"."PRODUCT_TYPE_CODE" =
"SLS_PRODUCT_TYPE_LOOKUP"."PRODUCT_TYPE_CODE" AND
"SLS_PRODUCT_DIM"."PRODUCT_COLOR_CODE" =
"SLS_PRODUCT_COLOR_LOOKUP"."PRODUCT_COLOR_CODE" AND
"SLS_PRODUCT_BRAND_LOOKUP"."PRODUCT_BRAND_CODE" =
"SLS_PRODUCT_DIM"."PRODUCT_BRAND_CODE" AND
#PROMPT ('FIELD','TOKEN','"SLS_PRODUCT_LINE_LOOKUP"."PRODUCT_LINE_EN"')#
LIKE #PROMPT ('VALUE','STRING')#
```

This is the same basic query that joins the product-related tables and fetches the required columns. The last statement in the WHERE clause uses two prompt macros. We will talk about it in detail.

How to do it...

We have already created a list report based on an SQL query subject as mentioned previously. To continue this recipe perform the following steps:

1. Drag the columns from the query subject onto the list over the report page:

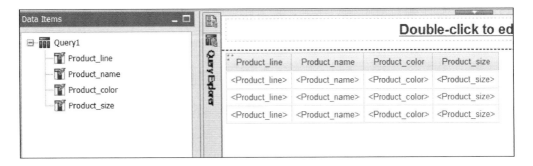

2. Now create a new prompt page.

3. Add a value prompt on the prompt page. Define two static choices for this:

Display value	Use value
Filter on product line	"SLS_PRODUCT_LINE_LOOKUP"."PRODUCT_LINE_EN"
Filter on product name	"SLS_PRODUCT_LOOKUP"."PRODUCT_NAME"

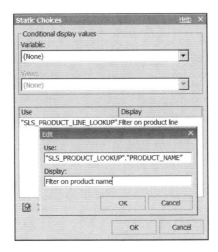

4. Set the parameter or this prompt to **Field**. This will come pre-populated as an existing parameter as it is defined in the query subject.

5. Choose the UI as radio button group and assign **Filter on Product Line** as the default selection.

6. Now add a textbox prompt on to the prompt page.

7. Set its parameter to **Value**; this comes as a choice in an existing parameter (as it is already defined in the query).

8. Run the report to test it. You will see an option to filter on product line or product name. The value you provide in the textbox prompt will be used to filter either of the fields depending on the choice selected using the radio buttons:

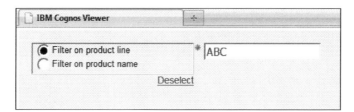

How it works...

The data type (second argument) of the PROMPT() function determines how the value is returned. For STRING type, the value is returned within a single quote. However, there is a data type called TOKEN. When you use this, the function accepts a STRING value and puts it literally within the expression, that is, without quotes.

Here, we have used this functionality to dynamically change the field on which the filter is applied. The two possible tokens are defined in the USE VALUE section of the radio button. Depending on the user's choice, one of the tokens will be placed in the query and will form the left part of the filter expression.

The right part of the filter is a standard string parameter. Whatever value the user types in the textbox prompt will be wrapped in single quotes and then placed in the SQL statement.

Effectively, the resulting expression will be something as follows:

```
"SLS_PRODUCT_LINE_LOOKUP"."PRODUCT_LINE_EN" = 'XYZ'
```

Using the prompt() and promptmany() macros in query subjects

This recipe will show you that macros can be used with standard query subjects as well.

Getting ready

Create a simple list report based on the **GO Sales Data Warehouse (Query)** package. Insert **Product line**, **Product**, **Product color**, and **Product size** as the columns.

How to do it...

In this recipe you will see how to use macros as filters in **Query Explorer** as follows:

1. Go to **Query Explorer** and open the query used by list.

2. Add a detail filter with the following definition:

   ```
   [Product line] = #prompt('ProductLine')#
   ```

3. Add another detail filter as follows:

   ```
   [Product] in #promptmany('Product')#
   ```

4. Run the report to test it. You will see two mandatory prompts. The one for the **Product line** will let you enter one value, whereas the other one will be on product and it will allow you to enter multiple values.

How it works...

This is the same Prompt macro which we used in prior recipes with native SQLs. As you can see, macros can be used in standard query subjects. You can utilize them in filters, a data items, or slicers.

The strength of this feature is seen when you use the other macros like `CSVIdentityNameList`, `TimeStampMask`, and so on in data item and slicer.

Showing the prompt values in a report based on security

This recipe combines the techniques learned in prior recipes to achieve a business requirement. Let's say that a report shows sales data by country and product line. Users can choose to see data for one or more countries.

However, we need to implement a security mechanism so that a user can choose only those countries to which they are supposed to have access. This is determined by the user group he/she belongs to.

Getting ready

Create a simple list report with **Country**, **City**, **Product line**, and sales **Quantity** as columns.

How to do it...

In this recipe, we will start by adding a filter for countries as follows:

1. Go to **Query Explorer** and insert a new detail filter and ensure that this filter is mandatory. Define it as:

   ```
   [Country] in ?Countries?
   ```

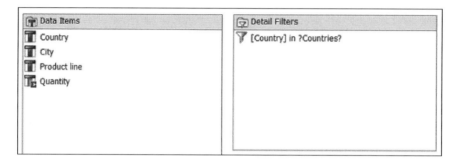

2. Now add a new prompt page. Drag a value prompt onto it.

3. Follow the prompt wizard to set the following:

   1. Link it to an existing parameter called **Countries**.

   2. Create a new query for this prompt and call it **Countries**.

4. Go to **Query Explorer** and open the **Countries** query subject.

5. Add a detail filter and define it as:

   ```
   [Country] in (#CSVIdentityNameList(',')#)
   ```

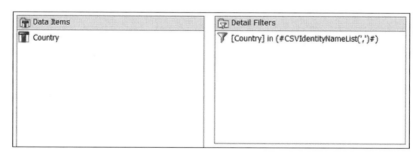

6. Run the report to test it. You will see that you can see only those countries in the value prompt to which the user is supposed to have access. For my account, I can see only 'Spain', as I have set the membership accordingly.

How it works...

This recipe simply combines the techniques we learnt in prior recipes. We use the `CSVIdentityNameList()` macro to retrieve the user group information.

We use this macro in the prompt query in order to restrict the values coming through in the value prompt. Whatever values are selected by users are then passed as a standard parameter for filtering to the report query.

String operations to get it right

We have seen one example of performing string manipulation in a macro to swap the columns of a slicer in *Chapter 7, Working with Dimensional Models*. In this recipe, I will show you more macro functions to manipulate the values and how to achieve the required functionality using them.

Let's say that a report is required to show sales by **Date** and **Product line**. This report should show data only for the current month (full month).

Getting ready

Create a simple list report with **Date**, **Product line**, and **Quantity** as columns:

Date	Product line	Quantity
<Date>	<Product line>	<Quantity>
<Date>	<Product line>	<Quantity>
<Date>	<Product line>	<Quantity>

How to do it...

In this recipe, we will see how to use some useful macro functions like `current_timestamp`, as follows:

1. Open **Query Explorer**. Go to the query used by the list object.

2. Add a new detail filter and define it as:

   ```
   [Date] between #timestampMask (_first_of_month(
      $current_timestamp),'yyyy-mm-dd')#  and #timestampMask(
      _last_of_month($current_timestamp),'yyyy-mm-dd')#
   ```

3. Run the report to test it. Unfortunately, the GO Sales database doesn't hold data for the year 2010. However, if you insert rows for the current month in the database, you will see that they are retrieved by the report.

How it works...

Here I am introducing you to four new elements usable in macros. The first one is a session parameter called `current_timestamp`. Session parameters are accessed in macros by putting a dollar sign ($) before them. `$current_timestamp` returns the current date and time on the Cognos server.

Then, we use functions called `_first_of_month()` and `_last_of_month()`. These functions accept the date-time value and return the corresponding first and last days of the month. For example, if today's date is 21st Jan 2010, then `#_first_of_month($current_timestamp)#` will return 1st Jan 2010.

Finally, we use the `timestampMask()` function to mask the time part and return the date in the required format. This function takes several format strings as a second argument, and we are passing `yyyy-mm-dd` for that. This way, we are using macros to determine the date range for the current full month. We use them to filter the data in our detail filter. You can use this concept to build up your own logic using different macro functions to achieve required functionalities that are not available as standard in Cognos Report Studio.

There's more...

I would highly recommend checking out the other macro functions using the Framework Manager.

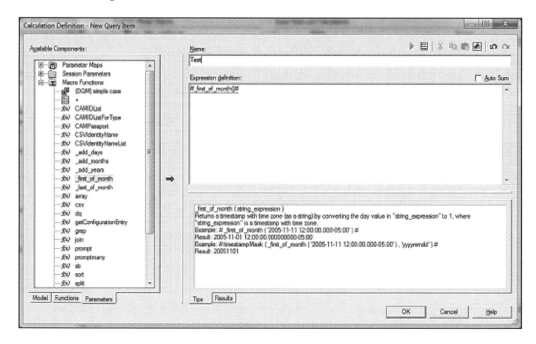

The Framework Manager gives you a ready list of available functions, their descriptions, and a place to quickly try and test them. If you are using Version 10, you can see this list of macro functions and syntax in the data editor, but you cannot quickly test a macro like you can do in the Framework Manager.

Showing a username in the footer

Let's examine two more session parameters which are very useful in real-life reports. Reports are often printed and handed over to other members/teams to have a look at. For a person who is looking at a printed report, the most important thing is to know the time when the report was run. That is why we usually put the timestamp in the report footer.

However, it is also useful to record who ran the report. This helps us to go back to the person in case of any queries. This recipe shows you how to display the user's name and the machine on which the report was run in the footer.

Getting ready

Pick up any of the existing reports.

How to do it...

In this recipe we will use a macro to show the user's username in the report footer, as follows:

1. Go to **Query Explorer** and create a new query subject called **User**.

2. In that query subject, add a new data item. Call it **Machine** and define it as:

   ```
   #sq($machine)#
   ```

3. Then, add another data item and call it **User**. Define it as:

   ```
   #sq($account.defaultName)#
   ```

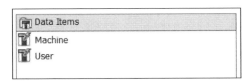

4. Now go to the report page. Select anything on the page. Using the **Ancestor** button, select the whole **Page** object.

5. For this, amend the **Query** property and link the page to the **User** query subject:

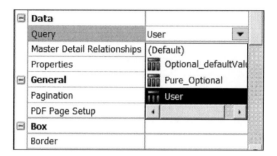

6. Now, drag the **User** and **Machine** data items from the **Data Items** pane in **Insertable objects** onto the report footer.

7. Run the report to test it:

How it works...

Here, we are using two session parameters, namely `$account.defaultName` and `$machine`. They are accessible from within a macro but that macro needs to be written within a query subject. Therefore, we create a new query subject to define these two items. Then, we link the page with it and drag the items onto the report footer.

There's more...

If the user directory is properly set up, you might be able to access more user information, such as e-mail ID, given names, and surname.

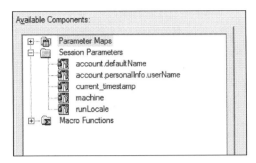

Please take your time to examine the other session parameters using the Framework Manager.

9
Using Report Studio Efficiently

In this chapter, we will cover the following topics:

- ▶ Using Report Studio's environmental options
- ▶ Copying and pasting partial or full reports
- ▶ Upgrading report specifications
- ▶ Setting the execution timeout
- ▶ Setting the maximum row limit
- ▶ Handling slow report validation
- ▶ Capturing a query
- ▶ Browsing values from the data expression window
- ▶ Viewing the page structure
- ▶ Picking up and applying styles
- ▶ Using the "grab them all" practice
- ▶ Using Default Data Formats

Introduction

A common issue when learning any rich tool is that we tend to miss out on some options or features that are not frequently used. We do routine development work without even knowing that there are some features that can improve our experience as a developer (report writer) or improve the deliverables.

This chapter will show you different customizable options and utilities within IBM Cognos Report Studio that can make a report builder's life easier. They will save you time and effort and some will reduce the number of defects as well.

Though I have made some recommendations throughout these recipes depending on my personal preference, I suggest that you try these options yourself and then decide. Please refer to the IBM Cognos manual for detailed information about each option and utility.

Using Report Studio's environmental options

In this recipe, you will learn about some environmental options that you can set in Report Studio to aid development.

Getting ready

Create a simple list report with **Product line** and **Product** as columns from the **Products** query subject.

How to do it...

In this recipe, we will examine some features in Report Studio that can be very helpful while creating your reports:

1. Select the **Product** column. Using the **Ancestor** button in the **Properties** pane, select the **List Column** object as shown in the following screenshot:

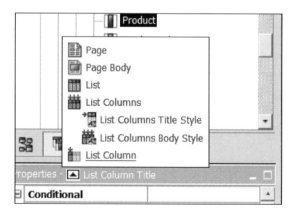

2. From the **Properties** pane, change the **Box Type** property to **None**:

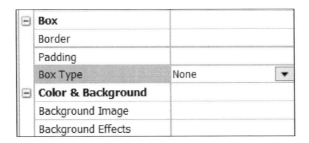

3. You will notice that you cannot see the **Product** column on the report page anymore. Now, assume that you want to change the **Box Type** property back to **default**. It is difficult to do it as you cannot select the column now.

4. From the menu, select **View** | **Visual Aids** | **Show Hidden Objects**. You will notice that the **Product** column becomes visible.

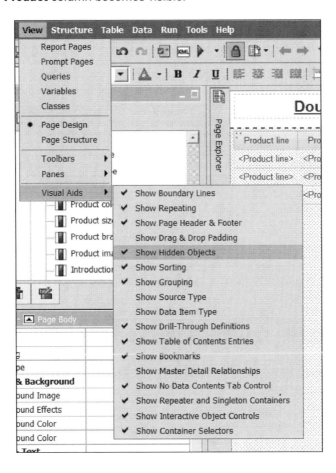

You can now select this column and change its properties as required.

Similarly, you can experiment with other options in **Visual Aids**.

Now we will see a crosstab-related feature:

1. Create a new page in the report and drag a crosstab with **Product** and **Product color** nested on rows, as shown in the following screenshot:

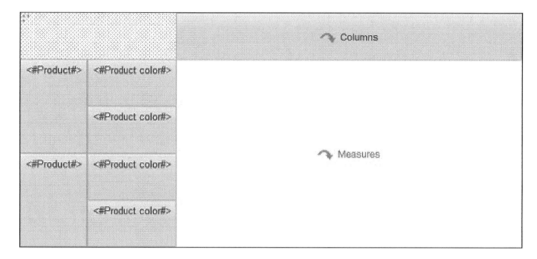

2. Now try to drag **Product size** beneath **Product**. You will see that it will create a new node without nesting **Product color** in it:

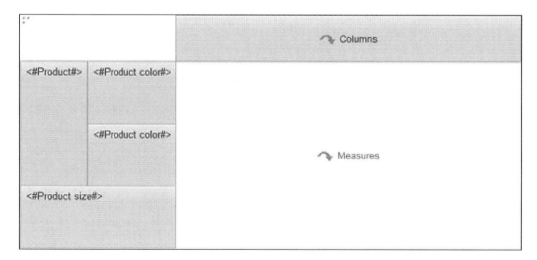

3. Now undo the last operation, and from the menu, select **Structure | Create Crosstab Nodes**. Uncheck this option.

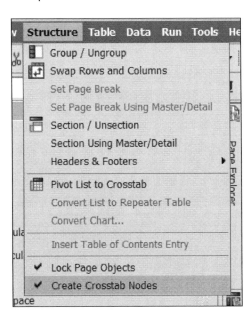

4. Try to drag **Product size** again beneath **Product**. You will notice that you can now insert it without creating a new crosstab node. It can be a peer of **Product** with **Product color** already nested in it, as shown in the following screenshot:

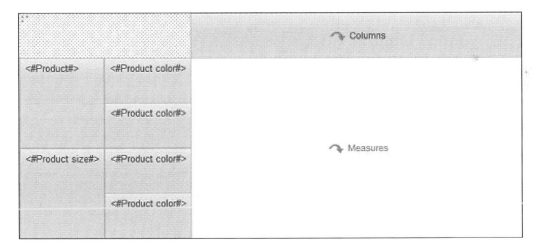

 We will discuss its usage in the *How it works...* section.

Now let us examine some options from the **Options** menu under **Tools**:

1. This dialog box has four tabs. The first tab is related to the look and feel of Report Studio. One important setting here is **Reuse IBM Cognos Viewer window**, shown in the following screenshot:

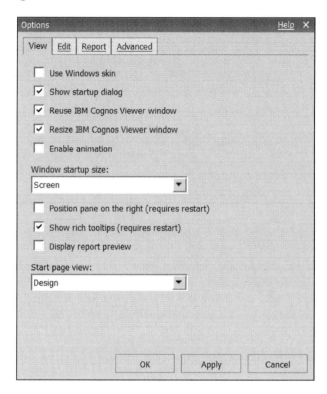

2. Toggle this option and run the report multiple times. You will notice that when this option is turned off, Report Studio creates a new window for every execution of the report.

3. Take your time to examine the options from other tabs as well. The **Report** tab has some useful options, which are discussed in the *How it works...* section.

How it works...

Now let us talk in detail about the options we visited in this recipe.

View | Visual Aids

As the name suggests, these are some visual aids to help the report writer during the development of a report.

We experimented with the option that toggled the visibility of hidden objects. Once an object is hidden, if it is not visible on the report page, the only way to manipulate it is to go to **Page Structure**. We will talk about this in another recipe in this chapter. However, I personally prefer **Show Hidden Objects** as it is very handy to select them from the report page and manipulate them.

Show Repeating is particularly useful when you have multiple levels of nesting and different group spans.

You should take your time to experiment with these options to decide on the ones you would like to keep.

Structure | Create Crosstab Nodes

As we have already seen, when this option is on and a new item is added to a crosstab, it is created as a crosstab node. When this option is off, the new item is added to the existing node and retains the existing nesting.

It is advisable to turn this option off. This will allow you to create discontinuous crosstabs. Also, you can manually add the same nesting as peer nodes anyway if you need to do so.

Tools | Options | View | Reuse IBM Cognos Viewer window

I prefer to turn this option off during development. By doing so, I can compare the report output with that of the previous execution and see the effect of whatever changes I performed. However, you might end up having loads of report viewer windows. So, you should remember to close the ones that are not needed. Again, it is your personal choice to keep or reject this option.

Tools | Options | Report

Let us examine some useful options from this tab:

Option	Description
Alias member unique names	This is useful when working with dimensional models. If turned on, Report Studio creates a separate data item (**alias**) for any member dragged into an expression.
	I prefer to keep this option off, as it unnecessarily increases the number of data items in a query subject.
Delete unreferenced query objects	When on, Report Studio automatically deletes the query objects linked to another object that is deleted. For example, if you delete a list, the query subject linked to the list is deleted as well. I like this one as it helps with housekeeping.
	If you want to remove an object from one place but still keep it in other places, you can "cut" it instead of "deleting" it.

Option	Description
Delete unreferenced conditional styles	This automatically deletes conditional styles when the last data item that refers to the conditional style is deleted.
Aggregation mode	This is a very useful option when working with a dimensional data source. It specifies the aggregation type to use when aggregating values in crosstabs and charts. ▸ **Within detail** aggregates the lowest level of visible details. ▸ **Within aggregate** aggregates the visible aggregates at the next lower level of detail. ▸ **Within set** aggregates the member sets. It considers members within the current content and is faster than **Within detail**. **Within set** can not only affect the result of the aggregation, but also the performance of report. This option has been taken off in Version 10.2.
Always Create Extended Data Items for new reports	I like to turn this option off. When turned off, any member dragged from **Source** to **Report** is created as an *expression-based* data item that can be modified by changing the expression. If this option is turned on, the items are "Extended Data Items" with extended properties but cannot be manually updated.
Limit on inserted individual members	This option works with a dimension source when you choose to insert children while dragging a member onto the data container. Instead of inserting all children, this allows us to specify how many children should be added, and the remaining children are grouped into **OTHER**.

There's more...

You should refer to the Cognos documentation to learn more about these options and then experiment with them to decide which are best for you.

Copying and pasting partial or full reports

Perhaps this is not something that is going to impress you. However, I was really impressed when I saw this feature. We will see how to copy part of a report and a full report and paste it into another instance.

We often need to copy part of a report or the full report from one Report Studio environment or instance, to another. This might be for re-use purposes or for promoting it to the next stage.

Getting ready

We will use the report created in the previous recipe for this one.

How to do it...

In this recipe we will see how to copy part of a report—in our case, a query and its list table—from one report to another report. We will also see how to copy the whole report to a new report. To do this, perform the following steps:

1. Open the report in Report Studio. We will call it the **Source** instance.

2. Now open another instance of Report Studio from the same connection portal for the same package, **GO Data Warehouse (query)**. We will call this instance **Destination**.

3. Now go to **Query Explorer** in both the instances.

4. Right click on **Query1** from the **Source** instance and choose **Copy**:

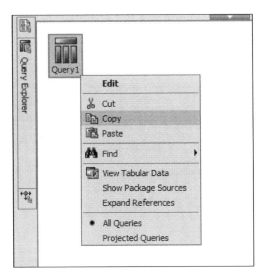

5. In the **Query Explorer** pane of the **Destination** instance, right-click and choose **Paste**.

   You will see that the query subject is successfully copied. You can open it and check the data items. They carry all the properties properly.

6. Now go to **Report Page** in the **Source** instance. Select the list object. This time hit *Ctrl + C* on the keyboard to copy it.

7. Switch to the **Destination** instance. Go to **Report Page**. Select the page body and hit *Ctrl + V* to paste the list object. Change the **Query** property of this list to **Query1** as shown in the following screenshot:

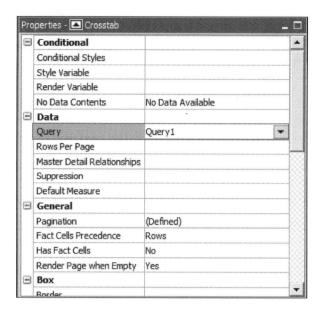

8. Run the report to test it. You will see that the list report is produced correctly.

9. Finally, we will see how to copy the whole report. For that, go back to the **Source** instance.

10. From the menu, choose **Tools | Copy Report to Clipboard**.

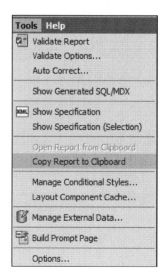

11. In the **Destination** instance, from the menu, choose **Tools | Open Report from Clipboard**.

12. You will see that the whole report has been copied to the **Destination** instance. Here, it is a new report that you can validate and save at an appropriate location.

How it works...

When a part of the report is selected and copied (right-clicking and then selecting **Copy** or *Ctrl + C*), its XML specification is copied on the clipboard. You can paste it in any XML or text editor and examine it. In the **Destination** instance, you can paste this XML specification and Report Studio properly parses it to create the objects.

When the copied object has some dependency, for example, a list that is dependent on the query subject, then the dependency object should be copied first. That is why we first copied the query subject and then the list.

 This feature is useful as it allows for the quick re-use of objects and saves time. Please note that this feature works only with IE up to Cognos 10.1.1. I have tested it on Firefox but it doesn't seem to work.

The **Copy Report to Clipboard** and **Open Report from Clipboard** options are particularly useful when copying reports across environments or servers. This comes in handy when the packages are promoted to the destination environment, and hence this saves the export-import hassles.

Upgrading report specifications

This recipe will examine whether we can use the copy and paste feature of Report Studio to promote a report from an older version to a newer version.

Getting ready

You might not be able to experiment with this. I will perform this recipe using two Cognos environments: 8.4 and 10.1.1. Both the environments are configured and have the **GO Data Warehouse (query)** package published.

How to do it...

In this recipe you will see how report specifications are upgraded when copying the report to a higher version of Cognos:

1. Open any report in Report Studio Version 8.4.

2. From the menu, choose **Tools | Copy Report to Clipboard**.

3. Open the Report Studio instance from a higher version of Cognos. I will open one from 10.1.1. Choose the **GO Data Warehouse (query)** package.

4. In this new instance, select **Tools | Open Report from Clipboard** from the menu.

   You will see the following dialog box:

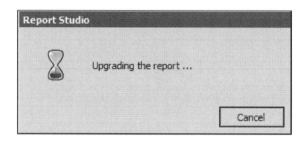

5. Run the report to test it. In most cases, the report will run fine.

How it works...

The newer versions of Cognos Report Studio are made backwards compatible when it comes to the XML specification of the report. That means we can copy the specification from an older version and paste it into a newer one. It will automatically detect the difference and will upgrade the specification accordingly.

Setting the execution timeout

Some reports are capable of firing quite resource-consuming queries on the data source. This can cause a bottleneck on the database and hence a problem for other users and jobs. This recipe will show you how to automatically get the report query killed if it takes longer than a certain time limit.

Getting ready

Create a simple list report based on the **GO Data Warehouse (query)** package. Pull Product line, Product type, and Product as columns.

How to do it...

In this recipe we will learn how to set the execution timeout for a query. To do this, perform the following steps:

1. Open the report in Cognos Report Studio.

2. Go to **Query Explorer** and select **Query1**.

3. From the **Properties** pane, open the **Maximum Execution Time** property.

4. Set it to a low number. For testing, we will set it to 1, as shown in the following screenshot:

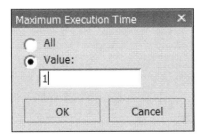

That means we are setting the maximum execution time for the query to one second.

5. Run the report to test it. In most cases, this will cross the threshold of one second and you will receive an error message such as the one shown as follows:

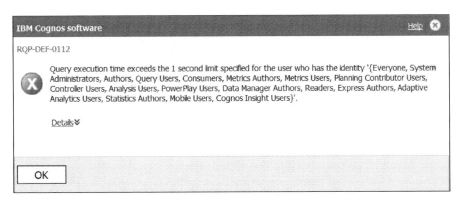

6. Now go back to Cognos Report Studio and increase the **Maximum Execution Time** value for the query to **30 sec** and run the report. It will run fine.

How it works...

In this recipe, we experimented with the **Maximum Execution Time** property of the query. As you can see, this property allows us to terminate the report execution automatically if the query is taking a long time.

It is a useful property for reports where users can accidentally or purposely put some highly resource-consuming selection parameters. For example, if a report is supposed to be run for a small date range, some users might mistakenly run it for months or years, therefore hammering the database. This can take up a lot of database time and might also affect other jobs running on the server.

By putting a time limit on it, we can ensure that the report is automatically terminated if it is going on for a certain length of time.

However, this time limit is not for the total time taken by the query on the database. It is for the time lapsed from query submission to the first result returned back. In an HTML output, often a page full of data is returned quickly, and hence the report might not show an error. However, when the same report is run in PDF or Excel, it might reach the threshold and result in an error.

Also, there is no easy way to customize the error message. As you can see, it is an ugly message, but we have to live with it.

There's more...

The maximum time limit can also be set at the package level in Framework Manager using the **governors**. Please refer to the Framework Manager documentation for the same.

The administrator can also define an environment-wide query execution time limit from the **connection portal** by configuring the report service. For that, please refer to the *Administration and Security Guide*.

Setting the maximum row limit

This is similar to the previous recipe. Instead of setting any limit for query execution time, here we will set a restriction on the number of rows returned by the query.

Getting ready

We will use the report created in the previous recipe for this recipe.

How to do it...

In this recipe we will learn how to set the maximum row limit for a query. To do this, perform the following steps:

1. Open the report in Report Studio.

2. Go to **Query Explorer** and select the report query.

3. From the **Properties** pane, open the **Maximum Rows Retrieved** property.

4. For testing purposes, set it to **50** as shown in the following screenshot:

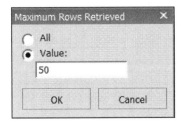

5. Run the report in HTML format.

6. Browse the report page by page. As soon as you hit the record count of 50 (usually on the third page), you will receive an error message saying that the query has reached the maximum row limit.

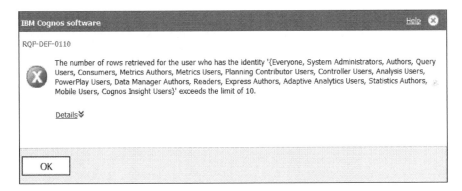

7. Go back to Cognos Report Studio and change the limit to the required row limit; for example, 2000.

How it works...

This option serves the same requirement as the last recipe. When you want to ensure that the data source is not burdened by heavy queries, you should set such limits.

The maximum row limit can also be set at the package level from Framework Manager.

Handling slow report validation

Sometimes when you try to validate a report in Cognos Report Studio, it takes a long time. You will see the validating alert and then a blank dialog box appears and the Studio will seem to have frozen.

This recipe will show you how to fix this problem.

Getting ready

Create a simple report with all the columns from **GO Data Warehouse (Query)/ / Sales/ / Products** as query subjects.

Product line	Product line code	Product type	Product	Product color	Product size	Product brand	Product image	Introduction date	Discontinued date	Product description
<Product line>	<Product line code>	<Product type>	<Product>	<Product color>	<Product size>	<Product brand>		<Introduction date>	<Discontinued date>	<Product description>
<Product line>	<Product line code>	<Product type>	<Product>	<Product color>	<Product size>	<Product brand>		<Introduction date>	<Discontinued date>	<Product description>
<Product line>	<Product line code>	<Product type>	<Product>	<Product color>	<Product size>	<Product brand>		<Introduction date>	<Discontinued date>	<Product description>

How to do it...

In this recipe you will learn a small trick that can help you to avoid slow report validation. To do this, perform the following steps:

1. We will start by replicating the scenario that I am talking about. For that, open **Query Explorer**.

2. Open the query associated with the list object. It is called **Query1** in the sample.

3. Add a detail filter with the following definition:

```
[Product line code] in ?PL?
and [Product type] in ?Type?
and [Product] in ?Name?
and [Product color] in ?Color?
and [Product size] in ?Size?
and [Product brand] in ?Brand?
```

4. Go back to the report page. Now click on the **Validate** button from the toolbar.

   Notice that you first get the validating alert. Then, a new dialog box appears, which is blank for a while.

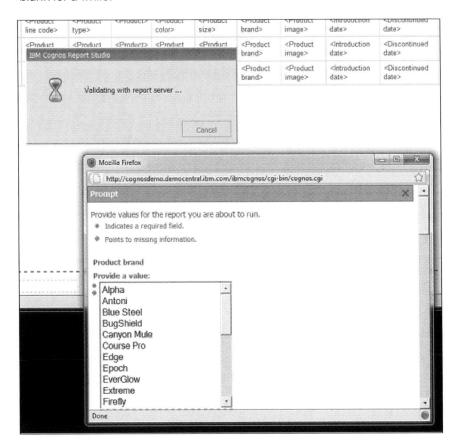

5. Finally, all the prompts are loaded in that dialog box. You need to select each of them as all are mandatory. After making the selection, the report validates.

6. Now go back to **Query Subject**. Disable the detail filter.

7. Try validating the report now. You will see that validation is very quick now. You are not prompted for any selection and also the time to bring the prompts up is saved.

How it works...

When we validate any report in Cognos Report Studio, it asks us to enter the values for all the mandatory filters. This is a good thing as it forms the query with more completeness before validating. However, the prompt query and type of prompt are not controlled, which can often result in a long time interval to generate the prompt. This is annoying for the report writer as he/she only wants to do a sanity check on the report code.

By disabling the filter, we exclude it from the validation process. Report Studio still validates everything else, that is, data items, slicers, calculations, other query subjects, and so on.

This way we can stop Cognos Report Studio from freezing or taking a long time to validate the report and still have peace of mind that most of the report is validated. After the validation is done, you should enable the filter again and then do test runs to ensure that the filters are working fine. You would do that anyway for unit testing.

There's more...

You can specify certain options related to report validation from the menu. Select **Tools | Validation Options**. Here you can decide what level of information you would like to receive during the validation process. By default, it is set to **Warning**.

I recommend setting it to the most detailed, that is, the **Information** level. This can provide some interesting and useful information about key transformations and query planning.

You can also decide whether you would like the query optimization to happen or not using the **Interactive Data** option. When this is selected, the optimization is done and the plan is created to retrieve the top rows depending on the **Execution Optimization** property of the query subject. By default, this option is unchecked. That means the query is planned for retrieval of all rows. I recommend keeping it as the default, that is, unchecked.

Capturing a query

Report Studio is a tool for a wide audience—right from business users, management personnel, and analysts, to the pure technical report writers. If you are a technical person who understands the SQL/MDX being fired on the database, you certainly want to examine one to optimize the report performance and sometimes to merely ensure that everything is fine.

This recipe will look at the right ways to capture the query fired on a data source.

Getting ready

We will use the list report created in the previous recipe for this recipe.

How to do it...

In this recipe we will learn how to extract the SQL/MDX query generated for a report. To do this, perform the following steps:

1. Open the report in IBM Cognos Report Studio.

2. Go to **Query Explorer** and set the **Usage** option of the filter item to **Optional**.

3. From the menu, select **Tools | Show Generated SQL/MDX**, as shown in the following screenshot:

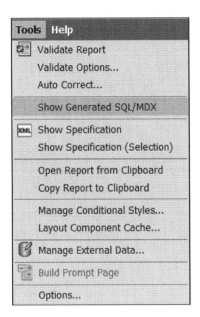

A new dialog box will appear with the SQL statements for each query subject (only **Query1** in this example).

4. Choose **Native SQL** from the drop-down list. Now, examine the SQL statement:

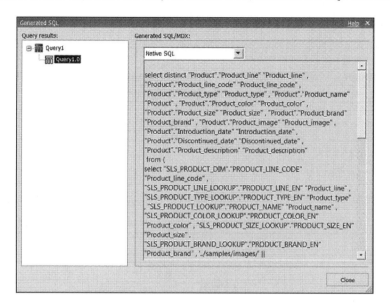

You will notice that there are no filters in the WHERE condition.

5. Now, close this dialog box. Change the **Usage** option of the filter to **Required**.

6. Again, choose **Tools | Show Generated SQL/MDX** from the menu. You will be asked to enter prompt values. Enter some and click on **OK**.

7. Check **Native SQL**. This time you will see that filters are included in the WHERE clause:

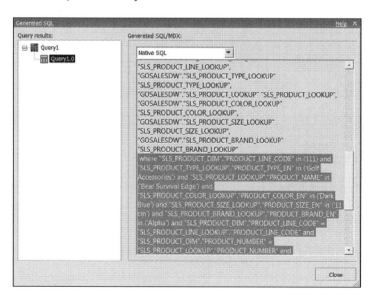

This is a query with more completeness, which gives a better idea of what statement will be executed on the database when users run the report.

How it works...

The **Show Generated SQL/MDX** option gives you two types of queries: **Cognos SQL** and **Native SQL**. Cognos SQL is a generic and more readable form that also uses some Cognos functions. However, it is not an exact query that is fired on the database. For that, we need to refer to Native SQL.

There's more...

The following are a few more important aspects of the recipe explained.

Why make filters mandatory?

In the previous recipe, I recommended that you disable the filters before validating. That was to exclude the query and speed up the validation. However, we have a different requirement here. Our report writing is almost done, and all data items, calculations, filters, slicers, and so on are defined. We now want to examine the actual query that will be fired on the database, to examine the correctness of joins and filtering, and to check any optimization possibilities.

For that purpose, we need the completeness of a query. Therefore, I am now asking you to change all the filters to **Required**. That way, we force Cognos Report Studio to prompt you for the values and then include all the filters in the query.

Query formatting

The native query in the dialog box is not formatted, and hence it is very difficult to read. I recommend using some query formatting tools for that.

Many database clients and utilities such as TOAD can be used to format SQL statements. You can also use online tools such as `http://www.dpriver.com/pp/sqlformat.htm`.

If you are writing a report against the dimensional source, the query will be of MDX type. Visit `http://formatmdx.msftlabs.com/` for information that can be useful for formatting it.

Capturing the query for the database

It is recommended that you use the tracing utilities to directly trap the query from the server. That way, you can examine the timing and behavior. When you run the report in the HTML format, Cognos might be asking for just a set of data. When you use **Sections** in the report, there will be multiple queries fired on the database for a loop of values. All this can be studied only by directly examining the activities on the database server. The **Session Browser** tab in TOAD and Profiler for SQL Server are classic examples of such utilities.

Browsing values from the data expression window

This recipe will show you a small feature of Cognos Report Studio that comes in handy and is often overlooked.

Getting ready

We will use the report used in the previous recipes for this recipe.

How to do it...

In this recipe we will see how we can browse the values in the data expression window to select a specific value to be used. To do this, perform the following steps:

1. Open the report in Report Studio.

2. Let's say we want this report to show only certain product lines (hardcoding). For that, we would want to add a **Product line** filter. So, add a new detail filter.

3. Now we are in the filter expression dialog. Enter the following expression:

   ```
   [Product Line] in
   ```

   This is shown in the following screenshot:

4. As this filter will do literal string comparisons, we need to enter the exact values of the required product lines. Select the **Product line** data item from the data items' pane. Click on the **Select Multiple Values** button in the upper-right corner of the page (located beside the cut icon).

    This will open a new dialog box.

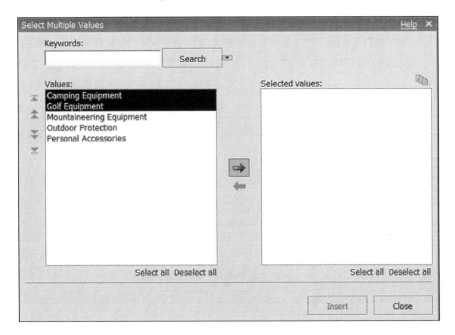

5. Select **Camping Equipment** and **Golf Equipment**. Click on the green arrow to add them to the list on the right. Finally, close this dialog by clicking on the **Insert** button.

6. You will see that the selected values are automatically populated in the filter expression, and the expression now reads like this:

    ```
    [Product line] in ('Camping Equipment', 'Mountaineering
    Equipment')
    ```

7. Close the dialog box and run the report to test it.

How it works...

We often need to hardcode some data values in reports. This may be to restrict the data set or to perform some conditional logic or some other requirements. In order to define the values correctly, we need to browse the data and make sure that we write them correctly in the expression.

Instead of opening a database client to browse these values, this utility in Cognos Report Studio comes in handy. Sometimes, the report authors don't even have the database clients installed and configured on their machine.

You will see these two buttons in Cognos Report Studio when you are in the data item expression or filter expression dialog box:

Both will let you browse the values of the selected data item or query item. However, the first one will allow you to select only one value to be inserted in the expression, whereas the other one will allow you to select multiple values and will add them to the expression as comma-delimited and within brackets.

There's more...

You can also test the data of the whole query subject (all query items with the filters and slicers applied on the results) by opening the query subject in **Query Explorer** and choosing **Run | View Tabular Data** from the menu, as shown in the following screenshot:

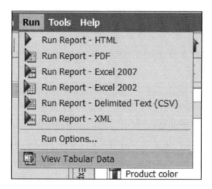

Please try this option to see how it works.

Viewing the page structure

This recipe will show you another view/option available in Cognos Report Studio to examine and edit the reports.

Getting ready

We will use the same report used in the previous recipe for this recipe.

How to do it...

In this recipe we will see how to view/use **Page Structure**. To do this, perform the following steps:

1. Open the report in Report Studio and go to the report page.

2. From the menu, choose **View | Page Structure** as shown in the following screenshot:

3. You will see that the report page transforms into a tree-type list object, as shown in the following screenshot:

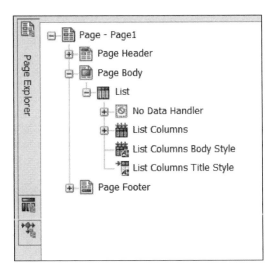

4. Open the different nodes and examine the objects.

How it works...

As you know, the report definitions in Cognos Report Studio are nothing but XML files. The report objects, Page, List, Columns, and so on, are all stored internally as nested tags.

By switching to the **Page Structure** view, you can actually see how the objects are contained within each other and how they are inter-related. You can select any object (for example, **List Columns Body Style**) and manipulate its properties. You can also delete them, copy the objects and paste them in another place, and move them around within the rules governed by Cognos Report Studio.

This is a great way to examine and manipulate some report objects that are not directly visible in the normal view. We had mentioned in the *Using Report Studio's environmental options* recipe that when you hide some objects on the report page, and if the hidden items are not made visible by changing the environment options, then the only way to select and manipulate them is to do it from the **Page Structure** view.

I would recommend that you familiarize yourself with this view. Do some browsing, copying/deleting of objects, and try changing properties of some objects. Later, you can go back to the normal view by selecting **View | Page Design** from the menu.

Picking up and applying styles

In this recipe, we will see a very useful utility within Cognos Report Studio that you can use to deal with styles in your reports.

Getting ready

We will use the same list report that we used in the previous recipe for this recipe.

How to do it...

In this recipe we will see how to pick up a specific style that is applied on a specific column and then apply it on other columns in the report:

1. We will apply certain formatting to the list columns. Start by applying the following to the `Product line` column:

   - **Font**: **12 pt**.
   - **Background Color**: **#FFFF99**.
   - **Border**: **1pt** solid lines on left and right. **None** for **Top** and **Bottom**.

2. Select the `Product line` column. Click on the Pick-Up Style button from the toolbar.

3. Now select the `Product type` and `Product` columns from the list (by holding the *Ctrl* key).

4. Click on the **Apply Style** button.

   You will see that all the formatting, font, background color, and borders are applied to the selected columns:

Product line	Product line code	Product type	Product	Product color	Product size	Product brand	Product image	Introduction date	Discontinued date	Product description
<Product line>	<Product line code>	<Product type>	<Product>	<Product color>	<Product size>	<Product brand>	<Product image>	<Introduction date>	<Discontinued date>	<Product description>
<Product line>	<Product line code>	<Product type>	<Product>	<Product color>	<Product size>	<Product brand>	<Product image>	<Introduction date>	<Discontinued date>	<Product description>
<Product line>	<Product line code>	<Product type>	<Product>	<Product color>	<Product size>	<Product brand>	<Product image>	<Introduction date>	<Discontinued date>	<Product description>

5. Now again select the `Product line` column.

6. This time, click on the little drop-down arrow beside the Pick-Up Style button. Choose the **Edit Dropper Style...** option as shown in the following screenshot:

7. This will open up a dialog box with the style already filled in. We don't want to copy the color for the rest of the columns. We need only font and borders. So, change the background color to **Default**.

8. Click on the **OK** button to close the dialog.

9. Now choose the rest of the columns from the list (the ones that are not formatted). Click on the **Apply Style** button. Notice that the fonts and borders are applied to these columns and the background color remains as default:

Product line	Product line code	Product type	Product	Product color	Product size	Product brand	Product image	Introduction d
\<Product line\>	\<Product line code\>	\<Product type\>	\<Product\>	\<Product color\>	\<Product size\>	\<Product brand\>	\<Product image\>	\<Introduct date\>
\<Product line\>	\<Product line code\>	\<Product type\>	\<Product\>	\<Product color\>	\<Product size\>	\<Product brand\>	\<Product image\>	\<Introduct date\>
\<Product line\>	\<Product line code\>	\<Product type\>	\<Product\>	\<Product color\>	\<Product size\>	\<Product brand\>	\<Product image\>	\<Introduct date\>

10. Run the report to test it.

How it works...

Pick-Up Style and **Apply Style** are buttons added to Cognos Report Studio from Version 8.3 onwards. They work in conjunction and are extremely useful to the report writer.

As you have seen in this recipe, it allows the writer to pick up or copy the styling of an object and then apply it to one or more objects in the report. You can choose to apply all the styles (colors, fonts, border, alignments, padding, formatting, data format, images, and so on) or just apply the selected ones.

From experience, it is seen that a lot of time is spent formatting reports that have a large number of columns, rows, aggregations, and so on. Also, this is the area causing cosmetic defects in the reports. Using this utility, we can save quite some time and prevent defects too.

Using the "grab them all" practice

This recipe will tell you about something that is good practice. I have put it under this chapter for two reasons. One: it builds upon the idea learned in the previous recipe. Two: it does help you use Report Studio better.

The previous recipe showed you how to apply styles to selected list columns. Here we will see the recommended way to apply the same style to all the objects (List Column Titles in this case).

Getting ready

We will continue working on the report that we modified in the previous recipe.

How to do it...

In this recipe we will show you how to apply the same style on multiple objects.

1. Say we want to apply the following style to all the list column titles:

   ❑ **Font**: **12 Pt**

   ❑ **Background Color**: **Silver**

   ❑ **Border**: **1pt Solid all sides**

2. We have two options. First apply this style to one column title, say, `Product line`, as shown in the following screenshot:

Product line	Product line code	Product type	Product	Product color	Product size	Product brand	Product image	Introduction
<Product line>	<Product line code>	<Product type>	<Product>	<Product color>	<Product size>	<Product brand>	<Product image>	<Introduc date>
<Product line>	<Product line code>	<Product type>	<Product>	<Product color>	<Product size>	<Product brand>	<Product image>	<Introduc date>
<Product line>	<Product line code>	<Product type>	<Product>	<Product color>	<Product size>	<Product brand>	<Product image>	<Introduc date>

3. Now, use the Pick-Up Style and Apply Style buttons to all the column titles as learned in the previous recipe.

4. Run the report to test it and you will see that it works:

Product line	Product line code	Product type	Product	Product color	Product size	Product brand	Product image	Introdu dat
<Product line>	<Product line code>	<Product type>	<Product>	<Product color>	<Product size>	<Product brand>	<Product image>	<Introd date>
<Product line>	<Product line code>	<Product type>	<Product>	<Product color>	<Product size>	<Product brand>	<Product image>	<Introd date>
<Product line>	<Product line code>	<Product type>	<Product>	<Product color>	<Product size>	<Product brand>	<Product image>	<Introd date>

5. However, if you drag a few more columns on the list, you will see that the formatting needs to be re-done on them.

Product line	Product line code	Product type	Product	Quantity	Unit cost	Unit price	Product color	Product size
<Product line>	<Product line code>	<Product type>	<Product>	<Quantity>	<Unit cost>	<Unit price>	<Product color>	<Product size>
<Product line>	<Product line code>	<Product type>	<Product>	<Quantity>	<Unit cost>	<Unit price>	<Product color>	<Product size>
<Product line>	<Product line code>	<Product type>	<Product>	<Quantity>	<Unit cost>	<Unit price>	<Product color>	<Product size>

6. To avoid this problem, let's learn another technique. Remember that we want to apply the same formatting to all column titles. So, undo all the changes we have made to the report in this recipe. Bring it back to the original state as we left it in the previous recipe.

7. Now select any one list column title.

8. Using the **Ancestor** button in the **Properties** pane, choose **List Column Title Style**. You will notice that all column titles are selected.

9. Now apply the required formatting (color, border, and font in this example):

10. Run the report to test it.

11. Add some new columns to the list. Notice that the column titles already have consistent formatting.

Product line	Product line code	Product type	Product	Quantity	Unit cost	Unit price	Product color	Product size
<Product line>	<Product line code>	<Product type>	<Product>	<Quantity>	<Unit cost>	<Unit price>	<Product color>	<Product size>
<Product line>	<Product line code>	<Product type>	<Product>	<Quantity>	<Unit cost>	<Unit price>	<Product color>	<Product size>
<Product line>	<Product line code>	<Product type>	<Product>	<Quantity>	<Unit cost>	<Unit price>	<Product color>	<Product size>

How it works...

What we are doing here is instead of selecting the column titles individually, we are making a general selection of **List Column Title Style** that applies to all column titles. In fact, it is a parent object, so even the new items added later on to the list will fall under it and will carry the same formatting.

This practice of selecting a generic or parent-level object not only saves time but also makes the formatting more future-proof. A report writer should follow this "grab it all" practice whenever formatting.

See also

Please don't miss the *Customizing classes for report-wide effect* recipe in *Chapter 13, Best Practices*, as it will further enhance the technique of applying a universal style to the report.

Using Default Data Formats

This recipe will show you how to specify default data formats to save time during development. This option is available in v10.2.

Getting ready

Create a new crosstab report.

How to do it...

In this recipe we will see how to define a default data format to be used within the report. To do this, perform the following steps:

1. From the **Data** menu, open **Default Data Formats...** as shown in the following screenshot:

2. Select the **Number** format and update the properties as you would like to commonly use throughout the report.

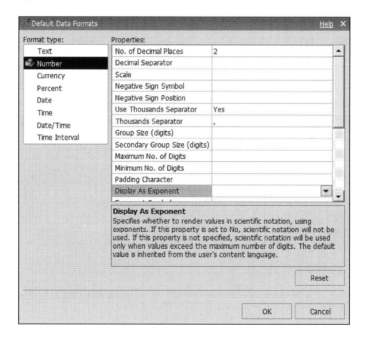

3. Go ahead with report creation as normal. For any numeric column or fact cells, select the data format as **Number** but don't specify any properties.

4. Run the report to test it. See that the item with the **Number** data format follows **Default Number Style**, that is, two decimal places, negative brackets, and the thousands separator.

How it works...

By defining the detailed properties (decimals, separator, negative sign, error characters, and so on) for each required data format (**Number**, **Date**, **Time**, **Currency**, **Percent**, and so on) under **Data | Default Data Formats**, Report Studio allows us to save time in development as well as maintain consistency in the report.

We can always override the properties for any individual item if required.

10
Working with
Active Reports

In this chapter, we will cover the following topics:

- ▶ Building tabbed reports
- ▶ Working with Decks
- ▶ Working with the Data Deck
- ▶ Filtering data using Data Check Box Group

Introduction

In this chapter, we will cover Active Reports. IBM Cognos Active Report is a new report output type that was introduced in IBM Cognos Business Intelligence 10.1. Active Reports allow professional report authors to create highly interactive and easy-to-use reports. These report outputs work as self-contained applications that allow users to go through the interactive contents even when they are offline. It is a great option for mobile workers who are often not connected to the network.

Active Reports make business intelligence easier for users on the go. Report authors build reports targeted at their users' needs, keeping the user experience simple and allowing them to explore their data and derive additional insight to their own convenience without being online and connected to the network.

IBM Cognos Active Report outputs are self-contained so all the data that is returned by the queries is included in the reports. As the amount of data increases, the output file **MHT** (**Microsoft Hypertext Archive**) file size increases.

Building tabbed reports

In this recipe, we will create our first Active Report. We will examine the Active Report's Tab control and see how to use it to create a multi-tab reports. Before Active Reports, these kind of reports could be done only by embedding a long HTML code in the report.

Getting ready

For this recipe, we will use the **GO Data Warehouse (query)** package. We will create a report with two tabs. In the first tab we will have a **Crosstab** report, while in the second tab we will have a **Chart** report.

Open the IBM Cognos Report Studio and select the **GO Data Warehouse (query)** package.

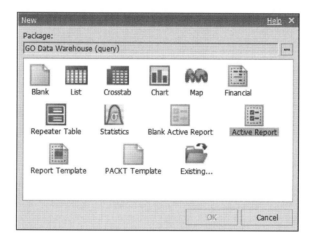

Select the **Active Report** template and click on **OK**. This will open a new Active Report that we will use through this recipe.

How to do it...

In this recipe, we will see how to use Tab control to build multi-tab reports. To do this, perform the following steps:

1. From the **Toolbox** items, drag the **Tab Control** object onto the report.

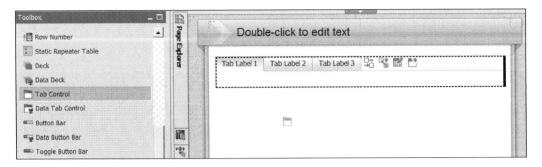

2. Click on the **Tab Control** object. In the **Properties** pane, rename the control to `Crosstab / Chart Tab Control`.

3. Click on the **Tabs Definition** button within the **Tab Control** object.

 If you don't see buttons, you will have to go to **View | Visual Aid | Show Interactive Object Controls**. After enabling, you will be able to see these buttons for Tab control:

4. In the pop-up window that will appear, delete **Tab Label 3** by clicking on the **X** icon that will appear when you hover over Tab Label 3.

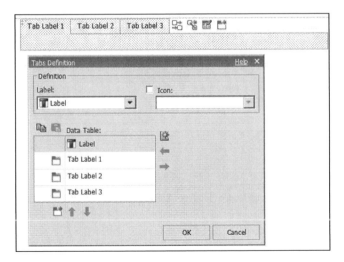

5. Rename **Tab Label 1** to `Crosstab` and **Tab Label 2** to `Chart`.

6. Click on **OK** to return to the report page. Now you can notice that the changes we have made are applied now to the Tab control.

7. Now from **Toolbox**, drag **Crosstab** onto the **Crosstab** tab.

8. From the **Source** pane, drag **Product line** onto the rows of the crosstab. Drag **Year** into the columns of the crosstab. Add **Revenue** as the crosstab measure.

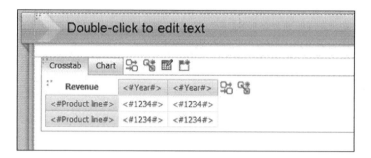

9. Now click on the **Chart** tab. Drag a chart from **Toolbox** and select **Line Chart** as the chart type and then click on **OK**.

10. From the **Source** pane, drag **Product line** onto the **Series:** of the chart. Drag **Year** onto **Categories:** of the chart. Add **Revenue** as the chart measure.

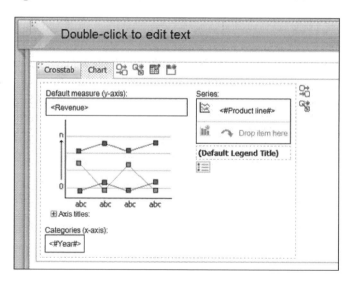

11. Now run the report to test it.

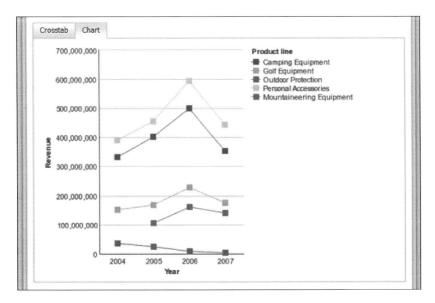

12. Finally, choose **Download Active Report** from Report Studio by selecting the option from the Run button as shown in the following screenshot:

This will download an MHT file that you can open anywhere (without being connected to the Cognos server or network) and it will show the same report with both tabs and data.

How it works...

Tab Control in Active Reports allows the report author to develop multi-tabbed reports. You use **Tab Definition** to define as many tabs as you want in your report. You can also edit the tab names as you wish or delete any of them if you don't need it any more in your report.

Once you add **Tab Control**, you can open each tab and work on it as if it's a separate report. You can add items such as lists, crosstabs, and charts.

There's more...

Another control to check out is the **Data Tab control**. A Data Tab control provides the report author with the ability to create tabs based on a number of records returned by a data item. A Data Tab control is used when you want to achieve dynamically generated tabs based on data items; for example, one tab for each product.

Working with Decks

As we saw in the previous recipe, it is easy to build multi-tabbed reports using Active Reports. Here, we will examine another technique that will give almost the same results. **Deck Control** allows the IBM Cognos report author to create cards.

A card is a data container. Each card in a Deck Control will have different data. You can think of cards as if they are tabs. In this recipe, we will create a report that contains a Deck with two cards, a crosstab, and a chart, just like the previous report.

Getting ready

As with the last recipe, we will use the GO Data Warehouse (query) package.

Open the IBM Cognos Report Studio and select the **GO Data Warehouse (query)** package. Select the **Active Report** template and click on **OK**. This will open a new Active Report that we will use through this recipe.

How to do it...

In this recipe, we will see how to use Deck Control to build data cards. To do this, perform the following steps:

1. From **Toolbox**, drag a **Radio Button Group** object into the new Active Report.

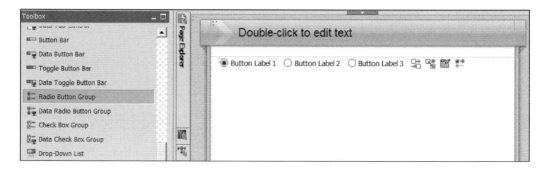

2. Click on the **Radio Button Definition** icon.

3. In the **Radio Button Definition** pop-up window, delete **Button Label 3** by clicking on the **X** icon that will appear when you hover over it.

4. Rename **Button Label 1** to `Crosstab` and **Button Label 2** to `Chart`. Click on the **OK** button to close the **Radio Button Definition** window.

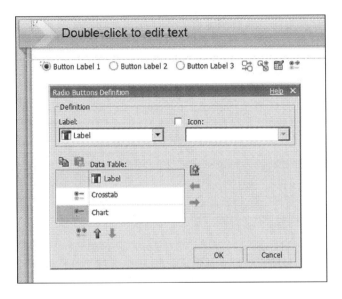

5. Click on **Radio Button Group**. In the **Properties** pane, rename the control to `Crosstab / Chart Radio Button Control`.

6. From the **Toolbox** items, locate the **Deck Control** object and drag it under the **Radio Button Group** control.

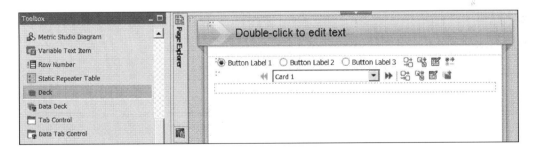

7. Click on the **Deck Cards Definition** icon in **Deck Control**. Within the **Deck Cards Definition** window, delete **Card 3**.

8. Rename **Card 1** to `Crosstab` and **Card 2** to `Chart`. Click on **OK**.

9. Rename **Deck Control** to `Crosstab / Chart Deck`.

10. From the **Toolbox** items, drag the **Crosstab** object onto the **Crosstab** card.

11. From the **Source** pane, drag **Product line** to the rows of the crosstab. Drag **Year** into the columns of the crosstab. Add **Revenue** as the crosstab measure.

12. Select the list from the **Deck** dropdown.

13. Now go to the **Chart** card. Drag **Chart** from **Toolbox**, select **Column Chart** as the chart type, and then click on **OK**.

14. From the **Source** pane, drag **Product line** to **Series:** of the chart. Drag **Year** into **Categories:** of the chart. Add **Revenue** as the chart measure.

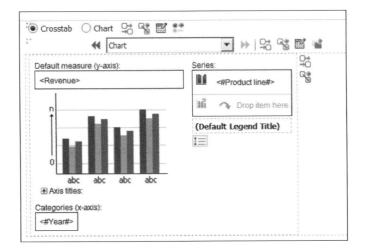

15. Now go back to **Radio Button Group**. Click on the **Create a New Connection** icon that looks like this:

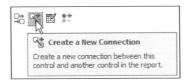

16. Within the **Create a New Connection** window, ensure that **Source Control:** is **Crosstab / Chart Radio Button Control** and **Target Control:** is **Crosstab / Chart Deck**. The Active Report variable should be **Label**.

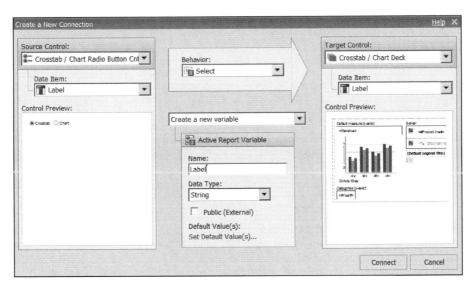

17. Click on the **Connect** button to make the connection and return to the report page.

18. Run the report to test it.

How it works...

Deck Control in Active Reports allows the report author to develop multi-tabbed reports. You use **Tab Definition** to define as many tabs as you want in your report. You can also edit the tab names as you wish or delete any of them if you don't need them any more in your report.

Once you have Deck Control in your report, you can deal with each card as if it is a separate report. It is almost the same like what we saw in Tab control.

By creating a connection between Radio Button Group and Deck Control, we define the interactivity between objects. When selecting different radio buttons, the end users will see different cards. All the code to show and hide the cards is automatically written behind the scenes and report developers need not worry about it.

While switching from one card to another, you can define an animated slide by selecting the Deck and choosing the **Slide Animation Direction** property.

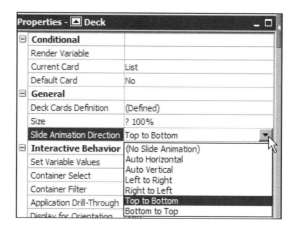

There's more...

Another control to check is the **Data Deck** object. This control is used to automatically create a card for each data item value used to drive the Data Deck. Data Decks are useful if the number of cards is unknown due to changing data. Data Decks are generally used to display the same report data container for different contexts.

In the next recipe, we will see the Data Deck Control in action.

Working with the Data Deck

We saw how to use the Deck Control in the previous recipe. The **Data Deck** is another great control in IBM Active Reports that has a similar functionality as the Deck Control.

The Data Deck Control is used to automatically create a card for each data item value used to drive the Data Deck. Data Decks are useful if the number of cards is unknown due to changing data. Unlike Decks, Data Decks are generally used to display the same report data container for different contexts.

Getting ready

In this recipe, we will use the GO Data Warehouse (query) package.

Open the IBM Cognos Report Studio and select the **GO Data Warehouse (query)** package. Select the **Active Report** template and click on **OK**. This will open a new Active Report that we will use through this recipe.

How to do it...

In this recipe, we will learn how to use the Data Button Bar in our reports. To do this, perform the following steps:

1. From the **Toolbox** items, drag the **Data Button Bar** object onto the report.

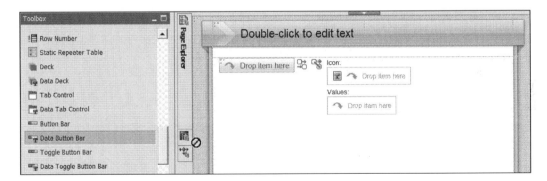

2. Click on **Data Button Bar**. Go to the **Properties** pane and change the **Name** property to **Product line Data Button Bar**.

3. Go to the **Query Explorer** tab and click on **Query1**. Change the name of the query from **Query1** to `Data Button Bar Query`.

4. Go back to the report page.

5. From the **Source** items, drag **Product line** into the **Labels** section of **Data Button Bar**.

6. From the **Toolbox** items, hold the right mouse button and drag the **Data Deck** object onto the report.

7. After releasing the right mouse button, a menu appears. Select the option **Insert using existing query**.

8. When prompted for a query, select **Data Button Bar Query** and then click on **OK**.

9. Click on **Data Deck**. Go to the **Properties** pane and change the **Name** property to `Product Line Data Deck`.

10. From **Toolbox**, drag a **List** object onto **Data Deck**.

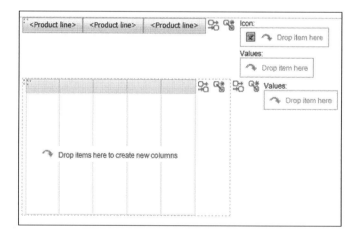

11. Go to the **Query Explorer** tab and click on **Query1**. Change the name of the query from **Query1** to `List Query`.

12. Return to the report page.

13. From the **Source** items, drag **Product line**, **Product type**, and **Product** onto the **List** object.

14. From the **Data Item** tab, drag **Product line** into the **Values:** drop zone of **Data Deck**.

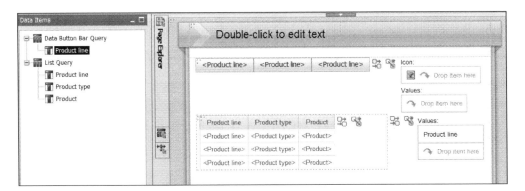

15. Select the **List** object and go to the **Properties** pane. Open the **Master Detail Relationships** property by clicking on it.

16. In the **Master Detail Relationships** dialog box, define a relationship between **Data Button Bar Query** and the **List Query** by clicking on **New Link**.

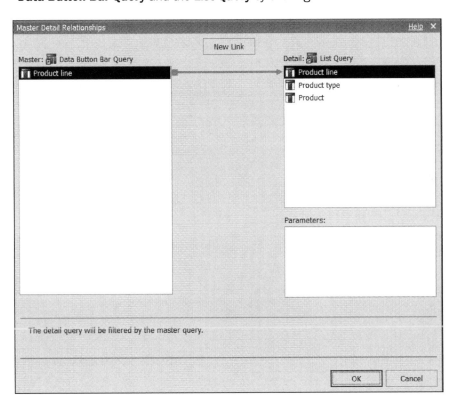

17. Click on the **OK** button to exit and then go back to the report page.

18. Select the **Data Button Bar** object and right-click to display the menu. Select **Create a New Connection**.

19. Ensure that **Source Control:** is **Product Line Data Button Bar** and **Target Control:** is **Product Line Data Deck**.

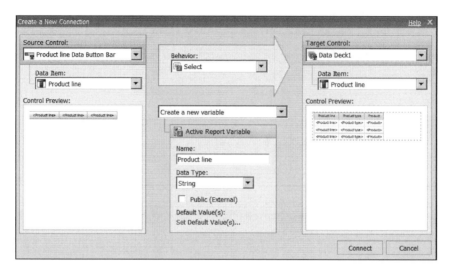

20. Click on the **Connect** button to create the connection.

21. Run the report to test it.

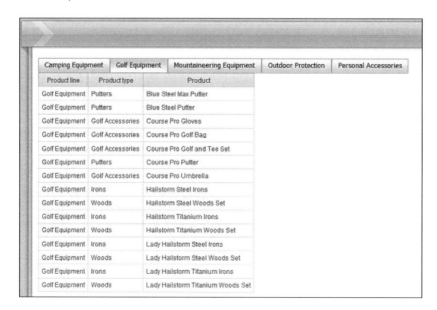

How it works...

A Data Deck is a data-driven control. Each card in the deck is determined by the data items inserted into the control.

To display the data that will be used in the Data Deck, we first defined a Data Button Bar where we added the reference to the Product line. This way we will have a button for each Product line that we have in our data. We then added the Data Deck that will use the same query used for the Data Button Bar.

In the Data Deck we placed our object, a list object in our case, and we created a Master-Details Relationship between the Product line in the Data Button Bar Query and the List Query, so that anything selected in the Data Button Bar will be reflected in the list.

The last step is to define the interactivity for the report between the Data Button Bar and the Data Deck by defining a new connection between them.

Filtering data using Data Check Box Group

In this recipe, we will have a look at a technique that you can use while working with Active Reports to filter the data in your report. This can be done using the **Data Check Box Group** control. This control provides the report author with the ability to display multiple selectable checkboxes based on the number of records returned by a data item. These checkboxes can be selected in multiples and used to dynamically filter a data container.

Getting ready

As usual, we will use the GO Data Warehouse (query) package for this recipe.

Open IBM Cognos Report Studio and select the **GO Data Warehouse (query)** package. Select the **Active Report** template and click on **OK**. This will open a new Active Report that we will use through this recipe.

How to do it...

In this recipe, we will learn how to use the Data Check Box Group control to filter the data. To do this, perform the following steps:

1. From the **Toolbox** items, drag the **Data Check Box Group** object onto the report.

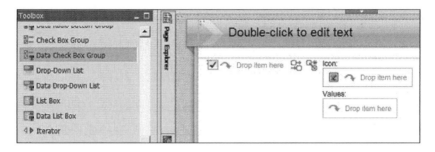

2. Click on **Data Check Box Group**. Go to the **Properties** pane and change the **Name** property to `Product Line Data Check Box Group`.

3. Go to the **Query Explorer** tab and click on **Query1**. Change the name of the query from **Query1** to **Data Check Box Group Query**.

4. Go back to the report page.

5. From the **Toolbox** items, hold the right mouse button and drag the **List** object onto the report.

6. After releasing the right mouse button, a menu appears. Select the option **Insert using existing query**.

7. When prompted for a query, select **Data Check Box Group Query** and then click on **OK**.

8. From the **Source** items, drag **Product line** and **Revenue** onto the **List** object.

9. From the **Data Item** tab, drag **Product line** into the **Values:** drop zone of **Data Check Box Group**.

10. Select the **Data Check Box Group** object and right-click to display the menu. Select **Create a New Connection**.

11. Ensure that **Source Control:** is **Data Check Box Group** and **Target Control:** is the **List** object.

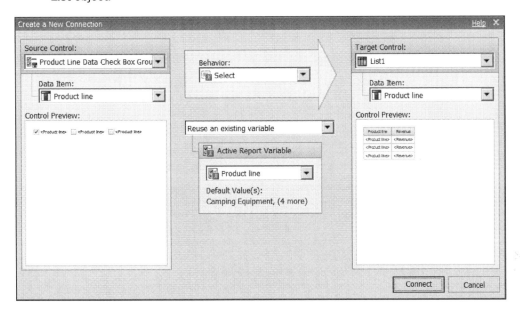

12. Click on the **Connect** button to create the connection.

13. Run the report to test it.

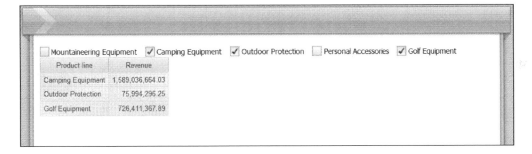

How it works...

Data Check Box Group is a nice way to filter data in your report. As you have seen in this recipe, by creating a connection between **Data Check Box Group** and the **List** object you can control the data that should be present in your report. The Master-Detail relationship allows filtering of list rows based on checkboxes, and you can build a more sophisticated logic using this feature. For example, you can filter Product Lines, yet display Products on the **List** report.

There's more...

There are some other controls to filter data. They are:

- ▸ Data Toggle Button Bar
- ▸ Data Drop-Down List

And it is very easy to change the control type that you want to use to filter data in your report. To do this, find the **Data Check Box Group** control and then right-click on it. In the menu, select **Convert Control**. In **Convert Control** you can find many options that you can convert the current control into.

Select the **Data Toggle Button Bar** control.

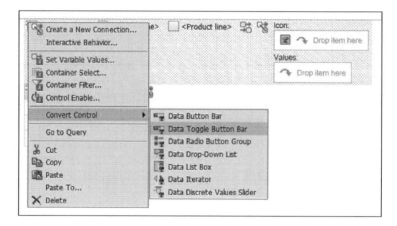

Run the report to test it.

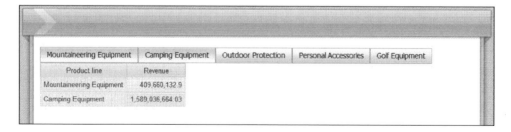

Try another option in **Convert Control** such as **Data Drop-Down List**. Run the report to check the output.

I would suggest that you spend some time trying the different controls that you can find in Active Reports. Also, check how you can convert between them using Convert Control if possible.

11
Charts and New Chart Features

In this chapter, we will cover:

- ▶ Chart formatting options
- ▶ Converting a chart to another chart type
- ▶ Working with pie charts
- ▶ Getting started with bullet charts
- ▶ Getting started with scatter charts

Introduction

Charts are without a doubt, a very powerful tool to deliver information. In IBM Cognos 10, charts got a lot of improvements. In fact, IBM Cognos 10 marks a significant improvement in a new charting engine that includes new chart types as well as many improvements in the chart properties and styles.

In addition to some new chart types introduced in Cognos 10 such as the bullet charts and tree maps, new chart properties are available such as the enhanced chart styles (colors, palettes, fills, shadows, and images), colored regions, enhanced pie/donut charts, summarizing small items, positioning and formatting notes, chart matrix layout control, and conditional formatting of items in the legend and greater control over Legend positioning.

One of the options available in Cognos 10 charts is the Summarize small items option, which can be used in pie, bar, and column charts. It allows us to focus data on top of reports; for example, the top three product lines.

In IBM Cognos 10, you have the choice either to work with the old legacy Cognos 8 charts or use the new improved charting engine introduced in IBM Cognos 10. By default, the new Cognos 10 charting engine is used. However, if you want to continue to use the Cognos 8 charting engine, you will have to change this in the Cognos options in Report Studio.

To choose a chart type, consider what you want the chart to illustrate. Different chart types and configurations emphasize different things. I got the following table from the Cognos Report Studio documentation to help you decide what kind of charts you can use based on your requirements:

Purpose	Chart type or configuration
Show contributions of parts to a whole	▶ Bar charts ▶ Pie charts ▶ Stacked charts, when you want to display measures of the whole as well as the parts ▶ 100 percent stacked charts
Show trends in time or contrast values across different categories	▶ Line charts ▶ Area charts ▶ Bar charts ▶ Column charts ▶ Always place time in the horizontal axis
Compare groups of related information against actual values	▶ Bar charts ▶ Radar charts
Compare different kinds of quantitative information	▶ Combination charts
Rank values in descending or ascending order	▶ Bar charts ▶ Column charts
Show correlation between two sets of measures	▶ Point charts
Show key performance indicators in an executive dashboard	▶ Gauge charts ▶ Bullet charts

Chart formatting options

In IBM Cognos 10 Report Studio, there are many options available to improve and enhance the chart objects based on the new charting engine.

In this recipe, we will check some of the formatting options available for charts in IBM Cognos Report Studio.

Getting ready

For this recipe, we will use the GO Data Warehouse (query) package.

How to do it...

In this recipe we will create a new chart report and will try to explore some formatting options. To do this, perform the following steps:

1. Open IBM Cognos Report Studio and select the **GO Data Warehouse (query)** package.

2. In the **New** pop-up screen, select **Chart** and then click on **OK**.

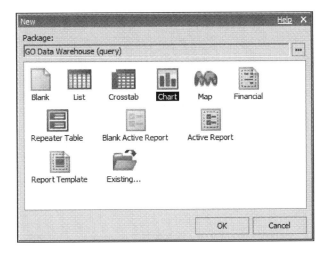

3. Another pop-up screen named **Insert Chart** appears. Select the **Clustered Column with 3-D Effects** chart and then click on **OK**.

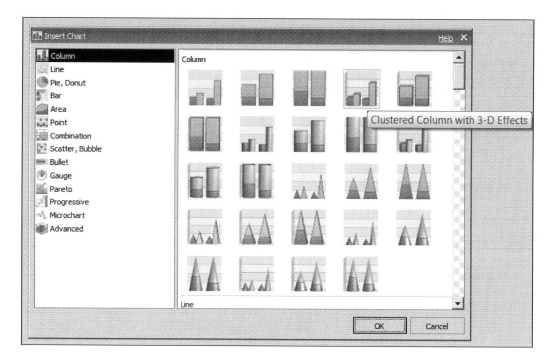

4. In the **Source** tab, open the **Products** dimension in **Sales (query)**. Drag-and-drop **Product line** to **Series (primary axis):**.

5. From **Sales fact**, drag **Revenue** to **Default measure (y-axis):**.

6. From the **Time** dimension, drag **Year** to **Categories (x-axis):**.

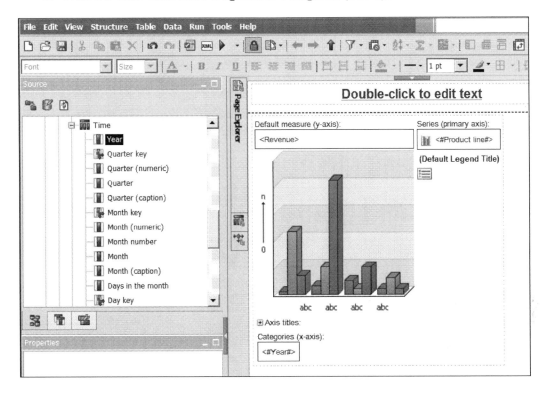

7. Run the report to test it.

8. Now we want to change the color of the columns in the chart. To do this, we simply choose a predefined **Palette** preset or create our own palette. In this recipe we will choose one of the Palette presets.

9. In the **Style** toolbar, click on **Chart Palette Presets**.

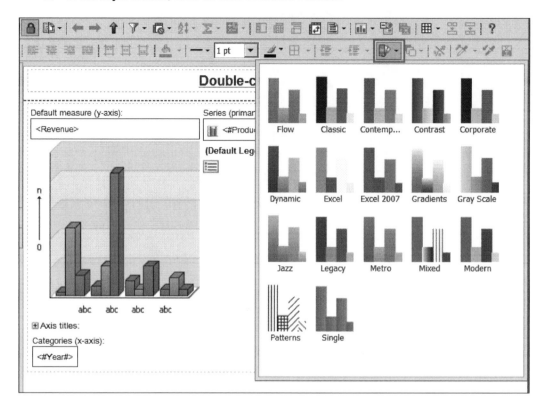

10. Select any palette such as the **Metro** palette and click on it.

11. To change the chart background effect, we can use **Background Effects Presets**.

12. In the **Style** toolbar, click on **Background Effects Presets**.

13. Select any effect such as the **Blue liner gradient with blue border** preset. Click on it to select it.

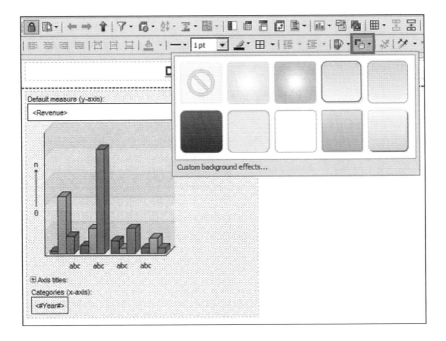

14. Finally, we want to change the width of the chart. In the **Properties** pane, locate the **Size and Overflow** property and click on it.

15. Set the width to 800 px and then click on **OK**.

16. Now run the report to test it.

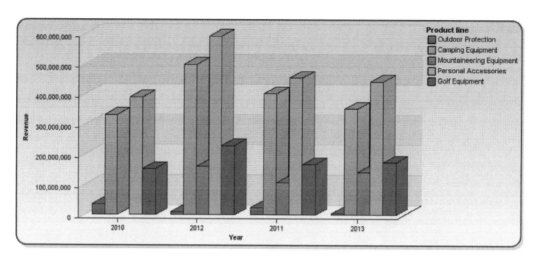

How it works...

As we see in this recipe, 3D effects in charts have improved a lot in the new version of IBM Cognos Report Studio. The look and feel of the new charts is much better than the older version (v8) charts thanks to the new charting engine.

We created a normal column chart but we selected the **Clustered Column with 3-D Effects** chart to get this shiny look. We defined the attribute of the chart as usual.

To enhance the look and feel of the chart, we used two new features in Cognos 10.

Chart Palette Presets

Though the palette concept was there in Cognos 8 Report Studio, it has changed completely in Cognos 10. Cognos now shows the palettes on the main toolbar on top so they are easy to locate.

The palettes in Cognos 10 are defined in ReportPresets.xml, which is located in <IBM Cognos install location>\webcontent\pat\res directory.

You can use any of the predefined palettes in **Chart Palette Presets**, or you can even create your own palette using your own colors that matches the whole report and company theme.

Background Effects Presets

This property is used to change background effects for data containers like charts. When you use **Background Effects Presets**, you can choose one of the predefined background presets or you can create your own background effects. This defines the background of the whole chart objects, including axis, legend, and so on.

You can also define a separate **Plot Area Fill** property to only fill up the background where the chart is plotted.

There's more...

You should spend more time to check the properties and the features of charts in IBM Cognos Report Studio 10.

Converting a chart to another chart type

You can convert a chart from one type (for example, a bar chart) to another type (for example, a line chart).

When you convert an existing chart to a new chart type, IBM Cognos Report Studio keeps the properties from the existing chart if those properties exist in the new chart type. For example, if you convert a pie chart to a bar chart, Report Studio maps your chart palette to the new chart, but does not map the exploding slices because the exploding slices property does not exist in a bar chart.

Getting ready

In this recipe we will use the column chart we created in the last recipe. So if it is not open, navigate in Cognos to the report created in the last recipe and open it in Report Studio.

How to do it...

In this recipe we will convert the column chart in our report to a bar chart. To do this, perform the following steps:

1. In IBM Cognos Report Studio, open the report created in the previous recipe.
2. Now, click on the **Chart** object that we created to select it.

3. Right-click on the **Chart** object and then click on **Convert Chart**.

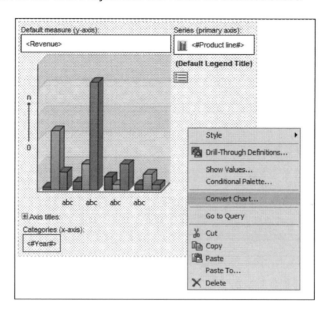

4. The **Convert Chart** screen appears.

5. Select the **Clustered Cylinder Bar with 3-D Effects** chart and then click on **OK**.

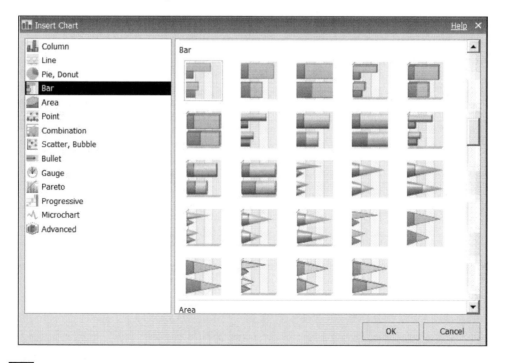

6. We want to change the measure used in the chart from revenue to gross profit. From **Sales fact**, drag **Gross profit** onto **Default measure (x-axis):** to replace **Revenue**.

7. We want to add a reference to the values of **Gross profit**. This reference will be on 25 percent of the scale.

8. In the **Properties** pane, locate the **Numeric Baseline** property and click on it.

9. In the **Baseline** screen, create a new baseline based on **Percent along axis**.

10. Enter 25 as the required percentage and then click on **OK**.

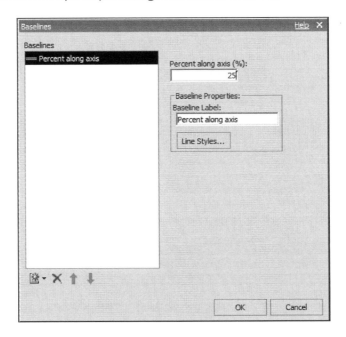

11. Finally, we want to change the width of the chart. In the **Properties** pane, locate the **Size and Overflow** property and click on it.

12. Clear the defined width, **800 px**, and then click on **OK**.

13. Run the report to test it.

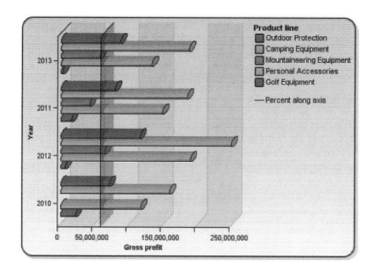

How it works...

We saw in this recipe how easy it is to convert from one chart type to another type.

While converting a chart to another type, Report Studio will keep the data used in the first charts as well as the properties and formatting option like palettes. The only concern here is that the second type, which we converted to, has to have these properties.

So here in our example, the new bar chart was created with the same data items used in the original column chart. We changed the measure for the chart to be Gross profit.

It is sometimes useful to have references in the chart that represent something meaningful to your data or your business. That's why you will need to use the baseline property.

Baselines are horizontal or vertical lines that cut through the chart to indicate major divisions in the data.

For example, you can add a baseline to show a sales quota or break-even point. Each baseline represents a value on an axis. By default, the baseline and its label appear in the legend.

Working with pie charts

Pie charts are useful for highlighting proportions. They use segments of a circle to show the relationship of parts to the whole. To highlight actual values, use another chart type such as a stacked chart.

Pie charts plot a single data series. If you need to plot multiple data series, use a 100 percent stacked chart. Reports in PDF or HTML format show a maximum of 16 pies or gauges per chart.

In this recipe, we will examine the pie chart and have a look at some of the new features available in IBM Cognos Report Studio 10.

Getting ready

For this recipe, we will use the GO Data Warehouse (query) package.

How to do it...

In this recipe we will create a new pie chart and will check some of its properties. To do this, perform the following steps:

1. Open IBM Cognos Report Studio and select the **GO Data Warehouse (query)** package.

2. In the **New** pop-up screen, select **Chart** and then click on **OK**.

3. Another pop-up screen named **Insert Chart** appears. Select the **Exploded Pie with 3-D Effects and Rounded Bevel** chart and then click on **OK**.

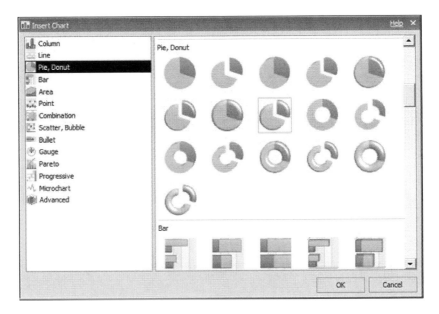

4. In the **Source** tab, open the **Products** dimension in **Sales (query)**. Drag-and-drop **Product line** to **Series (pie slices):**.

5. From **Sales fact**, drag **Revenue** to **Default measure:**.

6. At this stage, run the report to test it.

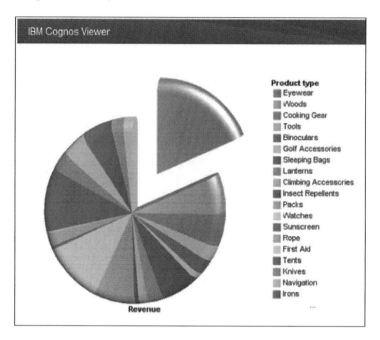

7. Now, go to the **Properties** pane and locate the **First Slice Angle** property. By default, the value is **90**. Change it to 60 and then click on **OK**.

8. Locate the **Exploded Slices** property. Make sure the value is **Slice 1 exploded 50**.

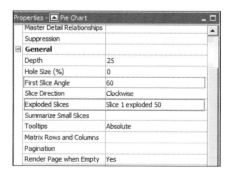

9. Go to the **Summarize Small Slices** property and click on it. The **Summarize Small Slices** screen appears.

10. Check the **Summarize slices smaller than a value** checkbox. Enter 5 as **Percentage values** and then click on **OK**.

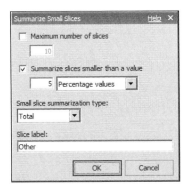

11. Run the report to test it.

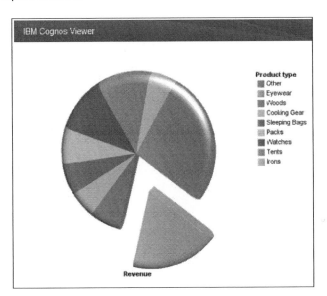

How it works...

As we saw in this recipe, pie charts are powerful visualization tools that got a lot of improvement in IBM Cognos 10. Let's check some examples for these improvements.

The Summarize Small Slices property

The Summarize Small Slices property specifies the summarization of small items, such as slices, lines, areas, bars, or columns in the chart and how they are summarized. You cannot summarize small items in charts that have matrix edges or in charts that have multiple numeric axes.

In our example, we summarize all slices in the pie chart that have values less than 5 percent to avoid displaying too many values in the chart that could make the chart unreadable. It is common that users want to focus on certain values while displaying the remaining items together as a separate category of **Other**.

The First Slice Angle property

The First Slice Angle property specifies the angle at which the first pie slice begins in a pie chart. This feature is used to enhance the pie appearance and to control the position of the first slice.

In our example we set the angle of the first slice to 60 degrees.

The Exploded Slices property

The Exploded Slices property specifies the slices that appear pulled out of a pie chart and their appearance. This feature is also used to enhance the pie appearance and to control which slice is to be exploded.

In our example we set the exploded slice to be the first slice, slice number 1, and also we specified that the slice should be exploded by 50 percent. This determines how far the exploded slice will be from the pie. The higher this percentage, the wider will be the space between the slice and the pie. If we choose 100 percent, the exploded slice will be at the maximum allowed space away from the pie.

Getting started with bullet charts

Bullet charts are a variation of bar charts. They compare a featured measure (the bullet) to a targeted measure (the target). They also relate the compared measures, Revenue for example, against colored regions in the background that provide additional qualitative measurements, such as good, satisfactory, and poor.

Bullet charts are often used instead of gauge charts in executive dashboards. Bullet charts can be horizontal or vertical.

A bullet chart contains the following components:

- ▶ A bullet measure, which appears as the blue bar in the chart
- ▶ A target measure, which appears as the black indicator in the chart

▸ From zero to five colored regions along the numeric scale to provide information about the featured measure's qualitative state

▸ A label that identifies the measures

▸ A numeric scale

Getting ready

For this recipe, we will use the GO Data Warehouse (query) package.

How to do it...

In this recipe we will create a bullet chart and check some of its properties. To do this, perform the following steps:

1. Open IBM Cognos Report Studio and select the **GO Data Warehouse (query)** package. Select a new **Chart** report and click on **OK**.

2. Another pop-up screen named **Insert Chart** appears. Go to the **Bullet** section, select **Horizontal Bullet**, and then click on **OK**.

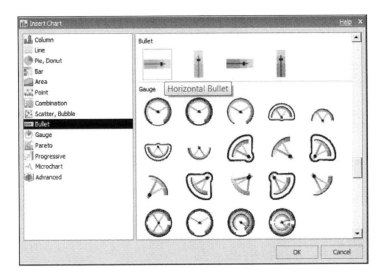

The bullet chart appears now in the Report Studio work area.

3. From the **Source** pane, open **Sales (query)** and then open **Sales fact**.

4. Drag **Revenue** to **Bullet Measure**.

5. Drag **Planned revenue** to **Bullet Target**.

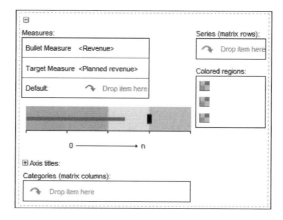

6. From the **Properties** pane, locate the **Legend** property and click on it.

7. The **Legend** pop-up screen appears. Check the **Show Legend** checkbox.

8. Select the required position for the legend and then click on **OK**.

9. At this stage, run the report to test it.

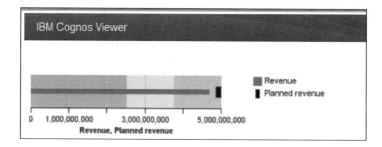

10. Again in the **Properties** pane, locate the **Colored Regions** property and click on it.

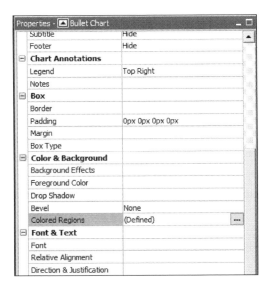

11. The **Colored Regions** pop-up screen appears. As you can see, there are three predefined colored regions: 0-50 percent, 50-75 percent, and 75-100 percent. You can customize these colors as per your requirements. Colored Regions can be defined based on any numeric value: **Percent on Axis**, **Mean**, **Statistical maximum or minimum**, or you can even define them based on a **Query calculation**.

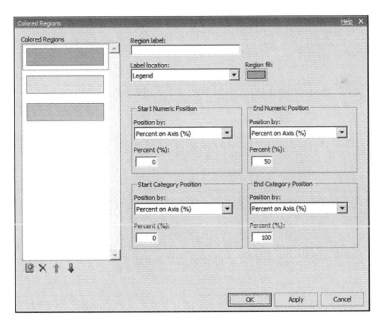

12. Make the necessary changes and then click on **OK**.

13. Now run the report to test it.

How it works...

Let's take a look at the previous chart.

First, we have the blue bar that indicates the actual revenue. The short black bullet indicates the planned revenue. By putting them in the same context, you can get the feeling of how close or far your sales are from the planned target, and this is what the bullet chart is all about.

When you combine this with colored regions in the background, you can have more insight. The colored regions can be numerical colored values or percentages (0-50 percent, 50-75 percent, and 75-100 percent) as we saw in our example. They can even be defined using query calculations. For example, you can define them to show the Gross Profit or the Product Cost. This way we can add even more data and value to this simple and concise chart. This single chart can help us compare measures as well as display additional information.

There's more...

The **Revenue** and **Target** revenue in our bullet chart are the overall values for our sales. Now, suppose that we want to get a bullet chart for each product line to get more insight about our data.

To do this, drag the **Product line** for the **Products** dimension into the bullet chart's **Categories**.

Now run the report to test it.

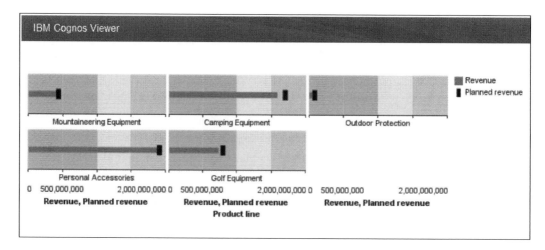

Getting started with scatter charts

Business is always decided on sales and marketing strategy by looking at the sales volume and the revenue generation for each product line.

Businesses would like to expand the product lines that generate high revenue despite low sales volume. They will keep the high sales, high revenue items as they are and discontinue the low selling, low revenue items.

For this sort of requirement, we will use scatter chart with colored regions.

Getting ready

For this recipe, we will use the GO Data Warehouse (query) package.

How to do it...

In this recipe we will have a look at how to create a scatter chart and how to define its properties. To do this, perform the following steps:

1. Open IBM Cognos Report Studio and select the **GO Data Warehouse (query)** package. Select a new **Chart** report and click on **OK**.

2. A pop-up screen named **Insert Chart** appears. Go to the **Scatter, Bubble** section, select **Scatter with 4 colored Quadrant and Transparent Markers** and then click on **OK**.

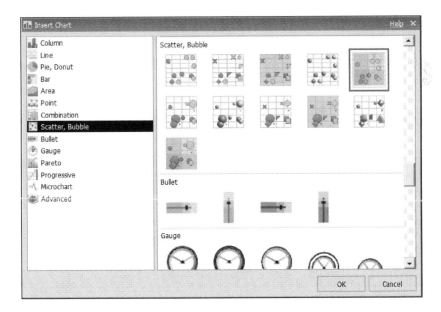

3. The scatter chart now appears in the Report Studio work area.

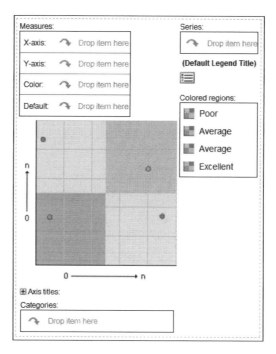

4. From the **Source** pane, open **Sales (query)** and then open **Sales fact**.

5. Drag **Revenue** to the **X-axis** measure.

6. Drag **Quantity** to the **Y-axis** measure.

7. Open **Products** and drag **Product line** to the chart's **Series** field.

8. In the **Colored regions** section, click on **Excellent** and in the properties, change the text from **Excellent** to `High Revenue - High Sales (Continue)`.

9. Again, change the text from **Poor** to `Low Revenue - Low Sales (Discontinue)`.

10. Finally, remove the first **Average** and change the text for the second one to `High Revenue - Low Sales (Expand)`.

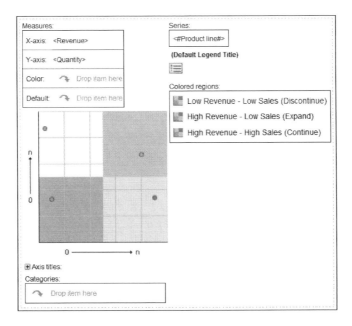

11. Now run the report to test it.

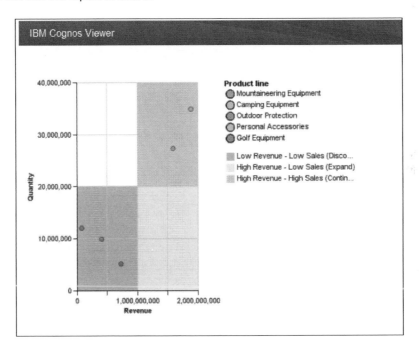

How it works...

The scatter chart is a very powerful chart that can show up to three measures. It is very useful for exploring correlations between different sets of data. By positioning dots over X and Y axes, it can quickly show a comparison of product lines over Revenue and Sales Volume. By adding colored regions to it, Cognos 10 has increased the expression power of this tool.

12

More Useful Recipes

In this chapter, we will cover the following:

- ▸ Timing report execution
- ▸ Missing values versus zero values
- ▸ Overriding data formatting using patterns
- ▸ Setting up conditional drill-throughs
- ▸ Dynamically switching between reports using an iFrame
- ▸ Freezing column titles

Introduction

In this chapter, we will have a look at some more useful tricks and techniques that will help us use the Cognos Report Studio more efficiently.

Timing report execution

We often want to record the exact time taken by a report to execute. This recipe will show you a technique that is tried and tested and can be used repeatedly to examine the performance of a report at different loads and volumes on the data source.

Getting ready

Take any report whose execution time is to be recorded. The steps for this recipe are to be carried out in Cognos Connection Portal, not Cognos Report Studio.

How to do it...

In this recipe, we will see how to get the time taken by the report to be executed by getting the start time and the completion time for the report from Cognos Connection Portal.

1. Go to IBM Cognos Connection Portal and locate the report.

2. Click on the **Create Report View** button and create a report view of this report in the desired location.

3. Open the **Properties** pane of the report view by clicking on the **Set Properties** button.

4. Go to the **Report View** tab. Uncheck the **Prompt for values** option.

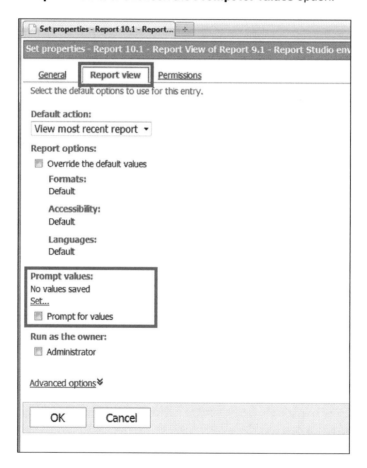

5. Click on the **Set** link for **Prompt values**. This will bring the prompt page up.

6. Select the prompt values and save them. Click on the **OK** button to come back to the list of reports and report views.

7. Now click on the **Run with options** button and choose the following options:

   ❏ **Format**: **PDF**

   ❏ **Delivery**: **Save the report**

   ❏ Uncheck the option **Prompt for values**

8. Click on the **Run** button.

9. Now from the administrator, open the **Past Activities** view. Once the report is executed, record the start time and completion time.

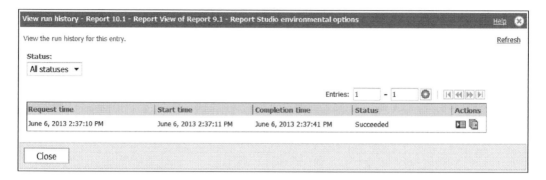

How it works...

Here we are creating a report view so that prompt values can be saved, and then we run it in the background so that timings can be noted from the schedule management.

The report view

The report view sits on top of the report. You can set different properties for it (delivery method, output format, and so on) as well as the prompt values, without affecting the actual report.

If the main report is updated, changes are automatically reflected in the view.

Scheduling

When we choose the delivery method Save Report Output, the report execution happens in the background using the batch processing service. Using the **Past Activities** view, we can see when exactly the report execution started and when it ended. This gives us the exact time taken by the report to execute.

When users use the report interactively, they prefer to see the output in the HTML format. This retrieves only a pageful of data at a time, and hence the time taken to produce the first page does not accurately reflect the time that will be required to generate the whole report. Also, checking the time manually can be error prone. Hence, it is advisable to use the scheduler as shown in the recipe, and do several runs with different prompt selections to record the execution timings.

There's more...

You can create multiple report views of the same report to choose different prompt values and output formats.

Also, whenever you want to run performance tests on a particular data source, you can create a job to run all the report views against that data source. This will allow you to record the timings for all and compare them with prior runs.

Please note that re-running the same report or report view with exactly same parameters immediately after a run will result in Cognos showing cached values instead of hitting the data source again. Hence, such situations should be avoided when checking performance.

Another way of checking report execution time is looking at `COGIPF_RUNTIME NUMBER` data items from the `Audit` package if you have access to the `Audit` package and if auditing is turned on at the server.

Missing values versus zero values

Missing values in the data source can mean two things in real business: either the data is zero or it is missing. For example, in the case of a sales transaction-based system, if there is no data for a product for a certain month, it means there was no sale of that product in that month. However, in some other systems, for example, yearly returns of different stocks missing data might just mean that data is not available for a certain reason. However, it certainly doesn't mean the return was zero.

Hence, it is important to clearly highlight the missing value as zero or missing in the report.

Getting ready

Create a simple crosstab report with all **Product line** on rows and **Month key** on columns from **GO Data Warehouse (Query)/Sales**. Choose **Quantity** and **Unit cost** as sales measures.

Quantity	<#Month key#>		<#Month key#>	
	<#Quantity1#>	<#Unit cost#>	<#Quantity1#>	<#Unit cost#>
<#Product line#>	<#1234#>	<#1234#>	<#1234#>	<#1234#>
<#Product line#>	<#1234#>	<#1234#>	<#1234#>	<#1234#>

How to do it...

In this recipe we will see how to avoid missing values in the report by replacing them with more meaningful values like zero or N/A.

1. Firstly, we will run the report to see if there are any missing values.

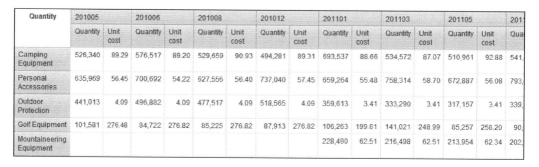

Quantity	201005		201006		201008		201012		201101		201103		201105		201
	Quantity	Unit cost	Quantity	Unit cost	Quantity	Unit cost	Quantity	Unit cost	Quantity	Unit cost	Quantity	Unit cost	Quantity	Unit cost	Qua
Camping Equipment	526,340	89.29	576,517	89.20	529,659	90.93	494,281	89.31	693,537	88.66	534,572	87.07	510,961	92.88	541,
Personal Accessories	635,969	56.45	700,692	54.22	627,556	56.40	737,040	57.45	659,264	55.48	758,314	58.70	672,887	56.08	793,
Outdoor Protection	441,013	4.09	496,882	4.09	477,517	4.09	518,565	4.09	359,613	3.41	333,290	3.41	317,157	3.41	339,
Golf Equipment	101,581	276.48	84,722	276.82	85,225	276.82	87,913	276.82	106,263	199.81	141,021	248.99	85,257	258.20	90,
Mountaineering Equipment									228,490	62.51	216,498	62.51	213,954	62.34	202,

We can see that the **Quantity** and **Unit cost** values are missing for certain columns.

2. Now go to Report Studio and choose the **Quantity** measure from the crosstab intersection.

3. From the **Properties** pane, open the **Data Format** dialog box. Set **Format type** to Number and **Missing Value Characters** to 0.

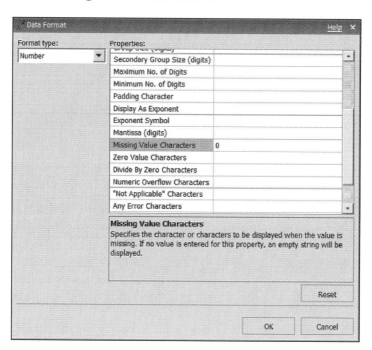

4. Similarly, set the data format for the unit price measure. However, this time set **Missing Value Characters** to **N/A**.

5. Run the report to test it.

Quantity	201005		201006		201008		201012		201101		201103		201105		201
	Quantity	Unit cost	Quantity	Unit cost	Quantity	Unit cost	Quantity	Unit cost	Quantity	Unit cost	Quantity	Unit cost	Quantity	Unit cost	Qua
Camping Equipment	526,340	89.29	576,517	89.20	529,659	90.93	494,281	89.31	693,537	88.66	534,572	87.07	510,961	92.88	541
Personal Accessories	635,969	56.45	700,692	54.22	627,556	56.40	737,040	57.45	659,264	55.48	758,314	58.70	672,887	56.08	793
Outdoor Protection	441,013	4.09	496,882	4.09	477,517	4.09	518,565	4.09	359,613	3.41	333,290	3.41	317,157	3.41	339
Golf Equipment	101,581	276.48	84,722	276.82	85,225	276.82	87,913	276.82	106,263	199.81	141,021	248.99	85,257	258.20	90
Mountaineering Equipment	0	N/A	0	N/A	0	N/A	0	N/A	228,490	62.51	216,498	62.51	213,954	62.34	202

How it works...

As discussed earlier, the missing values can mean different things. Here, when the sales quantity is missing, we know the sale was zero for the product for that period. However, the missing unit price doesn't mean it was zero. It just means that there is no data for that combination.

By setting the appropriate **Missing Value Characters** columns, we are ensuring that the correct message is conveyed through the report.

There's more...

You can also specify characters to be displayed in case of zero value, divide by zero, and some more conditions.

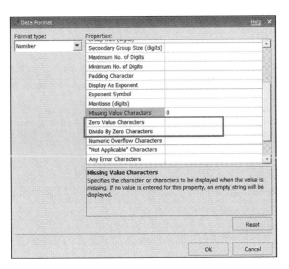

Overriding data formatting using patterns

In Cognos Report Studio, we can define the formatting of data items that we have seen in many recipes. However, sometimes the formatting defined in the report does not take effect. In this recipe, we will consider one such scenario.

Getting ready

Create a simple crosstab report with all **Product line** on rows and **Month key** on columns from **GO Data Warehouse (Query)/Sales**. Choose **Revenue** and **Planned revenue** as measures.

	<#Month key#>		<#Month key#>	
	<#Revenue#>	<#Planned revenue#>	<#Revenue#>	<#Planned revenue#>
<#Product line#>	<#1234#>	<#1234#>	<#1234#>	<#1234#>
<#Product line#>	<#1234#>	<#1234#>	<#1234#>	<#1234#>

How to do it...

In this recipe we will see how to use patterns in the data format. To do this, perform the following steps:

1. Firstly, let's run the report to check how the measured data are formatted.

	200501		200502		200503	
	Revenue	Planned revenue	Revenue	Planned revenue	Revenue	Planned revenue
Camping Equipment	34,337,564.76	37,266,188.19	35,112,266.68	38,504,624.69	31,851,160.4	34,018,609.9
Golf Equipment	14,471,129.43	15,436,205.11	15,382,962.82	16,553,586.11	15,731,334.61	17,176,989.99
Mountaineering Equipment	9,348,918.98	9,868,188.97	9,393,452.23	9,913,526.68	8,649,988.42	9,127,607.07
Outdoor Protection	2,186,828.57	2,271,963.21	2,193,995.43	2,279,765.16	2,024,751.14	2,100,711.66
Personal Accessories	34,653,760.87	35,058,886.22	37,405,365.5	37,814,275.89	40,484,980.69	41,077,933.9

2. You will notice that some numbers have two decimal places while some have one decimal place.

3. Now, go back to Cognos Report Studio. Select the measures and open the data format again.

4. This can be done in the data format using the **Number of Decimal Places** option, but this time we will check another functionality. Go to **Pattern** and define it as # , ### . 0 as shown in the following screenshot:

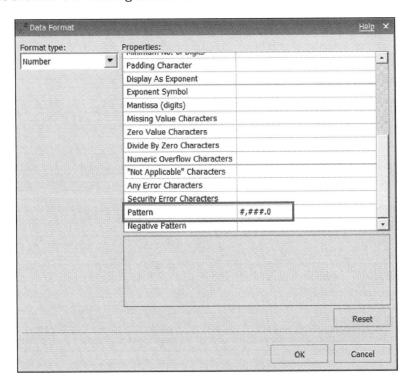

5. Run the report to test it. This time the report will show numbers up to one decimal point only.

	200501		200502		200503	
	Revenue	Planned revenue	Revenue	Planned revenue	Revenue	Planned revenue
Camping Equipment	34,337,564.8	37,266,188.2	35,112,266.7	38,504,624.7	31,851,160.4	34,018,609.9
Golf Equipment	14,471,129.4	15,436,205.1	15,382,962.8	16,553,586.1	15,731,334.6	17,176,990.0
Mountaineering Equipment	9,348,919.0	9,868,189.0	9,393,452.2	9,913,526.7	8,649,988.4	9,127,607.1
Outdoor Protection	2,186,828.6	2,271,963.2	2,193,995.4	2,279,765.2	2,024,751.1	2,100,711.7
Personal Accessories	34,653,760.9	35,058,886.2	37,405,365.5	37,814,275.9	40,484,980.7	41,077,933.9

How it works...

Using patterns can provide similar results as basic data formatting tasks. In this example, you can set the number of digits to appear after the decimal point. You can achieve these types of results with a pattern, or you can set the **No. of Decimal Places** property. Patterns allow flexibility for more complex requirements. You can format data so that it matches any pattern of text and numbers when default formats are not appropriate.

Setting up conditional drill-throughs

IBM Cognos Report Studio allows you to define **drill-through**. However, there is no facility to define conditional drill-throughs. This recipe will show you how to achieve it.

We will use the report created in the previous recipe for this recipe.

Getting ready

Create two dummy reports called `Drill 1` and `Drill 2`.

Open the report created in the previous recipe in Cognos Report Studio.

How to do it...

In this recipe we will create drill-through from the crosstab intersection to a dummy report (`Drill 1`). Then, we will try to achieve a conditional drill-through to another report (`Drill 2`) for certain months. To do this, perform the following steps:

1. First of all, create drill-through from the crosstab intersection to the first report (`Drill 1`). We saw how to create such a drill in earlier chapters of this book.

2. Now select the text item from the crosstab intersection, hold the *Ctrl* key and drag the text item a little to the left. This will create a copy of this text item within the same intersection.

Revenue	<#Month key#>	<#Month key#>
<#Product line#>	✤ <#1234#> ✤ <#1234#>	✤ <#1234#> ✤ <#1234#>
<#Product line#>	✤ <#1234#> ✤ <#1234#>	✤ <#1234#> ✤ <#1234#>

3. For this newly created copy of the text item, update the drill-through link to point to `Drill 2`.

4. Now, we will define the condition to switch between the links. Create a Boolean variable called `Is_2004`. Define the condition as: `number2string ([Query1].[Month key]) contains '2004'`.

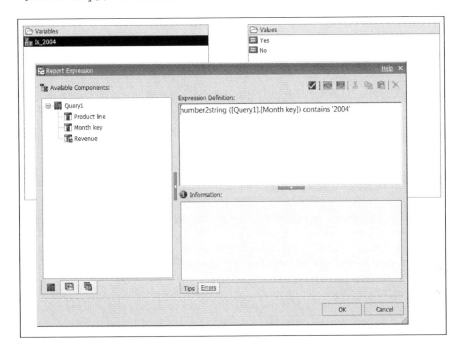

5. Go back to the report page. Attach the conditional variable `Is_2004` as **Style Variable** to both the drill links.

6. Using **Conditional Explorer**, set **Box Type** to **None** for the left link when `Is_2004` is **Yes**, and then do the same for the right link when `Is_2004` is **No**.

   That is, turn the visibility off for one of the links depending on the condition.

7. Run the report to test it.

How it works...

Within the drill-through definitions dialog box, there is no reference to the conditional variables. So, Report Studio provides no direct way to switch the drill target depending on a condition.

As a solution, we are creating a copy of the text item here and then we hide one of them based on a condition. As the text items go to different targets, we achieve conditional drill-through in the report.

There's more...

Instead of using **Style Variable** and **Box Type**, we can use **Render Variable** to directly set when the item should be visible. However, in order to use **Render Variable**, we will need to use **String Variable** instead of **Boolean**.

Dynamically switching between reports using an iFrame

In this recipe, we will have a look at how to use one report as a container to call or display different reports. We will use an HTML element called **iFrame** that allows the browser window to be split into segments. Each segment can be updated separately.

We will give users the ability to choose which report contents to display and allow them to toggle between two reports by clicking on the appropriate button. You can build upon this idea to create many practical solutions such as displaying help, toggling graphs, and providing tabs to display different reports.

Getting ready

Create a simple list report with product-related columns (the product query subject) and save it as `iFrame-Products`.

Product line	Product type	Product	Product color
<Product line>	<Product type>	<Product>	<Product color>
<Product line>	<Product type>	<Product>	<Product color>
<Product line>	<Product type>	<Product>	<Product color>

Create another simple list report with retailer-related columns (the retailer query subject) and save this report as `iFrame-Retailers`.

Retailer type	Retailer name
<Retailer type>	<Retailer name>
<Retailer type>	<Retailer name>
<Retailer type>	<Retailer name>

How to do it...

In this recipe we will see how to use the HTML element called iFrame to split the browser window into segments. Each segment will show a different report. To do this, perform the following steps:

1. Go to **Connection Portal** and locate the reports we created previously.

2. Click on the **Set Properties** button for `iFrame-Products`. From the **General** tab, click on the **View the search path, ID and URL** link.

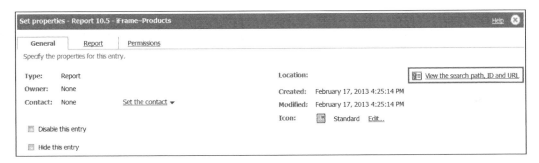

3. Copy the default action URL and save it somewhere for use in later steps. This URL will look similar to: `http://cognosdemo:80/ibmcognos/cgi-bin/ cognos.cgi?b_action=cognosViewer&ui.action=run&ui.objec t=%2fcontent%2ffolder%5b%40name%3d%27Samples%27%5d%2ffo lder%5b%40name%3d%27Models%27%5d%2fpackage%5b%40name%3d% 27GO%20Data%20Warehouse%20(query)%27%5d%2ffolder%5b%40na me%3d%27My%20Reports%27%5d%2ffolder%5b%40name%3d%27Chapt er%2010%27%5d%2freport%5b%40name%3d%27Report%2010.5%20-%20 iFrame%e2%80%93Products%27%5d&ui.name=Report%2010.5%20-%20 iFrame%e2%80%93Products&run.outputFormat=&run.prompt=true.`

4. Similarly, save the default action URL for the `iFrame-Retailers` report.

5. Now go to Cognos Report Studio and create a new blank report.

6. On the report page, drag a new **HTML Item** onto the page. Define the code as follows:

```
<script language="javascript" type="text/javascript">
function showReport(x)
{
switch(x)
{
```

```
/* Replace the URL in the following stmt with the one you saved
for iFrame-Product report */

case 1: document.getElementById("dynamic_report").src =
"http://cognosdemo:80/ibmcognos/cgi-bin/cognos.cgi?b_
action=cognosViewer&ui.action=run&ui.object=%2fcontent%2ffolder%
5b%40name%3d%27Samples%27%5d%2ffolder%5b%40name%3d%27Models%27%5
d%2fpackage%5b%40name%3d%27GO%20Data%20Warehouse%20(query)%27%5d
%2ffolder%5b%40name%3d%27My%20Reports%27%5d%2ffolder%5b%40name%
3d%27Chapter%2010%27%5d%2freport%5b%40name%3d%27Report%2010.5%20
-%20iFrame%e2%80%93Products%27%5d&ui.name=Report%2010.5%20-%20
iFrame%e2%80%93Products&run.outputFormat=&run.prompt=true";
break;

/* Replace the URL in the following stmt with the one you saved
for iFrame-Retailer report */

case 2: document.getElementById("dynamic_report").src =
"http://cognosdemo:80/ibmcognos/cgi-bin/cognos.cgi?b_
action=cognosViewer&ui.action=run&ui.object=%2fcontent%2ffolder%
5b%40name%3d%27Samples%27%5d%2ffolder%5b%40name%3d%27Models%27%5
d%2fpackage%5b%40name%3d%27GO%20Data%20Warehouse%20(query)%27%5d
%2ffolder%5b%40name%3d%27My%20Reports%27%5d%2ffolder%5b%40name%
3d%27Chapter%2010%27%5d%2freport%5b%40name%3d%27Report%2010.5%20
-%20iFrame%e2%80%93Retailers%27%5d&ui.name=Report%2010.5%20-%20
iFrame%e2%80%93Retailers&run.outputFormat=&run.prompt=true";
break;
}

}
</script>

<button type="button" onclick="showReport(1);">Products</button>
<button type="button" onclick="showReport(2);">Retailers</button>
```

For the URL shown in bold, you need to place the default action URLs that you saved for both the reports in the first step.

7. Now create another **HTML item** on the report page and define the code as:

```
<iframe name="dynamic_report" src="" frameborder="0" height="90%"
width="100%"></iframe>
```

8. The report will look like a blank page with two HTML items on it.

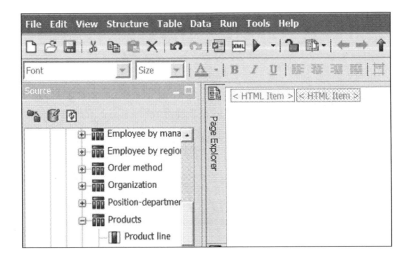

9. Run the report to test it. You should see two buttons called **Products** and **Retailers**. When you click on **Products**, the iFrame-Products report will be displayed. By clicking on the **Retailers** button, you can display the iFrame-Retailers report.

How it works...

Here, we are using the iFrame element of HTML to achieve dynamic content on the report page. In one HTML item, we define an iFrame element called `dynamic_report` and set it's source (`src`) property to blank. Then in another HTML item, we define two buttons and one JavaScript to dynamically change the source (`src`) property of the iFrame. Depending on which button is clicked, we set the source of iFrame to the default action URL of either the `iFrame-Product` report or the `iFrame-Retailers` report.

When the report first loads, the iFrame is empty (because the source property is blank). As soon as a user clicks on any of the buttons, the iFrame source is changed by the JavaScript. This causes either of the reports to execute and the output is loaded on the page. This way it allows us to dynamically switch between the reports contents while staying on the same page.

Please note that this recipe will work only on Internet Explorer.

There's more...

Please note that you should append `&cv.toolbar=false&cv.header=false` to the URLs in the JavaScript. This will hide the Cognos toolbar and header from showing up again in the iFrame.

Also, you should try and extend this concept to create other dynamic solutions, for example displaying help, toggling graphs, providing tabs to display different reports, and so on.

Freezing column titles

Let's say we have a report that is going to go over multiple pages when viewed online (HTML). Instead of users clicking on *Page Down* each time, we want to show all rows on one page so that users can simply scroll down.

However, when they scroll down, we want to keep the **Column Titles** frozen on top so the report can be easily read.

Getting ready

Create a simple list report with some data items such that it will produce a long-list report.

How to do it...

In this recipe we will see how to freeze the header of a list table by creating a specific style for this and applying it into the list headers. To do this, perform the following steps:

1. Drag a new **Block** from the toolbox and place it on the report page. Pull the **List Report** inside **Block**.

2. Select **Block** and define its height as 800 px and then select the scrollbar option for **Overflow**.

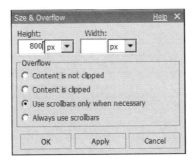

3. Then, select the **List data** container and set its **Rows per page** property to 500.

4. Now drag a new HTML item onto the page above **Block**. Define it as follows:

```
<style>
.frozenTitles{
        background-color: #E7E5E5;
        top: expression(parentNode.parentNode.parentNode.
parentNode.scrollTop-1);
        position: relative;
}
</style>
```

5. From **Page Explorer**, open **Classes**.

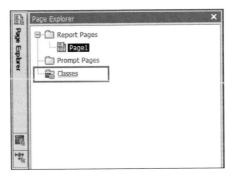

6. Paste the following fragment in **Local Classes** and it will create a new class:

```
RSClipboardFragment version="2.0">
<classStyle name="frozenTitles" label="My Frozen Headers"/>
</RSClipboardFragment>
```

You can see this in the following screenshot:

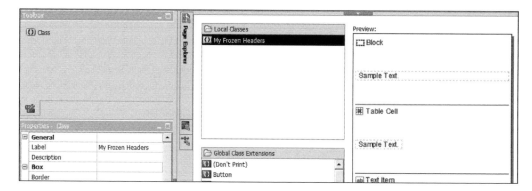

7. Now go back to the report page, hold down the *Ctrl* key and select all the individual **Column Titles** (headers). From **Properties**, open **Classes** and remove existing classes. Add the class that we created called `My Frozen Headers`.

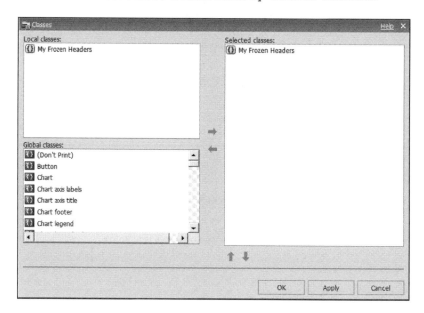

8. Run the report to test it. See that the report shows all the rows (maximum 500) on one page. When you scroll down, **Column Titles** on top remain frozen making it easy to go through the whole report.

How it works...

First of all, we have put the List Report in a block and defined the height of the block to be 800 px. As the report is going to be longer than that, we have defined the overflow behavior to display scrollbar. This way when the report is rendered, the block displays a scrollbar and the report scrolls within the block.

Now the only thing remaining is to keep the headers frozen so they always show when we scroll down. This is done by overriding the `style` header of the header cells with our hand-coded class that defines the top position of cells relative to `ScrollBar` `[top:` `expression(parentNode.parentNode.parentNode.parentNode.scrollTop-1);]`.

Hence, when we scroll down, the header cells also move down effectively looking frozen on the top of the page.

There's more...

In Cognos v10, Report Viewer now comes with a feature that users themselves can choose to freeze the titles without doing anything special in the report. This works with any report.

For that, when users view the report online in Report Viewer, they can right-click anywhere on the data container and choose to freeze the column heading as shown in the following screenshot:

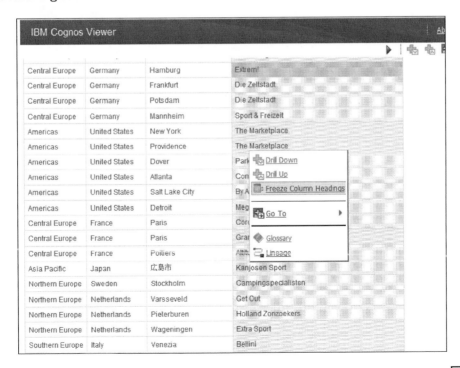

This is effective for only that time; so next time when they run the report, they will have to choose to freeze the heading again. In order to achieve the freezing by default for all users, please refer to the technique explained in this recipe.

13
Best Practices

In this chapter, we will cover:

- ▸ Reducing the number of query items
- ▸ Highlighting hidden items
- ▸ Using relative paths for images
- ▸ Controlling JavaScript file execution
- ▸ Customizing classes for report-wide effect
- ▸ Creating templates
- ▸ Regression testing
- ▸ Commenting the code
- ▸ Naming data containers (lists, crosstabs, and charts) for use in Cognos Workspace
- ▸ Enabling larger worksheet size for Excel 2007

Introduction

In this chapter, we will see some of the best practices followed in the world of IBM Cognos report development. Once you learn them and start using them in your day-to-day life, you will notice that these practices not only save your time but also reduce the number of defects and benefit the ongoing maintenance of reports.

Reducing the number of query items

From the maintenance and documentation perspective, it is advisable to keep the number of query items in report query subjects to minimal. In this recipe, we will see some good practices to ensure this.

Getting ready

We will use the dimensional **GO Sales (analysis)** package for this recipe.

From **Tools/Options**, check the option of **Alias member unique name** and uncheck **Delete unreferenced query objects**.

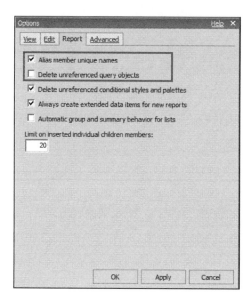

How to do it...

In this recipe we will see how to use some useful options available in Cognos Report Studio. This can be helpful and will make the reports more clear. To do this, perform the following steps:

1. We will start by creating a simple crosstab report. Open IBM Cognos Report Studio for a new crosstab report. Drag the **Time/Year** level onto columns.

2. From the **Toolbox** pane, drag a new **Query Calculation** onto rows.

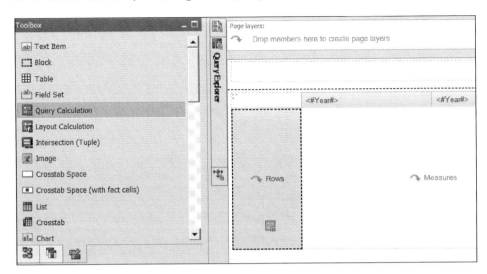

3. Give it a name, for example, `ProductLines` and choose the **Products** hierarchy.

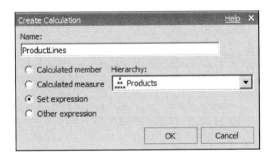

4. In the **Set Expression** window, expand the **Products** hierarchy to locate children of **Products**.

5. Select the three children of **Products** and drag them onto the expression definition. They will appear as comma-separated values. Put them within a SET() function.

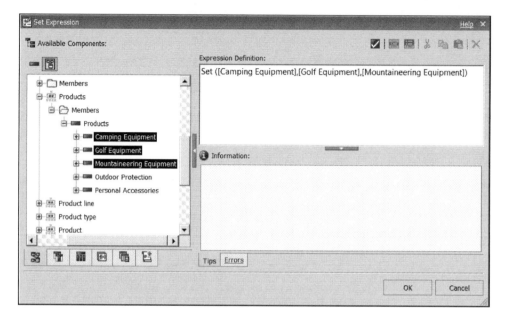

6. Pull **Revenue** from the measures into the crosstab intersection.

7. Run the report to test it. It should work fine. Now go back to the Studio and examine the report **Query Explorer**.

8. Now go back to the report page and delete **Year** from columns. Drag **Month** there instead.

9. Go back to **Query Explorer** to examine the query subject. Notice that both **Year** and **Month** are present.

10. Run the report to test it. It works fine. However, there is a redundant item in the query subject (that is, **Year**) that is not used anywhere in the report.

11. Now go back to Cognos Report Studio. From **Tools | Options**, uncheck the option of **Alias member unique name** and check **Delete unreferenced query objects** (opposite of what we had done at the beginning).

12. Delete the crosstab from the report page. Again create it by following steps 1 to 9. Examine the query subject this time. You will see that only three query items are present this time.

13. Finally, we will try one more thing. Select **Month** from columns and hit *Ctrl + X* to cut it. You will see that it is removed from crosstab.

14. If we want to bring it back, we have two places. Either we can drag it from the **Source** pane, or we can get it from the **Data Items** pane.

15. Drag it from the **Model** or **Source** tab. Notice that it is called **Month 1** now and a duplicate query item is created for it in the query subject.

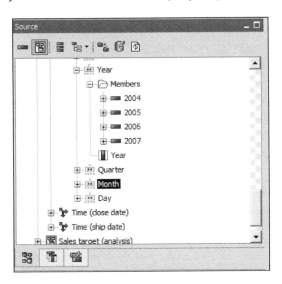

16. Hit the **Undo** button. Drag it this time for the **Data Item** pane. Notice that no new data item is created this time.

How it works...

We have already talked about the environment options in this book previously. This recipe highlights how these options can be useful in reducing the number of query items.

Alias member unique name

By checking this option, IBM Cognos Report Studio creates a new data item for each member used within any data item or filter. This means a greater number of query items. We uncheck this option to stop the creation of separate aliases.

Delete unreferenced query objects

When this is unchecked, the data items that you delete from the report page are still maintained within the query subject. Hence, we check this option to automatically clear the unused items. You can still cut the item from the report purposely to keep it in the query subject, if required.

Dragging items from the Data Items pane

Whenever an item is already present in the query subject, if it needs to be pulled again on the corresponding container, it should be pulled from the **Data Items** pane. Dragging it again from the model/source would mean creation of a duplicate query item. This duplicate query item will have name appended with the number **1**. Use this as an indication to identify the duplicate item and remove it.

Highlighting hidden items

We have seen that it is possible and in fact suggested to turn on the option of **Show Hidden Objects** from visual aids. This recipe will show you a best practice related to that.

Getting ready

We will use the GO Data Warehouse (query) package for this recipe. Open IBM Cognos Report Studio and turn on the **Show Hidden Object** feature from visual aids.

How to do it...

In this recipe we are going to highlight the hidden column with the yellow color. To do this, perform the following steps:

1. Create a simple list report with **Product line**, **Product type**, and **Product** as columns.

2. Select the **Product type** column and turns its **Box Type** to **None**. As we have chosen to show hidden items, we can still see the column on the report page.

3. Now from the **Background Color** property, select yellow.

Product line	Product type	Product
<Product line>	<Product type>	<Product>
<Product line>	<Product type>	<Product>
<Product line>	<Product type>	<Product>

4. Run the report to test it.

Product line	Product
Outdoor Protection	Aloe Relief
Personal Accessories	Astro Pilot
Personal Accessories	Auto Pilot
Personal Accessories	Bear Edge
Personal Accessories	Bear Survival Edge
Personal Accessories	Bella
Golf Equipment	Blue Steel Max Putter

How it works...

In this recipe, we have hidden a column by changing its **Box Type** property. As this item is now not going to appear on the report, we have the liberty to change its visual appearance. We changed its background color to yellow, which clearly distinguishes the item from the rest.

Next time, when any other developer opens this report in Report Studio or when you come back to it after several weeks, you don't have to refer to any documentation or check any object property to know which items are hidden. You can just turn on the **Show Hidden Items** feature and everything marked with yellow is part of the report but hidden in the output.

This is just a best practice to follow that helps in maintainability. It reduces the need for documentation and troubleshooting time.

Using relative paths for images

We have seen some recipes in this book where we displayed images on the report (for example, the traffic signal one). This recipe will show a best practice related to that.

Getting ready

We will use the report created in the last recipe for this one.

How to do it...

In this recipe we will learn how to use relative paths for images in our report. To do this, perform the following steps:

1. Open the report in Cognos Report Studio. From the **Insertable Objects/Source** pane, drag **Product image** onto the list as a new column.

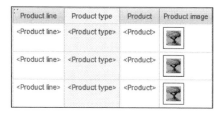

2. Run the report to test it.

3. It is possible that the images are not displayed.

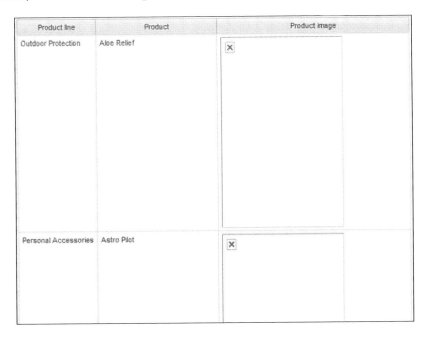

In that case, log on to the server and make sure the **Go Sales** sample images are located in the {installation folder}\webcontent\samples\images folder. If not, put them there from the sample provided with this book.

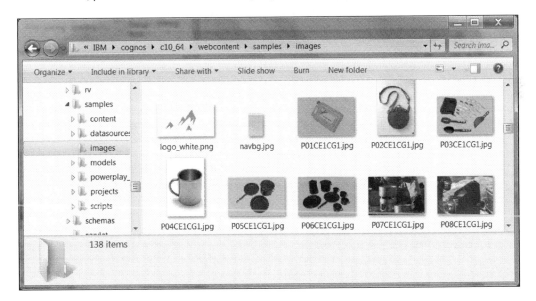

4. After putting the images in the correct folder, run the report and they should be displayed correctly.

Product line	Product	Product image
Camping Equipment	Canyon Mule Journey Backpack	#
Camping Equipment	Firefly Multi-light	Hemera Technologies/PhotoObjects.net (RF)/Jupiterimages

5. Now go back to IBM Cognos Report Studio. Double-click on the **Product image** column. This will open the data expression window.

6. Browse the model tree from left to locate the **Product image** column. Now click on the **Select Value** button to browse values from top.

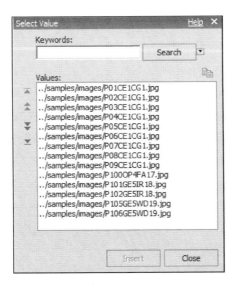

Notice that the values are relative paths and not absolute paths.

7. Now let's see how it works.

How it works...

The URL of the image object can be defined as **Absolute** or **Relative**. When we say Relative, it is with respect to the `Webcontent` folder within IBM Cognos Server's installation directory.

Hence, `./samples/images/P01CE1CG1.jpg` will translate to `C:\Program Files\ibm\cognos\c10_64\webcontent\samples\images\P01CE1CG1.jpg` (assuming that the installation directory on the server is `C:\Program Files\ibm\cognos\c10_64`).

It is best practice to always give a relative path for the images and put the images in the `Webcontent` folder, as it allows the report to be promoted to other environments (testing, UAT, production, and so on) without changing any code. If we had provided the absolute path and the images were hosted on the Cognos server itself, the promotion of the report to another environment would mean that the URL of the images would need to be changed.

There's more...

It is to be noted that if you have an organization-wide repository of images that are hosted on a different server to the IBM Cognos server, you can use an Absolute path. The path won't need any change when the report is promoted to a different Cognos environment.

Also for the Relative path to work in distributed installation with multiple application servers, the images must be copied on all Cognos application servers.

Controlling JavaScript file execution

In *Chapter 3, Using JavaScript Files – Tips and Tricks*, we saw many recipes to manipulate the prompts. However, it is to be noted that JavaScript files are executed every time the page loads. Hence, it is important to control the execution of certain scripts.

This recipe will show you why controlling the JavaScript file execution is necessary in certain cases and how to do it.

Getting ready

We will use the report created in the *Defining dynamic default values for prompts* recipe of *Chapter 3, Using JavaScript File – Tips and Tricks* for this one.

How to do it...

In this recipe we will have a look at how we can control the JavaScript execution by doing a simple modification to the original script. To do this, perform the following steps:

1. Open the report in IBM Cognos Report Studio and save it with a different name because we are going to change it.

2. Run the report to see what it is doing. We have already written the JavaScript in this report to default the date to second entry from top, where dates are sorted from recent to old. Hence, it defaults to **200711** as per the data available in the sample database.

3. Change the date to **200712** and run the report.

4. Once the report is rendered, hit the **RUN** button to re-run the report.

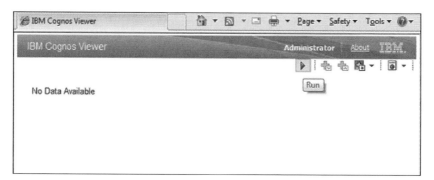

5. Notice that the date prompt goes back to **200711**. This can be quite annoying especially when you have multiple prompts on the page and all of them default to certain values.

6. Close the window and go back to IBM Cognos Report Studio.

7. In the prompt page, double-click on the **HTML** item kept in the report footer beside the **Finish** button.

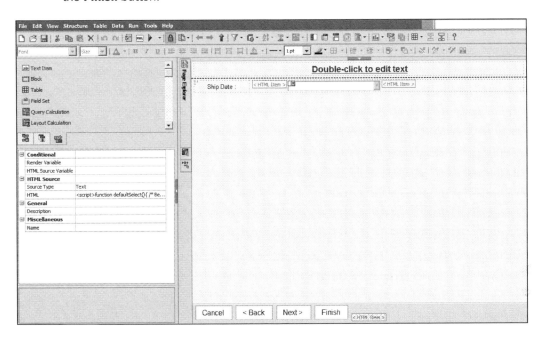

8. Replace the code with the following:

```
<script>
function defaultSelect()
{ /* Below is the original code to change selection. We just
encompassing it in a function */
var theSpan = document.getElementById("A1");
var a = theSpan.getElementsByTagName("select");
/* This stmt return an array of all value prompts within span */
for( var i = a.length-1; i >= 0; i-- )
/* now loop through the elements */
{var prompts = a[i];
if( prompts.id.match(/PRMT_SV_/))
{  prompts.selectedIndex = 3;
}
canSubmitPrompt();
}
}
</script>
<button type="button" onclick="defaultSelect()" class="bt"
style="font-size:8pt">Apply Defaults</button>
```

9. Run the report to test it. Observe that the date prompt is now not defaulting to any value. However, there is a new button called **Apply Default** in the footer. Hit that button and date will default to second from top (that is, **200711**).

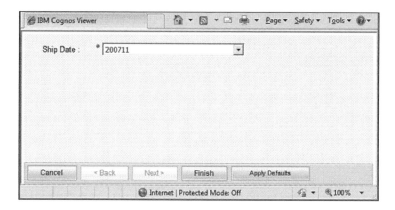

10. Change the date to `200712` and hit the **Finish** button to run the report. After the output is rendered, hit the **Run** button again and notice that the date is still `200712`. It does not automatically going back to `200711`, unless we hit the **Apply Default** button.

How it works...

Here we haven't written much new code. We have just put the existing JavaScript that selects the date into a function called `defaultSelect()`. Then, we have added one line of HTML code (the `BUTTON` tag) to generate a button in the footer.

When a user clicks on the button, the function is executed, thus changing the date selection to second from top. This way we are stopping the script from automatically executing when page loads.

This is very useful when there are many prompts on the page and many of them are commonly used for known values. Users can be educated to hit the button to default those prompts to the known values, thus saving their time. Then users can override the required prompt selections and on re-run those values are retained.

Customizing classes for report-wide effect

We will now see a best practice to apply standard formatting across the report and save development time at the same time.

Getting ready

Create a new report using the GO Data Warehouse (query) package. Pull multiple crosstabs onto the report page and populate them with valid rows, columns, and measures, similar to the one shown in the following screenshot. Create some drill links as well.

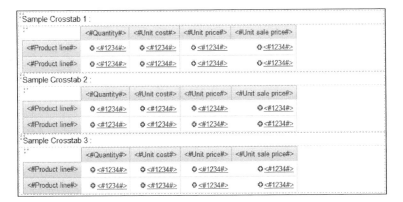

How to do it...

Let's work towards applying some standard formatting across the report. To do this, perform the following steps:

1. Open the **Page Explorer** pane and click on **Classes**.

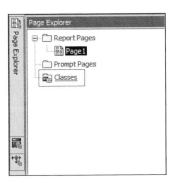

2. Locate **Crosstab member cell** from the **Global Class Extensions** list. Change its **Font** to **Bold** and **Background Color** to **#FFCC99**.

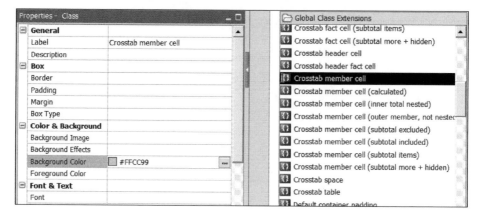

3. Similarly, locate the hyperlink object and change its **Foreground Color** to `Black`.

4. Go back to the report page. Notice that the changes you made have reflected everywhere and standard formatting is applied to all **Crosstab members** and **Drill links**.

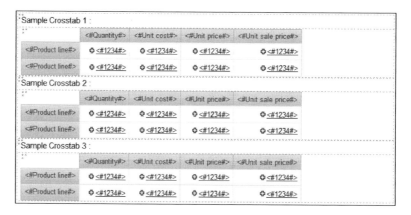

5. Run the report to test it.

How it works...

The objects on the report page inherit their properties from certain classes. Report Studio allows us to modify these classes. On doing so, the changes reflect on all the objects belonging to the class. This is a better way than selecting every object and changing their properties, which is error prone.

This way we can apply standard formatting across the report and also save time.

Creating templates

In all organizations, the reporting suite is required to follow the standard formatting. Similar to other tools and technologies, IBM Cognos Report Studio also allows you to create and use templates in order to maintain the standards, reduce cosmetic errors, and save time.

Getting ready

We will amend the report created in the previous recipe in this recipe.

How to do it...

We have already defined the formatting for crosstab members and hyperlinks. To create a template, you want to go ahead and define the standard report header and footer.

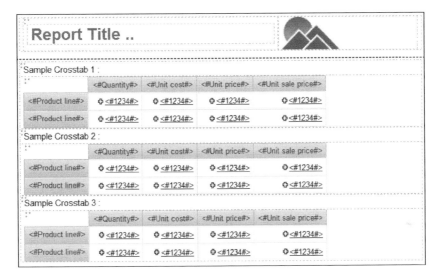

You might want to put the company logo in the header. To do this, perform the following steps:

1. From the menu, go to **File | Convert to Template**.

Notice that the **Model/Source** pane becomes empty and all data items are removed from the report.

2. From the menu, go to **File | Save As**. Give the filename **Template**. Notice that the icon created for this is different than other reports.

3. Now we will prepare the XML specification of this template to be inserted in the server files. For that, select **Tools | Copy Report to Clipboard** from the menu.

4. Go to any XML editor and paste the XML specifications that we just copied. Now perform the following:

    1. From the `<report>` tag, remove the `xmlns` and `template` attributes. So it should look like this:

       `<report expressionLocale="en ">`

    2. Add a `<template>` tag just above it:

       `<template name="PACKTSample "PACKT Sample Template">`

    3. Add `</template>` at the end of the file (just after `</report>`).

    4. Copy the whole specification on the clipboard.

5. Now, on the Cognos application server, open the Cognos installation directory. Locate the `C10_location/webcontent/pat/res/templates.xml` file.

6. Make a backup of the file for failover and then open this `templates.xml` file. Paste the specification that we copied in step 4 under the `<xmlFragment id="ReportTemplates">` tag. Save the file and close it.

7. The last step is to update the `Resources.xml` file. Locate `c10_location/webcontent/pat/res/Resources.xml` and open in the XML editor.

8. Find the `<listItems>` tag. Add following line in a similar fashion as the existing `<listItem>` tags:

   ```
   <listItem label="PACKT Template" icon="icon_blank.gif"
   templateName="PACKT Sample Template"/>
   ```

   You can also see this in the following screenshot:

```
<!--
This listView belongs in _7RF.xml but since the dialogs are renamed when packaged the
documentation for modifying templates can't refer to the file name.
-->
<listView id="New" view="icon" clipLabels="false">
        <listItems>
                <listItem idsLabel="IDS_LBL_NEW_BLANK_REPORT" icon="icon_blank.gif" templateName="Blank"/>
                <listItem idsLabel="IDS_LBL_NEW_LIST_REPORT" icon="icon_list.gif" templateName="List"/>
                <listItem idsLabel="IDS_LBL_NEW_CROSSTAB_REPORT" icon="icon_crosstab.gif" templateName="Crosstab"/>
                <listItem idsLabel="IDS_LBL_NEW_CHART_REPORT" icon="icon_chart.gif" templateName="Chart"/>
                <listItem idsLabel="IDS_LBL_NEW_MAP_REPORT" icon="icon_map.gif" templateName="Map"/>
                <listItem idsLabel="IDS_LBL_NEW_FINANCIAL_REPORT" icon="icon_financial.gif" templateName="Financial"/>
                <listItem idsLabel="IDS_LBL_NEW_REPEATER_REPORT" icon="icon_repeater.gif" templateName="Repeater"/>
                <listItem idsLabel="IDS_LBL_NEW_STATISTICS_REPORT" icon="icon_statistics.gif" templateName="Statistics"/>
                <listItem idsLabel="IDS_LBL_NEW_BLANK_APPLICATION" icon="icon_blankApplication.gif" templateName="BlankApplication"/>
                <listItem idsLabel="IDS_LBL_NEW_APPLICATION" icon="icon_application.gif" templateName="Application"/>
                <listItem idsLabel="IDS_LBL_NEW_TEMPLATE_RT" icon="icon_template_qs.gif" templateName="Template RT"/>
                <listItem label="PACKT Template" icon="icon_blank.gif" templateName="PACKT Sample Template"/>
                <listItem idsLabel="IDS_LBL_NEW_BROWSE" icon="browse_32x32.gif" idsTooltip="IDS_TOOLTIP_NEWBROWSE" isBrowse="true"/>
        </listItems>
</listView>
```

9. Save the file and close it.

10. Open a new instance of IBM Cognos Report Studio. Notice that a new option appears in the dialog box for **PACKT Template**.

Select this option and check that the template we created initially appears.

Now you can create a new report as usual. You are rest assured that formatting of objects and other components that you placed on the templates are maintained every time you create a new report using this method.

How it works...

This recipe looks like a long process but it is a one-time task that is extremely useful. We have already discussed the advantage of having templates.

If you are going to create many reports that need organization-standard formatting, some common scripts and components, and generic header and footer elements, it is highly recommended that you take time to prepare a template for it.

It is common to see a Cognos developer opening one existing report, making a copy of it and then updating it, thus using the base report as the template. While this serves the purpose very well, there are chances of accidently overwriting the templates. Especially in the case of multideveloper environment, it is suggested that one who has access to server installations performs this operation of defining a standard template and rest of the team uses it from the **New Report** dialog box.

Regression testing

Business Intelligence and Data Warehousing and Reporting systems need ongoing maintenance. New data comes in every day, volume grows, and business rules change. All this can impact the existing reports structurally and performance-wise. In this recipe, we will quickly see one way of doing regression test every time anything changes in the system.

Getting ready

We will just discuss the concept here and extend the *Timing report execution* recipe of *Chapter 12, More Useful Recipes*.

How to do it...

We saw in the *Timing report execution* recipe of *Chapter 12, More Useful Recipes* that we can create Report View, save certain parameters for it, and then run it in the background.

1. We will now add upon this concept. For regression, you will need to create report views for each report. Save all of them in one folder.

2. Create a new job by clicking on the new job icon.

3. Add all the report views to this job. Change **Submission of steps** to **In sequence** and **Continue on error**.

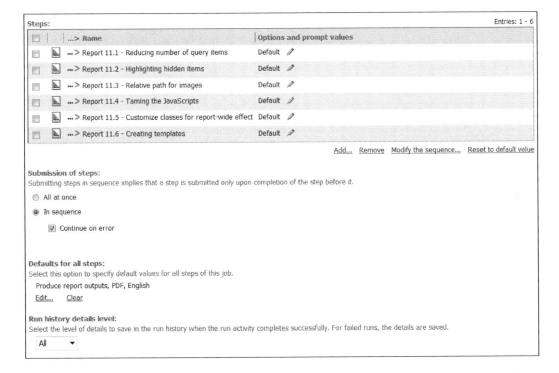

4. Change the defaults for all steps to **PDF** and **Save the Output**.

5. Save the job. Run this job every time you want to perform a regression test.

How it works...

Every time you run this job, each Report View will be executed with the saved parameter values. If anything is broken structurally in the system (for example, a table or view gone missing, columns renamed, account access removed, and so on), the execution will fail. You can refer to the **Schedule Management** or **Administration | Past Activities** from Connection Portal to check these.

Also, you can see the time taken by each report to execute. You can compare these timings with the prior runs. Thus, if the performance is affected due to any change in the system (grown volume, index dropped, and so on) it will be highlighted.

It is highly recommended that you create such a mechanism in your environment and run it weekly or on-demand to ensure that everything is working fine.

There's more...

It is possible to configure the Cognos server to produce the PDF outputs on the filesystem. You can use this and save the outputs and compare it with a previous run to check any purposeful or accidental change impact. You will need to write a small program to rename the PDF files appropriately.

Commenting the code

All applications need some kind of code commenting mechanism for maintenance purposes. With programming languages it is easier; however, with tools it can be a little tricky to put comments. In this recipe, we will see different options around putting comments within a report that will be invisible for users but accessible to the developers.

Getting ready

Open any existing report in IBM Cognos Report Studio.

How to do it...

In this recipe we will see some techniques that you can use to insert comments to your reports.

1. For the first technique to put comments and notes within a report and hide them from users, go to **Page Explorer** and create a new page. Call it Comments.

2. Open this new page and drag text items onto it. Write all comments about the report here (description, functionality, notes, special cases, and so on).

3. Now go to **Condition Explorer** and create a new Boolean variable. Define the expression as: 1=0. Name this variable as Render_Comments.

4. Go to the **Comments** page. Open the **Render Variable** property and connect it to the Render_Comments variable.

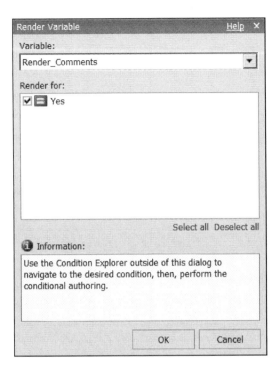

5. Run the report. Notice that the **Comments** page is never rendered.

6. Now we will see another place to put comments. For that go back to IBM Cognos Report Studio and open the main report page.

7. Drag a new **HTML** item onto the report header. Define the HTML code as follows:

```
<!-- This is HTML Comment -->
```

You can see this in the following screenshot:

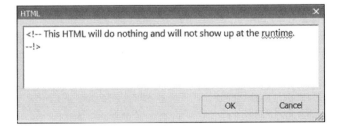

8. Run the report to test it. Notice that the comment doesn't appear in the report, but if you view the source code of the HTML output, you can see the comment.

9. Finally, let's see the XML commenting option. For that, copy the report to the clipboard.

10. Add the following line to the beginning of code:

```
<!-- This is XML Comment -->
```

You can see this in the following screenshot:

```
1    <!-- This is XML Comment -->
2    <report xmlns="http://developer.cognos.com/schemas/report/9.0/" expressionLocale="en"
3                    <modelPath>/content/folder[@name='Samples']/folder[@name='Models']/pa
4                    <drillBehavior/>
5            <queries>
6                <query name="Query1">
7                    <source>
8                        <model/>
9                    </source>
10                   <selection><dataItem aggregate="none" name="Product line" ro]
```

11. Copy the whole specification again and paste it back into Cognos Report Studio. Save the report.

12. Run the report to test it.

How it works...

We have seen three ways of putting comments and notes within the report in this recipe. All of them work fine and do their job.

Some developers don't like creating a new page or HTML item for storing the comments, as this means creating some objects on the report that are not required. These objects form a part of the XML specification and they are validated and parsed every time the report runs.

Following that belief, we can put the comments in the XML specification itself. That way comments are completely ignored by the Studio while validating and parsing. However, it does mean that each time we need to refer to or update the comments, we will have to copy the report specification in the XML editor.

Having a separate page (first approach) is a very clean method. However, it doesn't allow you to put comments inline. So if you have a comment or note specific to a column or prompt, you can't just put it near that object and make it noticeable.

I personally find the HTML comment method to be the best. By having one HTML item in the page header, I can put all the commentary about that page in there. Also, I can create specific HTML items to hold particular object-related notes and put them near that object. Also, later on if I am running any report and want to see the comments, I don't have to open it in Cognos Report Studio. Instead, I can just look at the HTML source code and it will have those comments inline.

I will leave it to your own experiments and preference to decide which one to follow in your team.

Naming data containers (lists, crosstabs, and charts) for use in Cognos Workspace

With IBM Cognos v10, there is a new tool introduced called IBM Cognos Workspace—Cognos Business Insight in Version 10.1. It is meant for end users to build their own dashboards by pulling required objects from prebuilt Report Studio reports.

This is great for end users because instead of running individual reports, they can bring together required contents from multiple reports (and hence multiple sources) onto their own dashboard and look them as and when required in one go. Also, each user can build their own dashboard without necessarily being trained on report development. All the report development can be done centrally, and end users can pull together their required objects as per individual demand.

Though the Workspace tool is not covered in this book, we will see a best practice when building Report Studio reports for use in Workspace.

Getting ready

Start a new report in Report Studio.

How to do it...

In this recipe you can see how can you name each data container with a meaningful name in your report so that you can use them in the Cognos Workspace. To do this, perform the following steps:

1. Drag new **List** and **Chart** items onto the report page.
2. Drag required items onto the list and chart to produce valid contents.

3. Now select the list using **Selector** (three orange dots) and check its **Properties**. Scroll down to **Name** and define it as `List of Products`.

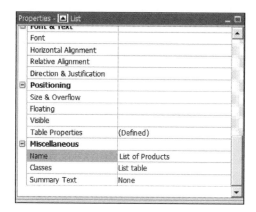

4. Similarly, select the chart and define the name as `Sales across Regions`.

5. Save the report as `Products-Sales Report`.

6. Now open the Cognos Workspace tool from Cognos Connection.

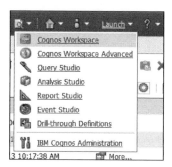

7. Create a new workspace and browse contents from the **Content** pane.

8. Locate our report called `Products-Sales Report` and expand it. You will notice that both list and chart are available with the names that we have given. You can now pull any or both of them onto the workspace.

How it works...

By defining appropriate names for the data containers in Report Studio reports, we make them user-friendly for Workspace users. They will exactly know what to expect while pulling any object from a report built by you.

There's more...

If you update the objects in underlying Report Studio reports, the object on Workspace will be marked with a dog-ear sign as shown in the following screenshot. Then, the user will have the choice to update the object in the Workspace or leave it as it is.

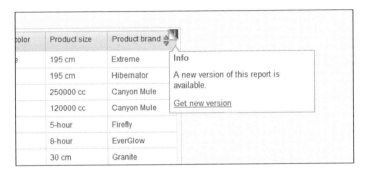

Please refer to the IBM documentation about the Workspace tool to understand its features and how to use it as a consumer of data.

Enabling a larger worksheet size for Excel 2007

Let's say that you have built a report that primarily is a data extract. It produces more than 65,000 rows. When users run it in Excel 2007, it is spread across multiple sheets though Excel 2007 supports over a billion rows. Let's see how to fix by changing server settings.

Getting ready

You require admin rights for this so you can change service settings.

How to do it...

In this recipe we will see how to enable a larger Excel 2007 worksheet by changing IBM Cognos BI server settings.

1. Open Cognos Administration from Connection Portal and go to **Configuration |
Dispatcher and Services**.

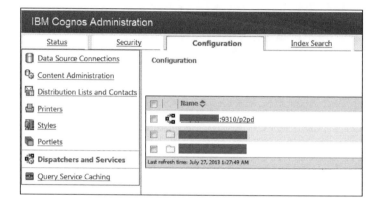

2. Click on the dispatcher and it should show you all services.

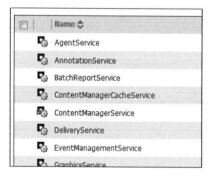

3. Go to the **Properties** pane of **Report Service** and open **Advanced Settings**.

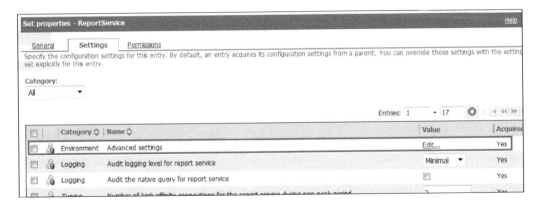

4. Define a new parameter called `RSVP.EXCEL.EXCEL_2007_LARGE_WORKSHEET` and set its value as **TRUE**.

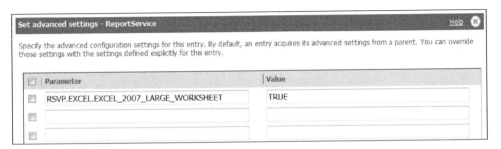

5. Do the same for the **Batch** report service. Restart the services.

How it works...

By defining this parameter, we enable Cognos to produce large worksheets with more than 65,000 rows in a sheet for Excel 2007 output.

There's more...

When the `RSVP.EXCEL.EXCEL_2007_LARGE_WORKSHEET` parameter is defined, you can also define the `RSVP.EXCEL.EXCEL_2007_WORKSHEET_MAXIMUM_ROWS` property to control the maximum number of rows Cognos created before spanning it over a new sheet; and you can also define the `RSVP.EXCEL.EXCEL_2007_OUTPUT_FRAGMENT_SIZE` parameter to solve any memory issues related to the Excel output.

Recommendations and References

In this chapter, we will cover the following topics:

- Version controlling
- Recommendations for prompt types
- Cognos Mashup Service
- SDK and third-party tools for Cognos
- IBM Cognos Analysis For Excel (CAFE)
- IBM Cognos for Microsoft Office
- IBM Cognos Workspace
- IBM Cognos Workspace Advanced
- IBM Cognos Cloud

Introduction

Let us now have a look at some topics that are very useful for a Cognos report developer to know about.

Version controlling

Cognos allows direct connection to certain version controlling software (Visual Source Safe being the most popular) for Framework Manager. However, there is no direct mechanism for reports.

The following methods are seen in different organizations for version controlling of reports:

▶ Copy the report specification to the clipboard, save it as an XML file, and store it in the version controlling system. This method allows easy comparison to prior versions of the report, and hence is good for code review during any changes. However, it can be tedious. Also, restoring to an older version needs to be done for one report at a time. This also breaks any existing report views defined at the target location.

▶ Export the whole suite of reports and store the export file (the ZIP format) in the version controlling system. This is less tedious compared to the previous one as only one file is created for the whole suite of reports. Reverting to an older and stable state is easy (the entire suite is reverted so that you can bring the system back to older and stable state, like baseline). However, this method is not particularly useful while troubleshooting a report to check what changed in it over the versions.

▶ Use third-party tools. It is possible to hook up to the content store to retrieve the information. There are some third-party tools available that use this method to retrieve report specifications and do certain jobs. You can consider the tools like MotioCI to automatically record report versions and track changes. They also allow you to revert to older versions (more information can be found at `http://www.motio.com/products/ci/overview.do`).

There are also similar tools from BSP Software (`www.bspsoftware.com`) and Envisn (`www.Envisn.com`) that provide version controlling as well as other administration tasks such as scheduling, migration, and monitoring.

Recommendations for prompt types

There are many types of prompts available for use in IBM Cognos Report Studio. Let's have a look at some information about when to use which kind of prompt.

Data	Suggested prompt	Description
Hierarchical	The tree prompt	This naturally supports hierarchical data.
2 to 4 values – single select, mandatory	The radio button group	The value prompt can be used in the radio button UI for this kind of requirement.
5 to 100 values – single select	The drop-down list	This is another UI of the value prompt. It saves space on the prompt page.
5 to 100 values – multi select	The listbox	This UI of the value prompt allows users to select multiple values by holding down the *Shift + Ctrl* keys.

Data	Suggested prompt	Description
More than 100 values	The search and select prompts	When more than 100 distinct values are available to choose from, it is advisable to use this prompt as users can search for required values which is much more simple than browsing. Also, it reduces the burden to populate all values when the prompt loads.

Cognos Mashup Service

Cognos Mashup Service is a web service that ships along with Cognos SDK (Software Development Kit) for Version 8.4.1 onwards. While Cognos SDK supports report authoring through programming, the Mashup Service is purely meant to run reports, access the report output, and expose the contents to other business applications in the UI and workflow.

Partner services talk to **Cognos Mashup Service** (**CMS**) using a REST or SOAP request. The contents are accessed in the XML, LDX, HTML, or JSON format. You can find more information about this in the IBM developerWorks library.

Some popular usages of CMS are embedding Cognos report contents into Google Maps, Google Earth, Adobe Air, and so on. Refer to the following link for one such example:

```
http://www.ibm.com/developerworks/data/library/cognos/page486.html
```

You can find more information and examples in the IBM developerWorks library and other discussion forums.

SDK and third-party tools for Cognos

As IBM Cognos provides a very open structure and easy access to contents and components through SDK and CMS, there are many products built over it. They use Cognos as the powerful application engine to generate contents, and then these tools present the contents in a visually appealing manner. When just Cognos Report Studio cannot meet your business requirement, you can consider using such third-party tools to enhance Cognos services and extract more values out of the investment made in Cognos.

There is one interesting third-party tool called MotioADF (www.motio.com) which provides a simple programming method than raw Cognos SDK. It has predefined routines/toolkits to provide a level of abstraction and ease of writing code to perform tasks on Cognos, such as executing reports, passing prompt values, and browsing contents.

By using such tools on top of Cognos, you can leverage the power of Cognos BI and extend/embed it into portals and websites very easily.

IBM Cognos Analysis For Excel (CAFE)

IBM's **Cognos Analysis For Excel** (**CAFE**) tool is quickly becoming popular among business and financial analysts. This Excel add-in is separately sold by IBM (doesn't ship with BI installation) and needs to be installed on the users' machines. It enables users to directly perform analysis in Excel with Cognos sitting as a layer between the data source and Excel.

Cognos Framework Model works as the modeling and security layer here. It allows multiple data sources to be pulled together into one business layer that is exposed in Excel using CAFE. Users can directly perform drag-and-drop, slice-and-dice operations to analyze the data.

They can put Excel calculations such as forecast on top of the figures and also create Excel charts. This brings the benefits of Cognos and Excel together and makes CAFE a killer application.

I would strongly recommend CAFE if your organization has data analysts who need to perform ad hoc analysis over data from warehouse and various other sources. You would need strong data modeling skills and this logic will sit in the Framework Model. IBM CAFE is suitable for dimensional models and **Dimensionally Modeled Relational** (**DMR**) schemas.

You can see how CAFE looks in the following screenshot:

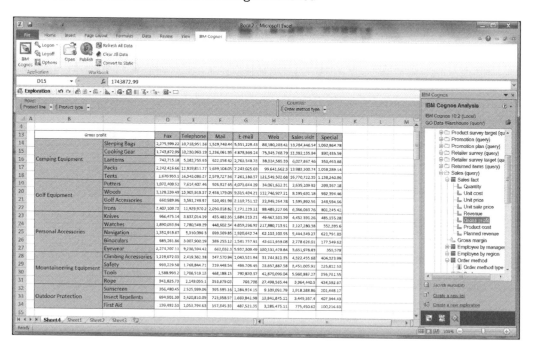

More information about CAFE can be found on the IBM website: `http://www-142.ibm.com/software/products/us/en/cognos-analysis-ms-excel`.

IBM Cognos for Microsoft Office

IBM CAFE that allows you to do data analysis in Excel, can be just too smart for the business users. Probably they only want to pull contents of predefined reports on their spreadsheets, Word documents, or PowerPoint presentations.

IBM Cognos for Microsoft Office is the way to go in such cases. It allows users to pull contents such as graphs, charts, tables, and crosstabs from existing reports into their MS Office documents. They can refresh contents on demand.

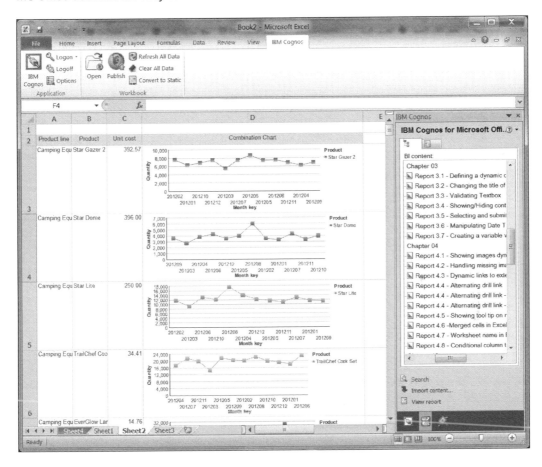

More information can be found on the IBM website: `http://www-142.ibm.com/software/products/us/en/cognos-microsoft-office/`.

IBM Cognos Workspace

Cognos Workspace provides a new way for end users to consume the required information from Cognos reports in their own hand-made workspace.

This tool was introduced in v10 and can be launched from the Connection portal from the right-top corner like other studios. Using this tool, you can create a workspace and then pull in required reports or parts of reports on it. You can also pull analysis and queries built using Analysis Studio and Query Studio respectively.

The whole idea is that rather than running tens of different reports, you can choose and pull in the required parts from all these reports together so that next time you just open your workspace to view them all in one go. This is a great tool for end users, as they can actually pull contents that are sourced from totally different databases/cubes on one screen and make use of that information. While Workspace won't let them create any new list, crosstab, or chart, it just allows them to collate the required parts from existing reports to make the best of it. This can also be used to quickly build dashboards and share them publicly.

Explore more about the Workspace tool using the IBM user guide from Info Centre. Look for *Cognos Workspace User Guide 10.2.0* on the IBM website.

IBM Cognos Workspace Advanced

With Cognos Version 7 and 8, users were often overwhelmed by the choices of "Studios" to create any report. There is Query Studio for basis relational reporting, Analysis Studio for dimensional reports, Report Studio Express mode for slightly advanced authors, and Report Studio Professional mode for fully trained professional authors.

In v10, IBM has tried to consolidate all these functionalities into one tool called **Cognos Workspace Advanced**. There is hope that the user community will embrace this tool as an ultimate do-it-all tool for end users so that Query Studio and Analysis Studio can be decommissioned over a period and Report Studio can be left as an IT tool or professional report authoring tool.

Explore more about Workspace Advanced from the IBM user guide. Look for *Cognos Workspace Advanced User Guide 10.2.0* on the IBM website.

IBM Cognos Cloud

Cognos Software and Analytics is now available as a service over the Cloud. IBM Cloud and Amazon Cloud are becoming very popular, as companies like the flexibility of borrowing resources as required rather than investing in processors, memory, storage, and software beforehand only to realize that they are either too less or too much for the requirement.

With Cloud-based BI, companies can now get access to Cognos BI software easily, quickly, and at lower entry costs. This comes with an option of scaling up as and when required. While Cognos software and services will be on the Cloud and you can bring down when required, the data sources and database will typically sit within your organization with a secured connection for the Cloud. You might choose the host content store on the Cloud and keep the actual query databases within your company behind the firewall.

More information about these can found on the IBM website if you intend to go Cloud!

Index

Symbols

A

B

B (continued)

C

Text property 100
Text Source Variable property 111
Time dimension 178
Time (ship date) dimension 178
timestampMask() function 198
TOAD 223
token
  adding, macro used 191-194
Tools | CopyReporttoClipboard option 118
Tools | OpenReportfromClipboard option 120
Tools | Options | View | Reuse IBM Cognos
    Viewer window 209
Tools | Show Generated SQL/MDX option 32
traffic light report 92-95

U

URL Source Variable dialog 93
user name
  displaying, in footer 199, 200
use value property 8

V

value prompt title
  changing 73-75
value property
  versus display value property 30-33

values
  selecting automatically 80, 81
  submitting automatically 80-82
variable width bar chart
  creating, JavaScript used 86-89
View | Visual Aids 208, 209

W

whole report
  filtering 165, 166
worksheet size
  larger worksheet size, enabling 327-330

X

XML
  about 115
  feature, row level formatting 128

Z

zero suppression
  achieving 169-171
zero values
  versus missing values 285-287

Thank you for buying
IBM Cognos 10 Report Studio Cookbook
Second Edition

About Packt Publishing

Packt, pronounced 'packed', published its first book "Mastering phpMyAdmin for Effective MySQL Management" in April 2004 and subsequently continued to specialize in publishing highly focused books on specific technologies and solutions.

Our books and publications share the experiences of your fellow IT professionals in adapting and customizing today's systems, applications, and frameworks. Our solution based books give you the knowledge and power to customize the software and technologies you're using to get the job done. Packt books are more specific and less general than the IT books you have seen in the past. Our unique business model allows us to bring you more focused information, giving you more of what you need to know, and less of what you don't.

Packt is a modern, yet unique publishing company, which focuses on producing quality, cutting-edge books for communities of developers, administrators, and newbies alike. For more information, please visit our website: www.packtpub.com.

About Packt Enterprise

In 2010, Packt launched two new brands, Packt Enterprise and Packt Open Source, in order to continue its focus on specialization. This book is part of the Packt Enterprise brand, home to books published on enterprise software – software created by major vendors, including (but not limited to) IBM, Microsoft and Oracle, often for use in other corporations. Its titles will offer information relevant to a range of users of this software, including administrators, developers, architects, and end users.

Writing for Packt

We welcome all inquiries from people who are interested in authoring. Book proposals should be sent to author@packtpub.com. If your book idea is still at an early stage and you would like to discuss it first before writing a formal book proposal, contact us; one of our commissioning editors will get in touch with you.

We're not just looking for published authors; if you have strong technical skills but no writing experience, our experienced editors can help you develop a writing career, or simply get some additional reward for your expertise.

IBM Cognos Business Intelligence

ISBN: 978-1-84968-356-2   Paperback: 318 pages

Discover the practical approach to BI with IBM Cognos Business Intelligence

1. Learn how to better administer your IBM Cognos 10 environment in order to improve productivity and efficiency

2. Empower your business with the latest Business Intelligence (BI) tools

3. Discover advanced tools and knowledge that can greatly improve daily tasks and analysis

IBM Cognos 10 Framework Manager

ISBN: 978-1-84968-576-4   Paperback: 186 pages

A comprehensive, practical guide to using this essential tool for modeling your data for use with IBM Cognos Business Intelligence Reporting

1. Your complete and practical guide to IBM Cognos Framework Manager

2. Full of illustrations and tips for making the best use of this essential tool, with clear step-by-step instructions and practical examples

3. All the information you need, starting where the product manual ends

Please check **www.PacktPub.com** for information on our titles

IBM Cognos Insight

ISBN: 978-1-84968-846-8   Paperback: 142 pages

Take a deep dive into IBM Cognos Insight and learn how this personal analytics tool can be integrated with other IBM Business Analytics products

1. Step-by-step, how to guide, for installing and configuring IBM Cognos Insight for your needs

2. Learn how to build Financial, Marketing, and Sales workspaces in Cognos Insight

3. Learn how to integrate and collaborate with IBM Cognos Business Intelligence

IBM Cognos Business Intelligence 10.1 Dashboarding Cookbook

ISBN: 978-1-84968-582-5   Paperback: 206 pages

Working with dashboards in IBM Cognos BI 10.1: Design, distribute, and collaborate

1. Exploring and interacting with IBM Cognos Business Insight and Business Insight Advanced

2. Creating dashboards in IBM Cognos Business Insight and Business Insight Advanced

3. Sharing and Collaborating on Dashboards using portlets

Please check **www.PacktPub.com** for information on our titles